The Song of the Vali....

The Song of the Valiant Woman

STUDIES IN THE INTERPRETATION
OF PROVERBS 31:10–31

Al Wolters

paternoster press

First published in 2001 by Paternoster Press

07 06 05 04 03 02 01   7 6 5 4 3 2 1

Paternoster Press is an imprint of Paternoster Publishing,
P.O. Box 300, Carlisle, Cumbria, CA3 OQS, UK
and
P.O. Box 1047, Waynesboro, GA 30830–2047, USA
Website: www.paternoster-publishing.com

British Library Cataloguing in Publication Data
A catalogue record for this book is available from the British Library

ISBN 1-84227-008-7

Cover Design by Campsie, Glasgow
Typeset by WestKey Ltd, Falmouth, Cornwall
Printed in Great Britain by
Bell & Bain, Glasgow

Contents

Preface

In this volume are collected six studies from my hand on the Song of the Valiant Woman (Prov. 31:10–31). Four of them have been previously published (between 1984 and 1994), one served as my MA thesis (1987), and one was written especially for this volume (2000). In chronological order they are as follows:

'Nature and Grace in the Interpretation of Proverbs 31:10–31', *Calvin Theological Journal* 19 (1984), 153–166. This is a study of the interplay between the history of exegesis and theological worldviews, illustrated with reference to the relationship between verse 30 (with its explicitly religious emphasis) and the rest of the poem (with its stress on this-worldly activities).

'Ṣôpiyyâ (Prov. 31:27) as Hymnic Participle and Play on Sophia', *Journal of Biblical Literature* 104 (1985), 577–587. As the title indicates, this essay argues that the anomalous participial form in verse 27 of the Song can be explained if we understand it as a heretofore unrecognized example of a 'hymnic participle', and as a clever bilingual pun playing on *sophia*, the Greek word for wisdom.

'The Song of the Valiant Woman (Prov. 31:10–31): A Pattern in the History of Interpretation (to 1600)'. Unpublished MA thesis in Religious Studies (Hebrew Bible), at McMaster University, Hamilton, Ontario, Canada. The thesis traces the history of interpretation of the Song up to the sixteenth century.

'Proverbs xxxi 10–31 as Heroic Hymn: a Form-Critical Analysis', *Vetus Testamentum* 38 (1988), 446–457. Here I argue that the Song, from a form-critical point of view, conforms to the standard pattern of the genre 'hymn', and that it also displays the characteristic features of 'heroic poetry'. (This article has also been reprinted in D.E. Orton [ed.], *Poetry in the Hebrew Bible: Selected Studies from Vetus Testamentum* [Leiden: Brill, 2000], 186–197.) Reprinted here with the permission of Brill Academic Publishers.

'The Meaning of *Kîšôr* (Prov. 31:19)', *Hebrew Union College Annual* 65 (1994), 91–104. It is argued in this philological investigation that the obscure *hapax legomenon* in question cannot mean 'spindle-whorl' or 'distaff' (*pace* the lexica), but probably designates a 'doubling spindle'. Reprinted with the permission of the Hebrew College Annual.

'The Song of the Valiant Woman since the Sixteenth Century'. Not previously published. This is essentially a supplement to the MA thesis, bringing the survey of the history of interpretation of the Song up to the end of the twentieth century.

In the present volume, these studies (copy-edited to fit this new context) have been grouped into two Parts. Part 1 comprises the four interpretive essays, ranging from broader issues of form criticism and worldview to detailed questions of philology. It is especially the first two which outline my own overall reading of the Song, stressing both its heroic character and its religious integrity. The second two illustrate what I believe to be the continued value of detailed, even microscopic exegetical investigation. Part 2 consists of the two essays on the history of interpretation of the Song, and connects with the emerging contemporary interest in the *Wirkungsgeschichte* or "post-history" of biblical texts.

My interest in the Song of the Valiant Woman dates back to a year-long interdisciplinary seminar on philosophical hermeneutics held in 1976–77 at the Institute for Christian Studies, Toronto. I thank the graduate students in that seminar, as well as my then-colleagues James Olthuis and Calvin Seerveld, for the stimulation of that seminar. I trust that something of the reformational hermeneutical vision which we explored at that time, notably the refusal to isolate faith from the specifics of interpretation, will come through in the following pages.

As is clear from the concluding part of the last essay, there has been a dramatic increase in scholarly interest in the Song in the last two decades – an interest only partly accounted for by the impact of feminism in biblical studies. It is my hope that the present collection of essays, which are themselves part of the evidence of this renewed interest, might serve as both a resource and a reminder in the ongoing discussion of this fascinating wisdom poem – a resource by making readily available some of the recent scholarship on the Song, and a reminder by pointing out that biblical scholarship cannot afford to ignore either the history of interpretation or the theological issues with which it is so intimately connected. It is time to wake up from the Enlightenment dream that genuinely critical biblical scholarship can safely dispense with either faith or its own history.

It remains for me to thank Craig Bartholomew and Pieter and Elria Kwant for helping to make this publication possible. I am very much indebted to the three of you.

I dedicate this volume to the memory of my mother, Luchiena Wolters-Seinen (1913–1959).

Al Wolters
Hamilton, Ontario
June 2000

Note. The bibliographical abbreviations used are those of the style sheet of the *Journal of Biblical Literature*.

Part One

1

Proverbs 31:10–31 As Heroic Hymn:
A Form-Critical Analysis

It is striking how little attention has been paid to the Song of the Valiant
Woman (Prov. 31:10–31) in form-critical discussions of ancient Hebrew
poetry. Although Gunkel had included a passing reference to it in his fundamental *Einleitung in die Psalmen*, under the heading 'Weisheitsdichtung
in den Psalmen',[1] his brief suggestion seems never to have been developed
in the later literature on Old Testament form criticism. Generally speaking, the concluding song of Proverbs has been left out of account altogether. Apart from one or two brief allusions – echoing Gunkel – to the
song as a wisdom poem,[2] general discussions of Hebrew poetic forms
ignore it. Specialized discussions devoted specifically to the genres of
wisdom literature either fail to mention it (so R.F. Schnell,[3] G. von Rad[4]
and J.L. Crenshaw[5]), or repeat the designation 'wisdom poem' (so R.E.
Murphy[6]), and even the numerous studies on the wisdom psalms, such as
those by S. Mowinckel,[7] Murphy,[8] K. Kuntz,[9] and L.G. Perdue,[10] scarcely

---

[1] Göttingen: Vandenhoeck & Ruprecht, 1933, 383.

[2] O. Eissfeldt, *Einleitung in das Alte Testament* (3rd edn, Tübingen: J.C.B. Mohr,
1964), 167, Eng. tr. *The Old Testament. An Introduction* (Oxford: Basil Blackwell,
1965), 125; A. Weiser, *Einleitung in das Alte Testament* (6th edn. Göttingen:
Vandenhoeck & Ruprecht, 1966), 46.

[3] *Form Criticism of Hebrew Wisdom, with Special Reference to the Book of Proverbs*
(unpublished PhD dissertation, University of Toronto, 1946).

[4] *Weisheit in Israel* (Neukirchen–Vluyn: Neukirchen, 1970), 39–73, Eng. tr.
Wisdom in Israel (London and Nashville: Abingdon, 1972), 24–52.

[5] 'Wisdom' in J.H. Hayes (ed.), *Old Testament Form Criticism* (San Antonio: Trinity
University Press, 1974), 225–64.

[6] *Wisdom Literature: Job, Proverbs, Ruth, Canticles, Ecclesiastes, and Esther* (Grand
Rapids: Eerdmans, 1981), 82.

[7] 'Psalms and Wisdom', *SVT* 3 (1955), 205–24; *The Psalms in Israel's Worship*
2 (Oxford: Basil Blackwell, 1962), 104ff.

[8] 'A Consideration of the Classification "Wisdom Psalms"', *SVT* 9 (1963), 156–67.

give it a nod. The commentaries on Proverbs follow the same remarkable pattern: when they come to the concluding pericope of the book they virtually cease to ask form-critical questions. Once it has been established that we are dealing with an alphabetic acrostic,[11] attention is turned to other things. Even the recent article by T.P. McCreesh devoted specifically to this song fails to address the form-critical question.[12]

This pattern of benign neglect is all the more striking when we observe that students of the Hebrew Bible, when their form-critical guard is down, so to speak, identify the Proverbs acrostic freely as the sort of poem which it obviously is, namely a song of praise. In the German literature, for example, I have seen it referred to as a *Preislied*,[13] *Lobpreis*,[14] *Lobpreisung*[15] and *Lobeshymnus*.[16] There is even a place where H.W. Wolff alludes to the song in passing as 'der grosse Hymnus auf die tüchtige Frau'.[17]

It is the thesis of the present chapter that Wolff's description of the song as a 'hymn to the capable woman' is correct – not only in the loose and informal sense in which Wolff no doubt intended it, but also in the technically precise sense given to the term *Hymnus* by Gunkel and his followers. I shall argue that the Song of the Valiant Woman in fact displays most of the formal characteristics of the hymnic genre.[18]

This is not to deny that the song also shows an affinity with the

---

[9] 'The Canonical Wisdom Psalms of Ancient Israel – Their Rhetorical, Thematic, and Formal Elements' in J.J. Jackson and M. Kessler (eds.), *Rhetorical Criticism: Essays in Honor of James Muilenburg* (Pittsburgh: Pickwick Press, 1974), 186–122.

[10] *Wisdom and Cult* (Missoula: Scholars Press, 1977), 329, n. 26.

[11] That 'alphabetic acrostic' is itself a genre designation has been argued by K.C. Hanson, *Alphabetic Acrostics: A Form Critical Study* (unpublished PhD dissertation, Claremont Graduate School, 1984). However, since most acrostics in the Hebrew Bible and the Dead Sea Scrolls clearly belong to other standard genres (hymn, complaint) Hanson is forced to conclude that the acrostic form constitutes a genre in its own right only in seven out of seventeen examples (including Prov. 31:10–31; see the discussion on 315–35).

[12] 'Wisdom as Wife: Proverbs 31:10–31', *RB* 92 (1985), 25–46.

[13] A. Wünsche, *Die Schönheit der Bibel. Erster Band: Die Schönheit des Alten Testaments* (Leipzig: E. Pfeiffer, 1906), 327.

[14] H. Rahner, *Maria und die Kirche* (Innsbruck: Marianischer Verlag, 1951), 86.

[15] O. Plöger, *Sprüche Salomos (Proverbia)* (Neukirchen–Vluyn: Neukirchen, 1984), 379.

[16] J. Obersteiner, 'Die Erklärung von Proverbia 31, 10–31 durch Beda den Ehrwürdigen und Bruno von Asti', *Theologisch–praktische Quartalschrift* 102 (1954), 1.

[17] *Anthropologie des Alten Testaments* (Munich: C. Kaiser, 1973), 250.

[18] This point is also made in passing in chapter 3.

'wisdom psalms', as a brief consideration will clarify. We need only compare it with Psalm 112, one of the few psalms that falls under everyone's definition of that elusive category,[19] to notice a number of striking parallels. Not only are both perfect alphabetic acrostics, but there is also considerable thematic correspondence. Proverbs 31 describes 'the woman who fears the Lord' (v. 30) by listing her God-fearing works. Psalm 112 describes 'the man who fears the Lord' (v. 1) by listing his God-fearing works. In the one case there is a concluding antithesis between the fear of the Lord and deceptive beauty (Prov. 31:30); in the other there is a concluding antithesis between the righteous and the wicked (Ps. 112:10). The woman and the man are both described in terms of wisdom (Prov. 31:26; Ps. 112:5), wealth (Prov. 31:16,18,29; Ps. 112:3), children to be proud of (Prov. 31:28; Ps. 112:2), compassion and liberality to the poor (Prov. 31:20; Ps. 112:4,5,9) and a fearless attitude to the future (Prov. 31:25; Ps. 112:7,8). It is clearly not without cause that some scholars have associated the song of the Valiant Woman with wisdom psalms. Moreover, a hitherto unnoticed word-play on the Greek *sophia*[20] only reinforces the thematic affinity.

Nevertheless, the comparison with Psalm 112 can also make clear that form-critical distinctions are not hard and fast, that features of one genre frequently do not exclude those of another. Psalm 112 is universally classified as a wisdom psalm, yet it is a kind of mirror image of its twin, Psalm 111, which is usually classified as a hymn.[21] It, too, is a perfect alphabetic acrostic, contains a list of praiseworthy deeds (including compassion and liberality), and culminates in the theme of the fear of the Lord. The difference is that here it is the Lord himself, not a human being, whose wonderful acts are recounted. As M. Dahood remarks in his commentary on the second of the twin psalms: 'Here ... the poet ascribes to the just man some of the attributes he assigned to Yahweh in Psalm 112. What was a hymn now becomes a Wisdom psalm'.[22]

If we learn from this example not to apply form-critical categories too rigidly or exclusively we can turn Dahood's words around when we consider the Song of the Valiant Woman: 'what was a wisdom psalm now

---

[19] As far as I know, only three other psalms (1, 37 and 49) share the distinction of being classed in the wisdom genre by all the authors who have dealt with the question of its definition.
[20] See chapter 3, § II. On the Valiant Woman herself as the embodiment of God-fearing wisdom, see chapter 2.
[21] A few authors (e.g. Mowinckel and Eissfeldt) take Psalm 111 to be a wisdom psalm.
[22] *Psalms III: 101–150* (Garden City: Doubleday, 1970), 127.

becomes a hymn'. After all, there is no good reason to restrict the term
'hymn' to songs in praise of God. Historically, at least, the Greek *hymnos*
applied to poetry 'in praise of gods or heroes',[23] and a similar point can be
made with respect to the Hebrew *těhillâ* and its cognates. Neither the
sapiential features nor the human subject should prevent us from reading
the Song of the Valiant Woman as illustrating the *Gattung* which Gunkel
gave the technical designation *Hymnus*.

There is first of all the overall structure of the hymn. This is generally
divided into the introduction, which announces the praise which will be
given and names its subject; then the body or *Hauptstück*, which enumer-
ates the praiseworthy attributes and deeds of the mighty one being
acclaimed; and thirdly the concluding exhortation to the audience and
others to join in the poet's praise.[24] In the acrostic poem of Proverbs this
corresponds respectively to verses 10–12, in which the subject of praise is
introduced as the Valiant Woman, a priceless asset to her husband; to
verses 13–27, in which are recounted the mighty deeds of the woman as
efficient manager, enterprising businesswoman and generous benefac-
tress; and to verses 28–31, in which first her children and husband praise
her, and then the audience and her own handiwork are exhorted to
join in the praise. To appreciate the last point, we must realize that the
imperative *těnû*, with which the last verse begins, is addressed to the audience (since the imperative is plural), and that it is to be read as a form of
the verb *tānâ*, 'celebrate in song', not of *nātan*, 'give'.[25] The song therefore
concludes with the words:

Extol her for the fruit of her hands,
And let her works praise her in the gates.

---

[23] H.G. Liddell, R. Scott and H.S. Jones, *A Greek–English Lexicon* (revised edn,
Oxford: Clarendon Press, 1940), s.v.
[24] Gunkel, *Einleitung*, 33–59. See also H. Gunkel, *The Psalms: A Form-Critical Introduction* (Philadelphia: Fortress Press, 1967), 10–12.
[25] See for example W.A. van der Weiden, *Le Livre des Proverbes: Notes philologiques*
(Rome: Biblical Institute Press, 1970), 155–6; J.P. Lettinga, 'Een bijbelse
vrouwenspiegel' in *Bezield Verband: Opstellen aangeboden aan prof. J. Kamphuis*
(Kampen: Van Den Berg, 1984), 121, 123; and *Tanakh. A New Translation of the
Holy Scriptures According to the Traditional Hebrew Text* (Philadelphia: Jewish Publica-
tion Society, 1985). Possibly the verb needs to be revocalized as the piel *tannû*, on
the analogy of its occurrences in Judg. 5:11 and 11:40; so L. Alonso–Schökel and J.
Vilchez, *Proverbios* (Madrid: Ediciones Cristiandad, 1984), 536; and the NEB (see
L.H. Brockington, *The Hebrew Text of the Old Testament. The Readings Adopted by the
Translators of the New English Bible* [Oxford/Cambridge: Oxford University
Press/Cambridge University Press, 1973], 168.) Note that *tānâ* is construed with *lě*
also in Judg. 11:40.

Given this concluding call to praise, the overall structural parallel with the hymns of the Psalter is striking.

The parallels also extend to points of detail. In the final colon just quoted it is the works of the Valiant Woman which are urged, in the third person, to give her praise. Presumably this refers to the fancy sashes and other woven products which she would offer for sale 'in the gates' to the traveling Phoenician merchant mentioned in verse 24.[26] Just as all animate and inanimate creatures of the Lord are enjoined to praise their maker in the hymns of the Psalter, so here the products of the woman's creativity are exhorted to praise her, to give her credit, to 'do her proud'. We are immediately reminded of familiar hymnic phrases like 'Let everything that breathes praise the Lord!' (Ps. 110:6) and 'All thy works shall praise thee, O Lord' (Ps. 145:10). The Proverbs song here echoes the theme of 'cosmic praise' which is such a characteristic feature of Israel's hymns.[27]

Another such characteristic feature, perhaps (if Gunkel is right) the original nucleus of the primitive hymn, is the use of the phrase *halĕlû-yāh* at the beginning or end of the song. It is inconceivable that an Israelite poet would use this phrase in a song praising a human being. Nevertheless, the author of the Proverbs song dares to use a verbal form which sounds very much like it in his concluding line. In the words 'and let her works praise her' the verb in Hebrew is *(wî)halĕlûhā*. In the context of the concluding call to praise, this cannot fail to have reminded the audience of the familiar hymnic *halĕlû-yāh*.

A grammatical peculiarity which distinguishes the hymn from other genres is the use of a participle where one would expect (and where the context often contains) verbs in the perfect or imperfect. These participles are used to describe the praiseworthy deeds recounted in the body of the hymn. Gunkel called them *hymnische Partizipien*, and F. Crüsemann has made a detailed study of them.[28] In the light of our discussion so far, it is not surprising that such a hymnic participle is also found in the Song of the Valiant Woman, although it was overlooked by Crüsemann and has not been recognized as such by the commentators. The form in question is *ṣôpiyyâ* in verse 27, where it is the verb in the sentence 'She looks well to the ways of her household.' As I argue in chapter 3, this is not only a hymnic participle, but also a pun on the Greek word *sophia*. The

---

[26] The word for 'merchant' there is *kĕnaʿănî*, 'the Canaanite'.

[27] M. Girard, *Louange cosmique. Bible et animisme* (Montréal: Bellarmin, 1973), especially 40–1.

[28] *Studien zur Formgeschichte von Hymnus und Danklied in Israel* (Neukirchen-Vluyn: Neukirchen, 1969), 81–154.

word-play was possible because the author knew and exploited this grammatical peculiarity of the hymnic genre.

It is possible to list a number of other points in the song which are reminiscent of the hymnic style. For example, when the poet writes 'Strength and dignity are her clothing,' (v. 25) this echoes the phraseology of the hymns in praise of Yahweh (see Ps. 93:1; 104:1). Particularly the use of *hādār*, 'dignity', or 'honour' is telling in this regard, since this word:

> as expression for God's regal dignity … plays a special role in the praise of Israel (Ps. xcvi 6; civ 1; cxi 3; cxlv 5, 12; 1 Chr. xvi 27). The hymnic praise of the "beauty" of Yahweh … arises out of the experience of his historical deeds (Ps. cxi 3; cxlv 5, 12).[29]

I might also mention the theme of God's incomparability, which is so frequent in Israel's hymns, and which finds its human counterpart in Proverbs 31:29, 'Many women have done valiantly, but you surpass them all.' But enough has been said to substantiate my main thesis that the Song of the Valiant Woman, from a form-critical point of view, is hymnic in character.

The failure to recognize this hymnic character in the past is no doubt due to a number of factors, including the failure to understand the significance of *ṣôpiyyâ* in verse 27 and *tĕnû* in verse 31. But the most important reason is undoubtedly the habitual association of 'hymn' with the praise of God rather than mortals. The Proverbs acrostic did not present itself to people's minds as a candidate for the hymnic genre because it was a song in praise of a human being – and a woman at that.[30] No matter how extraordinary her accomplishments were, they were necessarily incommensurate with the mighty acts of God. Moreover, since for Gunkel and his followers a literary form was strictly linked to its *Sitz im Leben* (the temple worship service in the case of hymns) it was difficult to imagine it as functioning in another setting. Certainly, one can hardly imagine the Song of the Valiant Woman as having its original situation in the cult.

A consequence of my thesis, accordingly, is that the hymnic form in Israel is not strictly tied either to the praise of God or to the temple liturgy. The acrostic poem in Proverbs, if its hymnic character is recognized, provides us with a unique perspective on the possible early history and function of the hymn in Israel – a perspective quite different from that afforded by the liturgical hymns.

---

[29] D. Vetter, '*hādār*', *THAT* 1, 471 (my translation).
[30] Cf. Hanson, *Alphabetic*, 330, 'One might call it a "hymn to the capable wife", but this would require extensive stretching of the genre "hymn".'

Obviously, this is a theme which is too vast to explore in the context of this chapter. Let me point out, however, that there are some aspects of the Song of the Valiant Woman which suggest that it stands in a tradition of heroic poetry – a tradition which may also underlie the hymns of the Psalter.

Heroic poetry is a type of literature which is found in many cultures. Examples are the Homeric epics of ancient Greece, the Old Norse poetry of the Vikings and the heroic songs of contemporary Yugoslavia. They are characterized by the recounting of the mighty deeds of heroes, usually the military exploits of noble warriors. Associated with the longer heroic narrative poem or epic are shorter forms such as the panegyric ode in praise of a victorious champion or the lament, celebrating the great feats of a fallen warrior.[31]

It has been pointed out that the literature of ancient Israel also contains poetry of this type. The Song of Deborah is a notable example, as is David's lament for Saul and Jonathan in 2 Samuel 1. We also hear of the song which the women sang when Saul and David came home victorious from battle against the Philistines (1 Sam. 18 and 21). Indeed, it has been argued that the time of the Judges and of David was Israel's Heroic Age, and that much of the literature associated with it is heroic in kind.[32]

Against this background it is striking that the Song of the Valiant Woman displays a number of features which are clearly reminiscent of poetry of the heroic type. I list the following items:

1. The subject of the song is called an *'ēšet ḥayil*, a term which has been translated in many different ways, but which in this context should probably be understood as the female counterpart of the *gibbôr ḥayil*, the title given to the 'mighty men of valour' which are often named in David's age. The person who is celebrated in this song is a 'mighty woman of valour'.

2. That this is the meaning intended emerges also from the recurrence of the word *ḥayil* in verse 29 near the end of the song, forming a kind of inclusio with *'ēšet ḥayil* at the beginning. There it occurs in the idiom *'āśâ ḥayil*, which regularly means 'to do valiantly' in a military context.[33]

---

[31] See H.M. Chadwick, *The Heroic Age* (Cambridge: Cambridge University Press, 1912); H.M. and N.K. Chadwick, *The Growth of Literature* 1 (Cambridge: Cambridge University Press, 1932–1940), chs. 2–5; and C.M. Bowra, *Heroic Poetry* (London: Macmillan, 1952), ch. 1.

[32] See Chadwick, *Growth* 2, 645. According to Bowra, true heroic poetry was never developed in Israel (*Heroic*, 14–15), but this is largely because he, unlike the Chadwicks, excludes panegyric and lament from his definition.

[33] The idiom can also mean 'gain riches' (see the lexica s.v. *ḥayil*), and the poet is probably exploiting this ambiguity in Prov. 31:29. The more common meaning, however, is the military one.

3. Besides these two occurrences of *ḥayil*, a word meaning basically 'power' or 'prowess', it is remarkable how often the woman's strength is mentioned in the song. 'She girds her loins with strength' (v. 17) and 'she is clothed with strength and honour' (v. 25), where the Hebrew word is *ʿōz* in both cases. The second line of verse 17 adds 'She strengthens her arms' (*ʾimmēṣ*).

4. A number of words and phrases besides *ʾāśâ ḥayil* seem to have a specifically military connotation. In the expression 'you surpass them all' (v. 29) the phrase *ʿālâ ʿal* is often used elsewhere in the sense of going out to do battle against an enemy. (In fact the meaning 'surpass' is assigned to it only here. See BDB and KB³ s.v. *ʿālâ*. In verse 19 the apparently innocent words 'she stretches out her hands to the distaff' translate the idiom *šālaḥ yād bĕ*, which (as Paul Humbert has pointed out) always has an aggressive connotation elsewhere, so that its use in this peaceful context is exceptional.[34] It is remarkable, moreover, that the same expression (with the preposition *lĕ*) is used in the heroic context of the Song of Deborah to describe Jael's grasping of the tent peg with which she kills Sisera (Judg. 5:26). I might mention also the use of the warlike words *šālāl*, 'plunder' (v. 11) and *ṭerep*, 'prey' (v. 15) in the unusual derived senses of 'profit' and 'food' respectively.[35]

5. It is necessary again to notice the use of *tānâ* in the concluding verse of the song, this time to point out that this rare verb occurs elsewhere only in the context of heroic poetry.[36] It is once used to describe the song in which the daughter of Jephthah was annually celebrated, either in lament or praise (Judg. 11:40). Its other occurrence is in the Song of Deborah, in the words:

> consider the voice of the singers at the watering places.
> They recite (*yĕtannû*) the righteous acts of the Lord,
> the righteous acts of his warriors in Israel.
>
> (Judg. 5:10)

According to F.F. Bruce in his comment on the verb here, 'the actual sense is "sing responsively", and the reference is to the song of victory sung by

---

[34] ' "Etendre la main" (Note de lexicographie hébraïque)', *VT* 12 (1962), 387: 'Or, avec *be* la tournure *šālaḥ yād* a toujours un sens préhensif ou agressif, sauf dans Prov. xxxi 19.' The idiom with *bĕ* occurs 21 times in the Old Testament. For a total of 57 instances of *šālaḥ yād* (with or without a preposition), the connotation is usually hostile, 'mais, très exceptionellement, pacifique' (388).

[35] These are the common interpretations, see e.g. KB³ s. vv.

[36] An exception is the *hitnû* of Hos. 8:9, if this is not a corrupt text or from another root.

the maidens at the wells in the following times of peace'.[37] Such songs may well have been the original nucleus of heroic poetry in general, and the verb used to describe them would mean to celebrate in song the mighty deeds of the victorious warriors. It is to such celebration that the audience is exhorted after hearing of the exploits of the mighty woman of valour.

6. A characteristic of heroic poetry is that it is a poetry of action. It does not dwell on the inner feelings or the physical appearance of the hero, but simply describes the mighty feats of valour which he accomplishes.[38]

In line with this, the Song of the Valiant Woman is a portrait in verbs. The only adjectives in the poem (there are just two) describe not the heroine but her merchandise (*ṭôb*, v. 13) and her rivals (*rabbôt*, v. 29). In a word, she is pictured as wisdom in action. When she is compared to the merchant ships in verse 14, it is not her appearance which is described, but her action of traveling long distances to acquire food for her household. In fact her physical appearance is alluded to only in verse 30, where the vanity of beauty is contrasted with the fear of the Lord.

7. Finally, heroic poetry typically describes the exploits of men belonging to an aristocratic class, a class in which honour and individual initiative rank high on the scale of values.[39] The hero is typically a nobleman. So too the valiant woman of Proverbs 31 is clearly a wealthy lady of the upper classes. She wears purple and fine linen (v. 22), expensive fabrics imported from Phoenicia and Egypt. Her husband sits as a respected member on the council of elders in the city gates (v. 23). She has maids, *nĕʿārôt* (v. 15), who are probably themselves of high social standing.[40] She has enough capital of her own to invest in the development of a new vineyard, a major agricultural project (v. 16). She has the resources to give to the poor and needy (v. 20). Moreover, dignity and honour (*hādār*), as we have seen, is her very garment (v. 25), and the personal initiative she takes in traveling for provisions (v. 14), developing new agricultural land (v. 16) and engaging in trade (v. 24) is truly remarkable. She is clearly the kind of aristocrat of pronounced individuality which is characteristic of the protagonists of heroic poetry.

All these traits in the poem give us reason to suppose that the Valiant

---

[37] See his contribution on Judges in F. Davidson et al. (eds.), *The New Bible Commentary* (London/Grand Rapids: Inter-Varsity Press/Eerdmans, 1954), 244.
[38] Bowra, *Heroic*, ch. 2.
[39] See Chadwick *Growth* 1, 64–7; 666–7; Bowra, *Heroic*, chs. 1 and 3.
[40] See J. MacDonald, 'The Status and Role of the *naʿar* in Israelite Society', *JNES* 32 (1976), 147–70.

Woman is deliberately described in terms borrowed from a tradition of heroic poetry. She is a heroine in the full sense of the word, and meant to be perceived as such. This impression is so effectively created that the heroic features of this portrait keep cropping up in translations and commentaries, despite the many misconceptions to which it has been subject. The LXX, for example, translated 'ēšet ḥayil as γυνὴ ἀνδρεία, which means not only 'manly woman' but also 'woman of courage'. And Jerome, baffled by the obscure word kíšôr which we translate 'distaff', produced the inspired guess *fortia*, 'gallant deeds'.[41] The translators of the King James Version were also sensitive to the heroic temper of the poem; their 'virtuous woman' in fact meant as much as 'heroic woman' in the English of that time.[42]

What conclusions are we to draw from all this? From the point of view of form criticism, the heroic characteristics of the Song, coupled with the recognition that its genre is that of a hymn, may provide us with a clue to the historical origins of the hymn. It may well be that the hymns of the Psalter, like the Song of the Valiant Woman, are both developments of an earlier heroic tradition in Israel or its environment which is largely lost but which is preserved, for example, in the Song of Deborah. It is particularly telling in that regard that the Song of Deborah, as we have seen, uses the verb tānâ of the celebration of both Yahweh and human heroes. The Song of the Sea, with its explicit statement that 'Yahweh is a man of war' (Ex. 15:3), may well represent the hymn at a stage still closely linked to specifically heroic poetry. In any case it is clear that heroic themes abound in the hymnic songs of the Psalter. If this hypothesis is correct, then it is not as unusual as it may seem that the Valiant Woman is celebrated in a literary form otherwise reserved for the praise of Yahweh. In other words, the hymnic form of the Proverbs acrostic is not so much an imitation of the liturgical genre (which might well have sounded blasphemous to a God-fearing Israelite), but a parallel development of another genre, the heroic panegyric. Whereas the liturgical hymn uses the formal resources of the heroic song to celebrate the mighty acts of Yahweh, the Proverbs acrostic draws on those same resources to extol the great deeds of a noble-woman who manages a large estate.

Finally, we must ask the question: what is the significance of this 'heroicizing' of the accomplishments of an enterprising and God-fearing wife and mother in Israel? Let me briefly suggest, by way of conclusion,

---

[41] See *Oxford Latin Dictionary* (Oxford: Clarendon Press, 1982), s.v. '*fortis*' 8 ('gallant,' 'heroic,' 'valiant,' with references to *fortia* as a substantive in this sense in Vergil and Livy).

[42] See *Oxford English Dictionary* s.v. 'virtuous', I. 1 a–c ('valiant,' 'heroic,' 'capable').

that an answer to this question must be found in the light of two factors: the twofold polemic which the Song embodies, and the emerging revaluation of military prowess which it exemplifies.

On an overt and explicit level the Song of the Valiant Woman constitutes a critique of the literature in praise of women which was prevalent in the ancient Near East. As a distinct tradition, this literature was overwhelmingly preoccupied with the physical charms of women from an erotic point of view – in a word, with their sex appeal. Against the ideal of feminine perfection reflected in this widespread erotic poetry, which was cultivated in the context of royal courts and harems, the acrostic poem glorifies the active good works of a woman in the ordinary affairs of family, community and business life – good works which for all their earthliness are rooted in the fear of the Lord. 'Charm is deceitful, and beauty is vain, but a woman who fears the Lord, she is to be praised' (v. 30).

On a subtle and more indirect level, the song also contains a polemic against the intellectual ideal of Hellenism (as I also suggested in chapter 3). It is widely recognized that the Song of the Valiant Woman portrays its heroine as the personification of wisdom,[43] the incarnation of what it means to be wise. That this involves a critique of Greek intellectualism becomes evident if we recognize *ṣôpiyyâ* in verse 27 as a word-play on the Greek word *sophia*. The point of the song then becomes: not abstract theoretical wisdom rooted in impartial rationality is the praiseworthy ideal, but concrete practical wisdom rooted in the fear of the Lord.

On both levels it is the heroic colouring of the hymnic genre which highlights the concrete and active dimensions of the alternative ideal of womanly worth which the song celebrates.

The second factor to consider is the emergence within Judaism of a new interpretation of the *gĕbûrâ*, 'heroic prowess', which is so prominent in the historical books of the Hebrew Bible. In a recent article, 'Dangerous Hero: Rabbinic Attitudes Toward Legendary Warriors', Richard G. Marks has pointed out that the rabbinic response to the *gibbôrîm* of Israel's Heroic Age:

> took two literary forms: one was to glorify them in legend while warning against reliance on them; a second was to redefine *gevurah* so that its associated glory applied to academic and moral victories.[44]

It would seem that the Proverbs acrostic is an early variant of this second literary tradition. The heroism of the battlefield is transposed in this case

---

[43] Most recently by C.V. Camp, *Wisdom and the Feminine in the Book of Proverbs* (Sheffield: Almond, 1985), 186–91.
[44] *HUCA* 54 (1983), 181.

not to the academic and moral sphere but to a woman's *vita activa* in home and community.

By way of conclusion, I submit that a form-critical analysis of the Song of the Valiant Woman shows it to be a heroicizing hymn adapted to a wisdom context. To ignore its literary form, or to focus only on its sapiential features, is to miss important dimensions of this extraordinarily rich and complex song of praise.

2

Nature and Grace in the Interpretation of Proverbs 31:10–31

A point which has often arrested the attention of interpreters of the Song of the Valiant Woman, which concludes the book of Proverbs, is the relationship of the body of the poem, with its catalogue of the down-to-earth exploits of the lady portrayed, to verse 30b, which describes her as 'the woman who fears Yahweh'. The poem as a whole describes such mundane and this-worldly activities, and the theme of *yir'at YHWH* is so emphatically religious, that their juxtaposition within the same tightly-knit poetic structure has often evoked comment in the history of interpretation.

The poles of the relationship in question are readily identified, within the tradition of Christian theology, with the themes 'nature' and 'grace'. On the one hand we have the 'natural' realm, the arena of ordinary and everyday earthly activities and concerns; on the other hand we have the 'spiritual' realm, the domain of religion and worship. It is no secret that the relationship between nature and grace has historically been conceived in fundamentally different ways, and that the differing paradigms for construing that relationship correlate with profoundly divergent Christian attitudes to the perennial questions of Christ and culture, church and world, faith and reason.[1] It is perhaps legitimate to speak in this connection of different Christian *worldviews*.

In chapter one we saw the interpretive tendency, in focussing upon the Song's sapiential character and setting, to miss its hymnic qualities. It will be the purpose of this essay to explore another factor with the potential to limit and shape our readings; to show how different worldviews, understood in the sense of *traditional paradigms relating nature and grace*, have influenced the history of the interpretation of Proverbs 31:10–31 from

---

[1] See H.R. Niebuhr, *Christ and Culture* (New York: Harper and Row, 1951) for a typology of such attitudes.

patristic times to the present. In this way I propose to illustrate the more general point, too often neglected in biblical studies, that one's basic stance on this fundamental religious issue is of decisive significance in the exegesis and interpretation of the Scriptures. On that score there is no essential difference between early patristic and contemporary critical students of the Bible.

For present purposes I will distinguish four such worldviews, recognizing, of course, that other classifications are possible and legitimate as well.[2] Roughly speaking, and at the risk of falling prey to all the dangers of schematization, I propose to distinguish conceptions which look upon grace as *opposing*, as *completing*, as *flanking*, and as *restoring* nature.

In the first view, salvation is essentially incompatible with the ordinary world of created human life and provides a radical alternative to it. In the context of modern western Christendom, we find this worldview strongly represented in the Anabaptist tradition. The second one is that of classical Roman Catholicism, which speaks of a natural and a super-natural *ordo*, related in such a way that the latter 'perfects' the former, and the former is oriented to the latter. The third view, often associated with Lutheranism, sees nature and grace (at least in the present dispensation) as two realms alongside each other with little intrinsic connection between them. The fourth worldview, finally, resists every distinction of realms between nature and grace and insists that grace throughout means re-creation, an internal healing and renewal of perverted nature. In the modern west this view has been strong in the Calvinistic tradition.[3]

To make a play on Latin prepositions, we could say that these four paradigms construe *gratia* as *contra*, as *supra*, as *iuxta*, or as *intra naturam*. Each has been influential in the way in which the Song of Proverbs 31 has been interpreted.

It should be noted that in describing the four worldviews, a variety of expressions is used to refer to their basic categories. On the one hand we speak of 'nature', 'the secular', 'the natural', 'the created world', and so on,

---

[2] For example, Niebuhr, *Christ*, distinguishes five paradigms. See also the fivefold typology of my colleague J.H. Olthuis, 'Must the Church Become Secular?' in *Out of Concern for the Church* (Toronto: Wedge, 1970), 120.
[3] My analysis owes a great deal to the work of the Dutch theologian Herman Bavinck (1854–1921). See J. Veenhof, 'Nature and Grace in Bavinck' (tr. A. Wolters), academic paper distributed by the Institute for Christian Studies, 229 College Street, Toronto, ON, Canada M5T 1R4. This is a translation of a section in J. Veenhof, *Revelatie en Inspiratie* (Amsterdam: Buijten en Schipperheijn, 1968).

and on the other of 'grace', 'the religious', 'the spiritual', 'supra-nature', etc. These cannot be said to be strictly synonymous, nor, indeed, equally legitimate, but they are comparable as various designations of the basic terms of the classical 'nature–grace' problem. That problem, dealing with the reality of both the sin-perverted created order and the salvation provided in Jesus Christ, is basic to all Christian thought, though its terms are construed in fundamentally different ways. It is this single trans-paradigmatic reality which makes the divergent categories of the various worldview paradigms comparable in principle.

I. Gratia Contra Naturam

The first perspective looks upon 'the fear of the Lord' mentioned in 31:30 as basically incompatible with such everyday earthly activities as spinning and weaving, planting and trading, as are listed in the body of the poem. The religious and the secular simply cannot be mixed in this way. Consequently, to retain the integrity of the Song, either the one pole of the relationship must be spiritualized, or the other one must be secularized.

The first alternative is that followed, with very few exceptions, in patristic and medieval exegesis. The domestic activities of the Valiant Woman are spiritualized by making her an allegory of some other, more clearly spiritual, reality. For roughly a thousand years there was a widespread consensus on this point. Whereas the Jews generally took the poem to refer to the Torah,[4] Christians generally read it as a description of the church. To be sure, a few Christian exegetes proposed alternative allegories (the woman as wisdom[5] or Scripture[6] or the Virgin Mary[7]), but from Origen to the Reformation (and longer in Catholic circles) the allegorical interpretation held virtually undisputed sway. This was very largely due to the authority of Augustine, who devoted his *Sermo 37* to

---

[4] A. Altman, 'Allegorical Interpretation,' s.v. 'Bible,' *Encyclopaedia Judaica*, vol. 4: 'Rabbinic *aggadah* and Midrash employed the allegorical method in an uninhibited homiletic rather than in a systematic manner … The only exceptions are the allegorical interpretations of Proverbs 31:10–31 (the "woman of valor" being understood as the Torah) and of the Song of Songs' (cols. 895–96).

[5] E.g. Adam of Perseigne (twelfth century), *Mariale*, in Migne, *Patrologia Latina* 211, col. 734.

[6] So Nicholas of Lyra under the influence of Rashi (see n. 13).

[7] E.g. Julien de Vézelay (twelfth century). See his *Sermons*, Sources Chrétiennes 192–193 (Paris: Editions du Cerf, 1972), vol. 1, 90.

[8] Augustinus, *Sermones de Vetere Testamento*, Corpus Christianorum, Series Latina, vol. 41 (Turnholt: Brepols, 1961), 446–73.

the Song,[8] and of his followers Gregory the Great[9] and the Venerable Bede,[10] reinforced in the thirteenth century by a separate book-length commentary on the Song from the hand of Albertus Magnus.[11]

Two points should be noted about this allegorical consensus. First, a new spiritual meaning is given only to the 'natural' activities of the Valiant Woman (for example the treatment of flax in verse 13 refers to the mortification of the flesh, the planting of a vineyard in verse 16 symbolizes church-planting on the mission field, and so on[12]), but no new sense is required for verse 30 since this already has a spiritual significance.

Second, we must not suppose that this allegorical interpretation was taken to be merely one of the traditional four senses of this scriptural passage, existing alongside an equally legitimate literal interpretation. The remarkable thing is that even those medieval exegetes who stressed the literal sense (such as Rashi, Albertus Magnus, and Nicholas of Lyra) nevertheless interpreted the Valiant Woman as Scripture or the church. As Nicholas of Lyra explains and approves, they held that the figurative meaning here *constitutes* the literal sense:

> In the last part of this book is placed the praise of the valiant woman. It is commonly interpreted by our teachers to refer to the church, which is metaphorically called the valiant woman, and her husband Christ, whereas her sons and daughters are called the Christian people of both sexes. And they say that this is the literal sense, the way it says in Judges 9: The trees went to the bramble bush, etc. The literal sense does not refer to the physical trees, but to Abimelech and the Shechemites who anointed him king over them.[13]

---

[9] Gregory has no commentary on Proverbs, but the allegorical interpretation of the Song of Proverbs 31 is found scattered throughout his writings; see for example his *Registrum Epistolarum* 5. 12 and *Homiliae in Hiezechihelem Prophetam* 2. 18.

[10] Beda Venerabilis, *Super parabolas Salomonis allegorica expositio* in Migne, *Patrologia Latina* 91, cols. 937–1040; cf. 1039–52. Beda's commentary on the Song is also printed under the name of Hrabanus Maurus in Migne, *PL* 111, cols. 780–93.

[11] *Liber de Muliere Forti*, in *Alberti Magni Opera Omnia*, A. Borgnet (ed.), vol. 18 (Paris: Vivès, 1893), 1–242.

[12] See J. Obersteiner, 'Die Erklärung von Proverbia 31, 10–31, durch Beda den Ehrwürdigen und Bruno von Asti', *Theologisch–Praktische Quartalschrift* 102 (1954), 1–12.

[13] *Biblia latina cum postillis Nicolai de Lyra* (1481), on Prov. 31:10: 'In ultima parte huius libri ponitur commendatio fortis mulieris. Et exponitur communiter a doctoribus nostris de ecclesia, quae metaphorice dicitur fortis mulier, et sponsus eius Christus; filii autem et filiae populus Christianus in utroque sexu. Et dicunt quod iste est sensus litteralis, sicut Iudicum IX dicitur: Ierunt ligna ad rhamnum, etc. Sensus litteralis non est de lignis materialibus, sed de Abimelech, et Sichimitis eum super se regem inungentibus.' See also the influential *Postilla super totam*

Like the parable of the trees told by Jotham, the literal meaning of the Song of Proverbs 31, in this view, is clearly allegorical.

If an exegete shrinks back from spiritualizing the secular activities of the Valiant Woman, and yet sees them as essentially incongruous as works of 'the woman who fears the Lord', he has the other option of reversing the process, that is, of 'secularizing' the sacred, in order to bring it into line with the 'worldly' tenor of the poem as a whole.

Generally speaking, this is the approach taken by modern critical scholars. Adducing the Septuagint translation of verse 30 in support of their view, they argue that the original redaction of the Song spoke not of a 'woman who fears the Lord', but simply of an 'intelligent woman'. Originally, in other words, the poem was 'a secular song',[14] but the emendation of a 'pious scribe' made it acceptable as part of the sacred writings.

To my knowledge, this hypothesis of a scribal *pia fraus* was first put forward by C.H. Toy in 1902,[15] and it has been widely accepted since.[16] It is reflected also in a number of recent versions of the Bible, notably the first edition of the Jerusalem Bible,[17] which translates not the Masoretic Hebrew text, but the postulated *Vorlage*.

Again, there are two observations that are in order here. First, it will not do to claim that the scholars who advocate this text-critical

---

[13] (*Continued*) *Bibliam* of the thirteenth-century Hugo of St. Cher (printed in Basel, 1504) on Prov. 31:10: '*A valiant woman, who will find*, etc. Although this could be expounded literally [*ad litteram*] in some way, according to the text in Ecclesiastes 7 [v. 28]: "one man among a thousand have I found; but a woman among all those have I not found", yet, since the commentators make no mention of a literal exposition (and we have no wish to assume the office of prophet [*vaticinari*] at this point), we shall proceed with a mystical [i.e., allegorical] interpretation.'

[14] C. Kuhl, *Die Entstehung des Alten Testaments* (Bern/Munich: Franke, 1960²), 270, on Proverbs: 'A *secular song* (31, 10–31) forms the conclusion of the whole …' (Kuhl's emphasis).

[15] *A Critical and Exegetical Commentary on the Book of Proverbs*, International Critical Commentary (New York: Scribner, 1902 [c. 1899]), 548–50.

[16] Cf. W.O.E. Oesterley, *The Book of Proverbs* (London: Methuen, 1929), 287; B. Gemser, *Sprüche Salomos*, Handbuch zum Alten Testament (Tübingen: J.C.B. Mohr, 1937), 84; M.B. Crook, 'The Marriageable Maiden of Prov. 31:10–31' *Journal of Near Eastern Studies* 13 (1954), 137; R.B.Y. Scott, *Proverbs–Ecclesiastes*, The Anchor Bible (New York: Doubleday, 1965), 186; H.P. Rüger, 'Zum Text von Prv. 31, 30', *Die Welt des Orients* 5 (1969), 96–99; R.N. Whybray, *The Book of Proverbs* (Cambridge: Cambridge University Press, 1972), 186.

[17] The Masoretic reading is restored in the second (French) edition: *La Bible de Jérusalem* (Paris: Editions du Cerf, 1980). The English version follows the first edition.

reconstruction are themselves committed to a *gratia contra naturam* perspective. They may very well be agnostic on the issue. Instead they *impute* such a perspective to ancient Israel, or at least to the redactors of the text. Such an imputation, in turn, may well be influenced by experience of the traditional worldview here under consideration.

Second, it should be noted that the use to which the Septuagint is put in this case is quite dubious. A number of scholars have pointed out that the Septuagint can plausibly be taken to reflect the Masoretic text at this point.[18] Moreover, quite apart from this, it is questionable whether a different Hebrew *Vorlage* for the Septuagint should necessarily be taken as evidence of a more authentic text.[19] Decisions on such questions are notoriously subjective and not immune from the influence of (imputed) worldview.

We see, then, how strong has been the influence of the paradigm which sees grace and nature as essentially in conflict with one another. With respect to the interpretation of the Song of Proverbs 31, both the consensus of the patristic and medieval church, and that of a good deal of modern critical scholarship, seem to have been decisively affected by this dualistic worldview.

II. Gratia Supra Naturam

In the second worldview, 'nature' is no longer an exclusively negative category. Though still depreciated with respect to 'supra-nature', it is now given a legitimate, if subordinate, place. Its legitimacy derives from its being a preliminary to the spiritual, which therefore constitutes its fulfillment or culmination. This is the paradigm of the *duplex ordo* of official Roman Catholic teaching.

Antoine Augustin Calmet, a Benedictine exegete of the eighteenth century, gives clear expression to this perspective when he writes in his commentary on verse 30:

> To this point Solomon had hardly praised anything in his mother but virtues which, though rare, *did not transcend the natural order*. He established, as virtually exclusive evidence of her praiseworthy qualities, the diligence, alertness,

---

[18] E.g. J. Becker, *Gottesfurcht im Alten Testament* (Rome: Pontifical Biblical Institute, 1965), 212; J. Haspecker, *Gottesfurcht bei Jesus Sirach* (Rome: Pontifical Biblical Institute, 1967), 93, n. 15.

[19] See E. Würthwein, *The Text of the Old Testament* (Grand Rapids: Eerdmans, 1979), 64.

discipline, and efficient administration of the famous lady; here, however, he teaches that all these qualities, indeed even her very beauty and her charms, are worthless and of no avail unless the fear of God, piety and true Wisdom *are added to them*.[20]

Particularly telling here is the idea that the fear of the Lord must 'be added' (*accedere*) in order to give value to the *naturalis ordo*. The spiritual is a kind of adjunct which elevates the status of the natural.

In the twentieth century this perspective comes through clearly in a popular book written by Michael von Faulhaber, a German cardinal trained in Old Testament studies. Commenting on Proverbs 31:30, he writes:

> The pearl of women has not forgotten the one thing needful amid all the Martha-cares of her busy life, but by her fear of God she has set the crown on all her life's work.[21]

Here the 'fear of God' and 'her life's work', correlated with 'the one thing needful' and 'Martha-cares' (an allusion to the story in Lk. 10:38–42), are clearly distinguished, and the former is conceived as *crown* in relation to the latter, a fitting image of the hierarchical subordination of the natural order.

Because this worldview makes such a clear distinction between the natural and the spiritual, it also lends itself to a combination with the critical view of the text mentioned under Section I above. We find such a combination, for example, in the article on Proverbs in the *New Catholic Encyclopedia* by W.G. Heidt:

> Apart from 31:30b, which could possibly be a later scribal modification, the virtues attributed to the ideal wife are wholly in the natural order: she seemingly has no other purpose than laboring for husband and household. However, these passages may be a final example of how secular compositions were taken over by the wisdom editors and spiritualized by being immersed in

---

[20] Augustinus Calmet, *Commentarius Literalis in Omnes Libros Veteris Testamenti*, Latinis literis traditus a Joanne Dominico Mansi vol. 6 (Wirceburgi: Rienner, 1792), 759 (my emphasis): 'Hactenus Salomon vix aliud in matre sua laudaverat quam virtutes, raras illas quidem, sed quae naturalem ordinem non superarent. Argumentum laudum suarum ferme unicum constituit industriam, vigilantiam, disciplinam, oeconomiam illustris foeminae: hic autem docet, hasce omnes laudes, quin et pulchritudinem ipsam et lepores, nisi Dei timor, pietas, et vera Sapientia accedant, inanes esse et nihil'.
[21] *The Women of the Bible* (Westminster, MD: Newman, 1938), 23.

the wisdom context, which oriented all human endeavor toward God. Verse 30b, then, would be an authentic expression of the sacred author's mind and purpose.[22]

It is especially expressions like 'the natural order', 'secular compositions', 'spiritualized', and 'sacred author', which reveal the structure of a nature/supra-nature framework, here ingeniously interwoven with a conjecture of redaction criticism. The 'scribal modification', in this view, does not *bring about* the spiritualization (as in Paradigm 1) but *expresses* a spiritualization which has already taken place by being 'immersed in the wisdom context'. The insertion of the poem into the spiritual order, therefore, is here more gradual and does not involve outright falsification. Grace is the *culmination* of nature.

III. Gratia Iuxta Naturam

Whereas the first paradigm has been most influential in the history of interpreting the Song of the Valiant Woman, and the second has had the greatest institutional authority, the third has perhaps had the smallest impact, at least in published commentaries. Moreover, it is closely akin to the second worldview in that it gives a separate and legitimate province to both the natural and the spiritual and could therefore (for some purposes) be classed with it.

I devote a distinct section to it here for two reasons: because as world-view it does have a distinctive structure which marks it off from the classical Roman Catholic view (notably the absence of hierarchical sub-ordination), and because Luther has supplied us with a particularly striking quote which gives apt expression to this kind of two-realm conception.

It must be remembered that it was probably Luther, or else (under his influence) Melanchthon,[23] who first broke the spell of the allegorical interpretation of the Song of the Valiant Woman. This must undoubtedly be understood in the context of the overall revalidation of natural life in

---

[22] *New Catholic Encyclopedia* vol. 11 (New York: McGraw-Hill, 1967), 916.

[23] See his *Nova Scholia in Proverbia Salomonis* (1529) reprinted in P.F. Barton (ed.), *Melanchthons Werke in Auswahl*, vol. 4 (Gütersloh: Mohn, 1963), 463, as well as his *Explicatio Proverbiorum Salomonis* (1555), found in C.G. Bretschneider (ed.), *Philippi Melancthonis Opera quae Supersunt Omnia*, vol. 14 (Halle: Schwetschke, 1847), col. 86: 'But this whole passage must be understood simply, without allegory, as the mirror of an honourable lady.'

the Reformation and particularly of Luther's doctrine of *Beruf* or vocation. This is clearly evident in Melanchthon's commentaries on the
Song.[24]

Luther did, however, maintain a clear duality between a natural realm
and a spiritual realm. This comes out plainly in a note which he jotted
down in the margin of his translation of Proverbs 31:30:

> That is to say, a woman can live with a man honourably and piously and can
> with a good conscience be a housewife, but she must also, in addition and next
> to this, fear God, have faith and pray. [25]

The Song's reference to the fear of the Lord, in other words, reminds us
that while it is perfectly legitimate to be engaged in the worldly realm,
there is another realm as well, distinct from the former and next to it
(*darneben*) where the fear of the Lord, faith, and prayer have their place.
Nature is not subordinate to grace, but neither does it have any intrinsic
connection with it.

The same perspective is reflected in Melanchthon's *Explicatio Proverbiorum Salomonis* of 1555, in which the Song is analysed in terms of two
kinds of virtues: those summarized in verse 30 (related to the first table of
the Decalogue) and those listed in the body of the poem (related to the
second table). The two kinds, once distinguished, are simply listed in
juxtaposition to each other:

> The third part [of the chapter] is a song about the virtues of an honourable
> mother of a household. Now as for all people the Decalogue must be the rule
> of life, so let the virtues in this panegyric be referred severally to the
> Decalogue. And the saying in this passage: 'The woman who fears God shall
> be praised,' belongs to the first table.
>
> By *fear*, however, we must understand all true worship, the true
> acknowledgement of God, fear, faith, prayer, love of God, and other
> associated virtues ...

---

[24] The *Nova Scholia* (1529) twice speak of woman's *vocatio* in commenting on the
Song, and the later *Explicatio* (1555) similarly states that in it 'the chief virtues and
duties of her *calling* are listed' (col. 86).

[25] *Martin Luthers Werke, Kritische Gesamtausgabe, Die Deutsche Bibel*, Band 10
(Weimar: Böhlau, 1957), 103: 'Das ist, Eine fraw kan bey einem Manne ehrlich
und göttlich wonen, und mit gutem gewissen Hausfraw sein, Sol aber darüber
und darneben Gott fürchten, glauben und beten.' This handwritten note was first
printed in the second 1543 edition of Luther's Bible translation. For its earlier
history, see ibid., Band 4, xxxiii and 29.

Next are listed the remaining virtues: chastity in marriage, love for her husband without crankiness, diligence in all the tasks about the house, thriftiness, frugality ...[26]

In Melanchthon's view the virtues enjoined by the first table of the Decalogue seem to be relatively detachable from those commanded in the second table.

IV. Gratia Intra Naturam

The fourth worldview is distinct from the first three in that it rejects any division of nature and grace into separate realms. In this view the spiritual penetrates into the natural, transforming it from within. Because of this, it has a more positive view of nature (the good creation) than any of the others since grace is here seen to serve its restoration.

Applied to the Song of Proverbs 31, this paradigm fosters an interpretation which looks upon the fear of the Lord as integral to the poem as a whole. Religion is not restricted to verse 30, but pervades the whole.

Historically, this interpretation has often been associated with interpreters of the Calvinist tradition. A good example is the note on the Song which is given by J.F. Ostervald, a Swiss Reformed theologian of the eighteenth century:

It must not be supposed that what is said in this chapter relates only to the maxims and duties of running a household. It is religion which enjoins on women these very duties, and the qualities which Solomon praises in the persons of this sex are those which recommend them in God's eyes.[27]

---

[26] *Opera*, vol. 14, cols. 85–86: 'Tertia pars carmen est de virtutibus honestae Matrisfamilias. Ut autem singulis hominibus vitae regula esse debet Decalogus, ita in hac laudatione distribuantur virtutes in Decalogum, et ad primam tabulam pertinet dictum hoc loco, Mulier timens Deum, laudabitur.

Timor autem intelligatur totus verus cultus, vera Dei agnitio, Timor, Fides, Invocatio, dilectio Dei, et aliae coniunctae virtutes ...

Deinde recitantur caeterae virtutes. Castitas coniugalis, amor erga maritum sine morositate, sedulitas in omnibus laboribus oeconomicis, Parsimonia, Frugalitas ...'

[27] See *La Sainte Bible ... avec Les Nouveaux Argumens et les Nouvelles Réflexions ...* par J.F. Ostervald (Amsterdam: F. Bernard et Herman, 1724), 543: 'Il ne faut pas croire que ce qui est dit dans ce Chapitre, ne soient que des maximes et des devoirs d'Oeconomie. La Religion impose aux femmes ces mêmes devoirs; et les qualitez que Salomon loüe dans les personnes de ce Sexe, sont celles qui les rendent recommandables devant Dieu.'

In other words, the good management of a household is itself a religious duty by which women please God.

The same point is made by Abraham Kuyper, the leader of Dutch Neocalvinism, in his discussion of the Song:

> In the beautiful song in which Lemuel drew for his son the picture of the vir-tuous woman, there is almost no mention of the quiet, inner virtues of this woman. To be sure, it does say that she 'feareth the Lord,' but this too is understood of the outside, not the inside. A woman who demonstrates in her *home management* that she does not pursue vanity but fears the Lord, she shall be *praised.*[28]

Here the woman's household activities are seen, not as something opposed to, or even distinct from, her fear of the Lord, but rather as its *external manifestation*.

The exegetes of this tradition are quite conscious of bringing a distinct perspective to bear on the interpretation of the Song, especially as regards the value and status of 'natural' life. The English Puritan Thomas Cartwright, for example, in his influential seventeenth-century commentary on the book of Proverbs, after pointing out that the Valiant Woman is pictured at 31:19 as personally engaged in the lowly task of spinning, adds the comment:

> This passage must be given careful attention in order to establish us more firmly in the common duties of this life as duties pleasing to God, against the Anabaptists, who judge them to be too lowly to be engaged in by Christians, and against the Papists, who, although they do not condemn this kind of work, nevertheless, in that they exalt so highly the works of their own devising belonging to their innovations, which have never been approved by the Holy Spirit, slacken the hands of godly women.[29]

---

[28] A. Kuyper, *Als gij in uw huis zit* (Amsterdam: Höeveker en Wormser, 1899), 66: 'In den schoonen zang toch, waarin Lemuel voor zijn zoon het beeld der deugdelijke huisvrouw uitteekende, staat over de stille zielsdeugden van deze vrouw bijna niets. Er staat wel "dat ze den Heere vreest," maar ook dit wordt niet van den binnenkant, maar van den buitenkant genomen. Een vrouw die in *haar huishouding* toont, niet de ijdelheid na te jagen, maar den Heere te vreezen, zal *geprezen* worden.'

[29] T. Cartwright, *Commentarii succincti et dilucidi in Proverbia Salomonis* (Amsterdam: Laurentius, 1638), col. 1318: 'Hic locus observandus est ad nos in communibus hujus vitae officiis, tanquam Deo gratis confirmandum, contra Anabaptistas, qui abjectiora esse statuunt, quam ut christiani se in iis exerceant, et Pontificios, qui, tametsi hujusmodi opera non damnent, dum tamen commentitia suarum novarum opera nusquam a Spiritu Sancto probata tantopere efferunt, manus piarum foeminarum remissiores faciunt.'

The polemic against the Anabaptists and the Roman Catholics is here directed at their depreciation of the *communia huius vitae officia*, that is, the everyday tasks of natural life, such as the humble work of spinning thread. Cartwright clearly distinguishes the radical perspective of the Anabaptists (Paradigm 1) from the more moderate one of the Roman Catholics (Paradigm 2). He does not mention the third worldview, probably because in the Reformation Lutherans and Calvinists made common cause against what they perceived as the downgrading of the intrinsic creational goodness of natural life on the part of Anabaptist and Catholic writers.

It would be a great mistake, however, to suppose that the type of worldview reflected in the interpretation of the Song of the Valiant Woman is simply a reflex of an exegete's ecclesiastical affiliation. To be sure, this does largely seem to be the case in the time of the Reformation and the three centuries which followed it, but there is no such neat correlation between worldview and confessional tradition in the last hundred years or so. Increasingly, traditional paradigms relating nature and grace are transdenominational, no doubt under the influence of the rise of critical scholarship and the ecumenical movement. This is not to say, however, that the basic worldview paradigms no longer play a decisive role; instead they show up in less predictable contexts.

Linked to this weakening in the correlation of worldview and ecclesiastical communion is another trend that can be observed in the last century of interpretation of Proverbs 31:10–31. Although, as we have seen, Paradigms 1 and 2 are still very much alive in scholarly interpretation, and though Paradigm 3 is probably still operative in many devotional commentaries, there does seem to be a movement away from these on the part of the majority of biblical scholars.

This is evidenced by a kind of ecumenical convergence toward Paradigm 4 in modern interpretations of Proverbs 31:10–31. This growing consensus finds expression in two interrelated themes which have been repeatedly emphasized by exegetes of the Song since the late nineteenth century. The first theme is that all the Valiant Woman's actions are rooted in (or even constitute) her fear of the Lord; the second is that she represents the concrete embodiment of that wisdom whose beginning is the fear of the Lord.

As an example of the first theme we can quote Franz Delitzsch, the great Lutheran exegete of the nineteenth century. In his commentary on the Song he writes:

the poet … refers back all these virtues and accomplishments of hers to the fear of God as to their root.[30]

This is an emphasis which we find repeated in such Old Testament scholars as H. Schultz,[31] A.B. Ehrlich,[32] B. Gemser,[33] W.H. Gispen,[34] and M.A. Klopfenstein,[35] as well as in devotional commentaries.[36]

The second theme is that of the Valiant Woman as the personification of Wisdom – not in an allegorical sense, but in the sense of an earthly embodiment of what it means to be wise. We find this interpretation expressed, for example, in the commentary of G. Currie Martin, who writes that the Song was probably added to Proverbs because 'it embodied some of the ideals of practical wisdom that had been already inculcated'.[37] This theme is echoed in a number of subsequent commentators of various confessional allegiances. These include A. MacLaren,[38]

---

[30] F. Delitzsch, *Das Salomonische Spruchbuch* (Leipzig: Dorffling und Franke, 1873), 527: 'der Dichter führt alle diese ihre Tugenden und Leistungen auf die Gottesfurcht als ihre Wurzel zurück.'

[31] H. Schultz, *Alttestamentliche Theologie, Die Offenbarungsreligion auf ihrer vorchristlichen Entwickelungsstufe* (Göttingen: Vandenhoeck und Ruprecht, 1889⁴), 196: 'Prov. 31:10–31 shows us the exemplary housewife, and looks upon such a faithful fulfillment of duty as *fear of the Lord* (30).' This statement is made under the general heading 'The root of all morality is *fear of the Lord*.'

[32] A.B. Ehrlich, *Randglossen zur Hebräischen Bibel*, fünfter Band (Leipzig: Hinrichs, 1912), 179: 'Our heroine's fear of the Lord consists chiefly in the fact that she frees her husband from all the cares of life.'

[33] B. Gemser, *De Spreuken van Salomo*, Text en Uitleg, vol. 2 (Groningen/Den Haag: Wolters, 1929–31), 50: 'he looks upon the fear of the Lord as the foundation and summary of all virtues' (on 31:30).

[34] W.H. Gispen, *De Spreuken van Salomo*, Korte Verklaring, vol. 2 (Kampen: Kok, 1952–54), 350: 'Also the pluckiness [*flinkheid*] celebrated in this poem is rooted in the fear of the Lord' (on 31:30).

[35] M.A. Klopfenstein, *Die Lüge nach dem Alten Testament* (Zurich: Gotthelf, 1964), 174: 'not her charm and beauty, but her fear of the Lord, from which all the acclaimed virtues must spring as from their root, if they are to be true virtues' (on Prov. 31:30).

[36] E.g. the *Stuttgarter Jubiläumsbibel* (Stuttgart: Württembergische Bibelanstalt, 1953) on Prov. 31:30: 'Such a woman, whose domestic excellence and virtue is rooted in the fear of the Lord …'

[37] G.C. Martin, *Proverbs, Ecclesiastes and Song of Songs*, The New Century Bible (New York/Edinburgh: H. Frowde, 1908), 12.

[38] A. MacLaren, *Expositions of Holy Scripture*, vol. 3: *II Kings–Ecclesiastes* (Grand Rapids: Eerdmans, 1942), 294.

A. Barucq,[39] B. Lang,[40] P.E. Bonnard,[41] and H. Schüngel–Straumann.[42]

The two themes we have discussed come together in a summary statement by Helmer Ringgren in his commentary on the Song. Having pointed out how highly the poet prizes the value of a good housewife, he writes:

> This comports well with the general theme of Proverbs, for wisdom in the broad sense of the word is precisely all that enables a person to succeed in life. The excellent housewife, too, stands as an example of such wisdom. And just as wisdom and fear of the Lord were one in the eyes of the collectors of Proverbs, so also the virtues of the good housewife have their roots in her fear of the Lord.[43]

In this view, the 'fear of the Lord' of verse 30 is both the root of the Valiant Woman's actions and the 'beginning' of the wisdom which they exemplify. In other words, her praiseworthy deeds in home and community *flow from* her religious confession and allow no opposition or dichotomy between the secular and the sacred, between nature and grace.[44]

I conclude by observing that the main thesis, the influence of worldview on (the history of) exegesis, can be effectively illustrated in the case of Proverbs 31:10–31. I do not claim that worldview is always decisive in questions of interpretation, nor that other factors do not play a

---

[39] A. Barucq, 'Proverbes, Livre des' in *Dictionnaire de la Bible, Supplément*, Tome huitième (Paris: Letouzey et Ané, 1972), cols. 1466 and 1468.

[40] B. Lang, *Anweisungen gegen die Torheit, Sprichwörter-Jesus Sirach* (Stuttgart: KBW Verlag, 1973), 52–53.

[41] P.E. Bonnard, 'De la Sagesse personnifiée dans l'Ancien Testament à la Sagesse en personne dans le Nouveau' in M. Gilbert (ed.), *La Sagesse de l'Ancien Testament* (Louvain: Duculot, 1979), 127–128.

[42] H. Schüngel-Straumann, 'Die wahre Frau' in *Christ in der Gegenwart* 33 (1981), 385.

[43] H. Ringgren, *Sprüche*, Das Alte Testament Deutsch, 16/1 (Göttingen: Vandenhoeck und Ruprecht, 1962), 121: 'Das passt gut zum allgemeinen Thema der Sprüche, denn Weisheit im weiteren Sinne des Wortes ist eben alles was den Menschen zum Erfolg im Leben befähigt. Als ein Beispiel solcher Weisheit steht auch die tüchtige Hausfrau da. Und ebenso wie Weisheit und Gottesfurcht den Sammlern der Sprüche eins sind, so haben auch die Tugenden der guten Hausfrau ihre Wurzeln in ihrer Gottesfurcht.'

[44] Cf. also Barucq, 'Proverbes', col. 1467: 'The vignette which he engraves at the bottom of the page is intended as an idealized projection of the blossoming [*épanouissement*] into the everyday of a life grounded in a Yahwist wisdom.' If we delete the words 'a life grounded in,' this formulation is freed from all suspicion of a lingering nature–grace duality.

crucial role. But at least in the selected test case – and perhaps elsewhere – the dimension of worldview, understood in the sense defined in this essay, is shown to be a significant determinative factor in biblical interpretation. This is of interest not only to the historian of exegesis, but also to the practising exegete who accepts the Bible's claims to authority. For my thesis leads to the conclusion that biblical interpretation can only be properly done if it is informed by a worldview which is itself biblical, and so provides a legitimate two-way link between biblical studies and systematic theology.

3

Ṣôpiyyâ (Prov. 31:27) as Hymnic Participle and Play on Sophia*

It is well known, as we have already seen, that the Song of the Valiant Woman at the end of the book of Proverbs (31:10–31) is an alphabetical acrostic. According to the rules of this genre, the eighteenth verse of the poem (31:27) must begin with the eighteenth Hebrew letter, ṣādê, a requirement that the poet meets by composing the following two hemistichs:

> She looks well to [ṣôpiyyâ] the ways of her household,
> and does not eat the bread of idleness (RSV).

It is the verb form ṣôpiyyâ, also translated 'she watches over' or 'supervises', that is here chosen to fit the acrostic pattern.

But the initial word of this verse is of interest for two further reasons – because it is a *participle* and because it is an uncommon *form* of the participle. All the other verbs describing the praiseworthy deeds of the Valiant Woman are in the perfect and the imperfect (regularly of the qāṭĕlâ form, occasionally followed by a *wattiqṭōl*),[1] so that we would expect 'she watches over' to be expressed as ṣāpĕtâ, the regular feminine singular form of the perfect, analogous to 'āśĕtâ ('she makes') in verse 24, lĕbûšâ ('she is clothed') in verse 25, and pātĕḥâ ('she opens') in verse 26. Instead, in verse 27, we are confronted with a participle. Moreover, the form of the participle is also not what we would expect. The regular qal form of the feminine singular would be ṣôpâ, but the poet at this point chooses instead

* I would like to thank R.K. Harrison (Wycliffe College, Toronto) and R. Van Leeuwen (Calvin Seminary, Grand Rapids, Michigan) for reading an earlier draft of this paper.
[1] See P. Joüon, 'Les temps dans Proverbes 31, 10–31 (La femme forte)', *Bib* 3 (1922), 349–52.

to use the much rarer inflection *ṣôpiyyâ*.[2] In other words, *ṣôpiyyâ* in verse 27 is unusual not only from a syntactical but also from a morphological point of view.

This double anomaly has led to some confusion in the ancient versions. The LXX, Peshitta, and Targum construe the Hebrew word (presumably in its unvocalized form *ṣwpyh*) as the predicate of a nominal sentence. The Greek translation has *stegnai hai diatribai oikōn autēs*, 'the occupations of her households are strict', which is reflected also in the VL,[3] whereas the Syriac and Aramaic render the Hebrew form with words meaning 'open' or 'manifest'.[4] Although it has been suggested that these renderings presuppose another Hebrew *Vorlage*, it is more likely that they are unsuccessful attempts to interpret the puzzling form *ṣwpyh*.[5] It is not until the translations of Symmachus (*skopeuei*)[6] and Jerome (*consideravit*) that the Hebrew word is correctly construed and vocalized as a less common participial form of the verb *ṣāpâ*, 'to keep watch (as a lookout)', so that the Valiant Woman is here being said, quite appropriately, to be 'keeping a sharp eye on' the activities of her household.[7]

---

[2] See E. Kautzsch, *Gesenius' Hebrew Grammar* (Oxford: Clarendon, 1910), 212 (§ 75v). This form of the feminine participle is found only in *lamed-he* verbs.

[3] 'Severae conversationes domorum eius' (see Augustine *Sermo* XXXVII, CCSL 41, 467).

[4] According to A. Vööbus (ed.), *The Didascalia Apostolorum in Syriac* (CSCO; Louvain: Secrétariat du Corpus-SCO, 1979), 23, n. 41 (Peshitta) and P. de Lagarde (ed.), *Hagiographa chaldaica* (Leipzig, 1873; reprinted Osnabrück: O. Zeller, 1967) (Targum).

[5] A.J. Baumgartner very ingeniously takes an original *ṣĕpúyôt* (passive participle agreeing with *hălikôt*, 'ways') to underlie all three versions, suggesting that the Peshitta and Targum reflect one sense of *sph* ('watch') and that the LXX reflects its other attested meaning ('overlay', 'plate') (*Etude critique sur l'état du texte du livre des Proverbes* [Leipzig: W. Drugulin, 1890], 246). In the first case, the postulated semantic development is 'watched' – 'open to view' – 'manifest'; in the second it is 'overlaid (with metal)' – 'impervious' (cf. 'iron-clad'). Though this reconstructed *Vorlage* meets with a number of objections (a passive participle *ṣāpúy* is unattested in the OT, whereas 'plated' is expressed with the pu'al *mĕṣuppeh*; the semantic development is merely guessed at in any case), it may well represent a *varia lectio*. However, it is not to be preferred to the MT, since the meaning 'she keeps watch' comports better with the Song's emphasis throughout on the woman's valiant *deeds*.

[6] As cited in F. Field (ed.), *Origenis Hexaplorum quae supersunt Fragmenta*, vol. 2 (Oxford: Clarendon, 1875), 375.

[7] Compare the cognate words *ṣôpeh*, 'watchman,' 'lookout', and *ṣippiyyâ*, 'watch-tower'. The connotation of the word seems to be 'overseeing from a high lookout post'.

This reading of the word (now enshrined in the vocalization of the MT) is almost universally accepted by modern translators and exegetes, who take it to mean simply 'she watches over', parallel to the other main verbs of the context. Only rarely does a commentator point out that the form of the verb is unusual, although it is true that on one occasion the morphological peculiarity has led to a proposal to emend the text.[8] Most commentaries ignore the verb's anomalous form altogether,[9] as does the article by Joüon, which is specifically devoted to the verbal forms used in the poem.[10]

Although we have no reason to suspect the MT at this point, and although some such translation as 'she watches over' is entirely appropriate, the double oddity of the form *ṣôpiyyâ* does call for some explanation. It will be our contention that it can in fact be explained: first as a so-called 'hymnic participle', and second as a Hebrew pun on the Greek word *sophia*.

I. *Ṣôpiyyâ* as Hymnic Participle

The discussion in chapter 1 showed that, as a rule, form-critical studies have tended to neglect the acrostic poem of Proverbs 31, usually mentioning it, if at all, only in a passing reference in discussions of *Weisheitsdichtung*,[11] particularly of the so-called wisdom psalms.[12] Yet, as we saw, there can be no doubt that the poem in fact shows many features of the genre 'hymn' or song of praise. Indeed, outside of form-critical discussions, it is often described in the German literature by such words as

---

[8] See M.T. Houtsma, 'Aanteekeningen op het boek der Spreuken', *Theologisch Tijdschrift* 53 (1919), 31: 'De Grieksche en Arameesche vertalingen zagen in *ṣwpyh* een part. pass., behoorende bij *hlykwt*, waarvoor ook de vorm van het woord pleit, te meer omdat men volgens de gewone opvatting evenals in de vorige verzen een Perf. moest verwachten (*spth*).' It would seem that Houtsma is here dependent on Baumgartner (see note 5).

[9] An exception is F. Delitzsch, who refutes F. Hitzig's proposal to construe *ṣôpiyyâ* with the suffix of the preceding *lĕšônāh* by referring to the participles in Is. 40:22–23 and Ps. 104:13–14. See his *Das Salomonische Spruchbuch* (Leipzig: Dörffling und Franke, 1873), 537.

[10] Joüon, 'Les temps', 349–52.

[11] H. Gunkel, *Einleitung in die Psalmen* (Göttingen: Vandenhoeck & Ruprecht, 1933), 383; A. Weiser, *Einleitung in das Alte Testament* (Göttingen: Vandenhoeck & Ruprecht, 1966⁶), 46.

[12] O. Eissfeldt, *The Old Testament: An Introduction* (Oxford: Blackwell, 1965), 125; L.G. Perdue, *Wisdom and Cult* (Missoula, MT: Scholars Press, 1977), 329.

Preislied,[13] *Lobpreis,*[14] *Loblied,*[15] and *Lobeshymnus.*[16] H.W. Wolff even speaks
explicitly of 'der grosse Hymnus auf die tüchtige Frau'.[17]
Nor is it only the content of the poem that justifies such a description.
A number of the formal features of the genre *Hymnus,* as described by
Gunkel and his followers, are also found in the song in praise of the Valiant
Woman. Its overall structure, for example, conforms to the pattern of the
classic hymn: introduction (vv. 10–12); body [*Hauptstück*], enumerating
praiseworthy attributes and deeds (vv. 13–27); and concluding call to
praise (vv. 28–31).[18] Individual words and phrases also recall the hymnic
style, such as 'let her works praise her' (v. 31), which in its Hebrew
form (*wî*)*halĕlû-hā* is strongly reminiscent of the familiar *halĕlû-yāh* which
characterizes the hymns of the Psalter.

Having explored them in chapter 1, we need not point out all the
hymnic features of the song of Proverbs 31 here. Our immediate concern
is to show that it shares another characteristic feature of the hymn: in
describing the praiseworthy deeds of the mighty one being acclaimed, the
hymn typically uses a participial form of the verb, frequently when the
context is dominated by the tenses of description or narration.[19] Gunkel
calls such forms 'hymnische Partizipien'.

F. Crüsemann has made a careful study of the participle used in this
way.[20] He provides an almost exhaustive list of over a hundred instances of
this usage in the OT, failing only to mention *ṣôpiyyâ* in Proverbs 31:27. It
is interesting that his list does include the participles in Isaiah 40:22–23
and Psalm 104:13–14, the places to which Franz Delitzsch refers to
account for the unusual participle describing the watchfulness of the
Valiant Woman.[21] Crüsemann's list includes also Psalm 113:6a, where
God is described in a hymn as one 'looking down from on high', just as

[13] A. Wünsche, *Die Schönheit der Bibel. Erster Band: Die Schönheit des Alten Testaments* (Leipzig: E. Pfeiffer, 1906), 327.
[14] H. Rahner, *Maria und die Kirche* (Innsbruck: Marianischer Verlag, 1951), 86.
[15] Ibid.
[16] J. Obersteiner, 'Die Erklärung von Proverbia 31, 10-31, durch Beda den Ehrwürdigen und Bruno von Asti', *TPQ* 102 (1954), 1.
[17] H.W. Wolff, *Anthropologie des Alten Testaments* (Munich: Kaiser, 1973), 250.
[18] Gunkel, *Einleitung,* 33–59. See also H. Gunkel, *The Psalms: A Form-Critical Introduction* (Philadelphia: Fortress, 1967, 10–12).
[19] Gunkel, *Einleitung,* 44–45. See also S. Mowinckel, *The Psalms in Israel's Worship* (Oxford: Blackwell, 1962), 1. 83, n. 19.
[20] F. Crüsemann, *Studien zur Formgeschichte von Hymnus und Danklied in Israel* (Neukirchen–Vluyn: Neukirchener Verlag, 1969), 81–154.
[21] See n. 9.

ṣôpiyyâ suggests a looking down from a watchtower.[22] Often the hymnic participle, as in Proverbs 31:27, is an isolated form among the finite verbs of the context.

II. Ṣôpiyyâ as Play on Sophia

Consequently, although we may still wonder why a hymnic participle is used only at this particular point of the song, the syntactical oddity of ṣôpiyyâ can be said to be accounted for, at least in the sense that it is shown to fit a wider pattern of formal characteristics of the hymnic genre. But what of the morphological peculiarity? Why did the composer of the song of Proverbs 31 choose the participial form ṣôpiyyâ rather than the more usual inflection, which would have been ṣôpâ?

In the absence, as here, of considerations of meter or euphony which would clearly favor one form over the other, such a question would normally be unanswerable. Even the circumstance that one form can be construed as a Hebrew transliteration of a key word in a neighboring language (here the Greek *sophia*) could be dismissed as a curious but trivial statistical fluke, comparable to the coincidence that *lābûš* in verse 21 can be read as the French *la bouche*. But the situation changes if it can be shown that the homonymous foreign word designates the very concept that exegetes have found, on other grounds, to be the central theme of the poem in question. In other words, if it is true that many different interpreters of Proverbs 31:10–31 have taken the Valiant Woman to be the personification of *wisdom*, then it can hardly be dismissed as accidental that the doubly unusual form ṣôpiyyâ should spell the Greek word precisely for *wisdom*. This conclusion becomes even more compelling when we note that the hemistich in which the word appears makes good contextual sense whether ṣôpiyyâ is construed as the Hebrew verb or the Greek noun, and that deliberate syntactical ambiguity following this pattern is a recurring feature of the poem as a whole. We turn to each one of these points in turn.

It would carry us too far afield to discuss all the evidence that has been or can be adduced to show that the Valiant Woman of Proverbs 31 is pictured as the personification of wisdom. We will limit ourselves to naming a number of those exegetes, ancient and modern, who have come to this conclusion, and we refer the reader to the works of the more recent interpreters for the details of the argumentation.

Before we do so, we must point out an ambiguity in the phrase

---

[22] Crüsemann, *Studien*, 144; see n. 7.

'personification of wisdom'. This can mean either the *allegorical symbol* or the *concrete embodiment* of wisdom. Bearing in mind both this double meaning and the impact upon the interpretation of the Song that various worldviews were shown to have in chapter 2, we can say that almost every age and persuasion in the history of exegesis has yielded examples of the interpretation of the Valiant Woman as the personification of wisdom.

In the tradition of allegorical interpretation, the Valiant Woman has been taken as representing wisdom[23] since patristic exegetes like Hilary of Poitiers[24] and Ambrose of Milan.[25] Recently this interpretation has been revived by Edmond Jacob, the well-known French OT scholar. In an article entitled 'Sagesse et Alphabet: A propos de Proverbes 31:10–31',[26] he presents an independent argument in favor of viewing the Valiant Woman as an allegory of wisdom, apparently unaware that he is thereby perpetuating a long subtradition in the history of interpretation.[27]

The *non*-allegorical interpretation of the Valiant Woman as personification of wisdom seems to begin with the twentieth century. This is the view that the Valiant Woman represents wisdom in action and that her deeds are the practical and concrete incarnation of what it means to be wise. We find brief expressions of this interpretation in Martin (1908), MacLaren (1942), Ringgren (1962), Heidt (1967), Barucq (1972), Lang (1973) and Schüngel-Straumann (1981).[28] A more sustained argument in

---

[23] Note that this tradition much more commonly takes the Valiant Woman as representing the Torah (among Jewish exegetes) or the church (among Christian exegetes).

[24] *PL* 9, 708.

[25] *PL* 14, 669 and 788–89.

[26] In *Hommages à André Dupont-Sommer* (Paris: Adrien-Maisonneuve, 1971), 287–95.

[27] Also including, for example, Pseudo-Procopius of Gaza (*PG* 87, 1, 1535–44), Adam of Perseigne (*PL* 211, 734), and notably R. Stier, *Die Politik der Weisheit in den Worten Agur's und Lemuel's. Sprüchworter Kap. 30 und 31* (Barmen: Lange-wiesche, 1850).

[28] G. Currie Martin, *Proverbs, Ecclesiastes and Song of Songs* (NCB; New York and Edinburgh: H. Frowde, 1908), 12: the acrostic was added to Proverbs 'by some scribe who felt that it embodied some of the ideals of practical wisdom that had been already inculcated'; see also Martin's notes on Prov. 31:11,13–16 (203–4). A. MacLaren, *Expositions of Holy Scripture*, vol. 3, *II Kings–Ecclesiastes* (Grand Rapids: Eerdmans, 1942), 294: 'The old legend of the descending deity who took service as a goatherd, is true of the heavenly Wisdom, which will come and live in kitchens and shops'. Helmer Ringgren, *Sprüche* (ATD; Göttingen: Vandenhoeck & Ruprecht, 1962), 121: 'Als ein Beispiel solcher Weisheit steht auch die tüchtige Hausfrau da.' W.G. Heidt, 'Proverbs, Book of', *NCE* 11, 916: 'wisdom exemplified in the ideal housewife'; A. Barucq, 'Proverbes, Livre des', *DBSup* 8,

favor of this interpretation is found in a recent major article by P.-E. Bonnard, who makes his case in the context of the overall theme that wisdom in the OT is 'incarnated' in various degrees.[29]

This second interpretation of the Valiant Woman as wisdom has the advantage that it not only takes seriously the clues in the text that hint at the theme of wisdom (as pointed out especially by Stier and Jacob) but also does justice to the everyday and down-to-earth character of the Valiant Woman's mighty deeds as manager of a large estate.

We may conclude that workaday wisdom rooted in the fear of the Lord is a central concern of the Song of the Valiant Woman, and it may well be this concern that led to its inclusion in the book of Proverbs. If wisdom is a central theme, then the phonetic correspondence of *ṣôpiyyâ* and *sophia* can hardly be coincidental. This conclusion is reinforced by the fact that *ṣôpiyyâ*, if taken as a noun meaning 'wisdom', makes for a completely different but entirely plausible re-construal of the sentence in which it occurs. If it is construed as the predicate of a nominal sentence (as in the LXX, Peshitta, and Targum), then verse 27a does not signify 'She looks well to the ways of her household,' but 'The ways of her household are wisdom,' a perfectly idiomatic Hebrew construction,[30] which drives home the point that everything in the Valiant Woman's sphere of action embodies wisdom. Furthermore, it balances the statement in the previous verse that 'she opens her mouth with wisdom'. She personifies wisdom in both word and deed.

Is such an interpretation not oversubtle? Granted for a moment that *ṣôpiyyâ* is a clever pun on *sophia*, is it not too much to find here a calculated grammatical ambiguity as well? One would be inclined to think so if

---

[28] (*Continued*) 1395; see also 1466: 'Serait-ce une autre façon de personnaliser la Sagesse? Ce n'est pas à exclure', and 1468: '… que la femme … puisse être une représentation de "la Sagesse".' B. Lang, *Anweisungen gegen die Torheit: Sprichwörter – Jesus Sirach* (Stuttgart: Katholisches Bibelwerk, 1973), 52: 'Die einzelnen Aussagen sind als einzelne Erweise der vollkommenen Weisheit der Frau gedacht: die Weisheit wird im Tun erkannt.'; H. Schüngel-Straumann, 'Die wahre Frau' in *Christ in der Gegenwart* 33 (1981), 385: 'Dass das Gedicht am Schluss des Sprüchebuches steht, konnte zudem darauf hindeuten, dass diese Frau eine Verkörperung der "Weisheit" überhaupt ist'.

[29] P.-E. Bonnard, 'De la Sagesse personnifiée dans l'Ancien Testament à la Sagesse en personne dans le Nouveau' in M. Gilbert (ed.), *La Sagesse de l'Ancien Testament* (Louvain: Duculot, 1979), 117–49, esp. 128. It is somewhat surprising that there is no reference to the Valiant Woman as the personification of wisdom in W. McKane, *Proverbs: A New Approach* (London: SCM, 1970), 665–70.

[30] Cf. Deut. 32:4 'all his ways are judgment'; Ps. 25:10 'all the paths of the Lord are mercy and truth'; Prov. 3:17 'all her paths are peace' (said of Wisdom).

the rest of the song, in fact the very same verse, did not provide us with evidence that such studied ambiguity is found also outside the line in which ṣôpiyyâ occurs. The immediately following hemistich (v. 27b), for example, is usually construed to mean 'and does not eat the bread of idleness', but it can with equal validity be taken to mean 'and idleness will not eat bread', if one understands 'idleness' in the concrete sense of 'idlers'. This interpretation, which emphasizes the strictness of the Valiant Woman as mistress of the household – and thus puts verse 27b in synonymous parallelism with verse 27a – is preferred by a number of translators and commentators,[31] and the sentiment it expresses can be backed up by biblical parallels.[32] In this construction, 'aṣlût as the subject of verse 27b (= 'idleness') balances ṣôpiyyâ as the subject of verse 27a (= sophia).

Another example of artful ambiguity is provided by verse 25a, where lĕbûšâ(h) can be read as either a verb ('she is clothed with strength and honor') or a noun ('her clothing is strength and honor'). Moreover, if read as a noun, it can be construed as either the subject or the predicate, so that it refers either to literal or metaphorical clothing, that is, to either textile products or character traits. All these construals make eminently good sense in the context.

A number of other examples of what appears to be a deliberately ambiguous choice of words occur in the poem. We will do no more, in the present context, than mention two further striking instances. In verse 11b we have another case of two possible constructions (šālāl, 'plunder', as either subject or object), and in verse 29 the phrase 'āśâ ḥayil bears the double meaning 'do valiantly' and 'gain riches'. In both cases, again, either of the two possible interpretations fits the context and finds defenders among reputable exegetes and translators.[33]

---

[31] See W.A. Van Der Weiden, *Le Livre des Proverbes: Notes philologiques* (Rome: Pontifical Biblical Institute, 1970), 154–55. This interpretation is already anticipated by J.G. Herder in his *Geist der ebräischen Poesie* (1783); see B. Suphan (ed.), *Herders Sämmtliche Werke* (Berlin: Weidmann, 1877–1913), 12. 112 ('Die Trägheit isst bei ihr kein Brot'). Cf. also the Vg: 'Panem otiosa non comedit.'

[32] Cf. Prov. 19:15: 'the idle soul shall suffer hunger'; and 2 Thess. 3:10: 'if any would not work, neither should he eat'.

[33] In 31:11 šālāl is usually taken as the object, but it is taken as the subject by the Peshitta, Luther, Herder (*Geist*, 112), D. Winton Thomas ('Textual and Philological Notes on Some Passages in the Book of Proverbs' in M. Noth and D. Winton Thomas (eds.), *Wisdom in Israel and in the Ancient Near East*, VTSup 3 [Leiden: Brill, 1955], 292), and the NEB.

In 31:29 we find the meaning 'do valiantly' or an equivalent in most modern Bible versions, but the meaning is 'gain riches' in the Vg, Luther, and Van Der Weiden (*Proverbes*, 155); similarly, H.J. Van Dijk, *Ezekiel's Prophecy on Tyre (Ez.*

In the light of this recurring pattern of studied semantic ambiguity within the poem, the assumption of a double meaning and construal of ṣôpiyyâ in verse 27a is not without warrant. What makes the latter case unique, both in the acrostic song and (as far as I know) in the OT as a whole, is that it appears to involve a bilingual play on words.[34]

Yet this too, within the context of ancient Near Eastern literature, is not without parallels. The complicated cuneiform system by which Akkadian was written in signs originally designed for Sumerian provided scribes with the opportunity of making elaborate bilingual puns.[35] The same cuneiform character could be read as both a Sumerian logogram and an Akkadian phonogram. A well-known example is found in the Babylonian creation epic *Enuma elish*, in which the supreme god Marduk, preparatory to giving an exhibition of his power, 'places a cloak' before the other gods. This placing of a cloak is at the same time an allusion to the Sumerian meaning of the cuneiform signs for *mar* (i.e. 'place') and *duk* (= *tug*, i.e. 'cloak'), which in Akkadian spell the god's name – Marduk.[36]

We do not know whether the author of the acrostic poem of Proverbs 31 was acquainted with cuneiform writing and its complicated word-plays. We do know that he (or she) was a very sophisticated literary craftsman,[37] living in an international literary environment where cuneiform was very much alive.[38] It is at least possible, and perhaps probable, that he had some experience of Sumero–Akkadian literary punning.

In the light of all of the above – the fact that a hymnic participle is used precisely and exclusively at this point in the song, the rarity of the participial inflection chosen, the pattern of calculated ambiguity, the cuneiform precedents of bilingual wordplays, and above all the poem's

[33] *(continued) 26,1–28,19): A New Approach* (Rome: Pontifical Biblical Institute, 1968), 105. That the idiom can also bear this sense is not in dispute (cf. Deut. 8:17–18; Ezek. 28:4). The LXX gives both senses: *pollai thygateres ektēsanto plouton, pollai epoiēsan dynamin* (v.l. *dynata*).

[34] See J.M. Sasson, 'Wordplay in the Old Testament', *IDBSup*.

[35] See G. Contenau, *Everyday Life in Babylon and Assyria* (New York: Norton, 1966), 167–71.

[36] See G. Dossin, 'Le vêtement de Marduk', *Le Muséon* 60 (1947), 1–5. As Dossin points out, the poet exploits other Sumerian meanings of the cuneiform signs as well.

[37] This is shown also, for example, by the intricate chiastic construction both of the song as a whole and of its pivotal v. 19. See M.H. Lichtenstein, 'Chiasm and Symmetry in Proverbs 31', *CBQ* 44 (1982), 202–11.

[38] Although Akkadian, written in cuneiform characters, was gradually superseded as the major international language in the Near East by Aramaic and Greek, it did survive into the Christian era.

thematic concern with *wisdom* – the theoretical possibility that *ṣôpiyyâ* is a deliberate play on the Greek *sophia* becomes an almost inescapable probability, the kind of probability that is characteristic of all *double entendre*.

A final question must be raised and answered. Is *ṣôpiyyâ* in fact a plausible Hebrew transliteration of the Greek *sophia*? Would the two words have been pronounced in recognizably similar ways?

We must bear in mind that ancient Greek had no stress accent, and that the letter *phi* was an aspirated bilabial stop (as in English 'pea'), not yet a fricative (as in English 'fee'). In other words, on these points the Hebrew *ṣôpiyyâ* represents a more accurate rendering of the sound *sophia* than the modern pronunciation of the Greek would suggest (in fact, the *peh* without *dāgēš*, as here, also represents an *aspirated* bilabial stop).

It is significant, moreover, that the Hebrew word is written *plene*; all three vowels of the Greek word are represented by a *mater lectionis,* so that the spelling of the Hebrew consonantal text represents the vowels of *sophia* as unambiguously as was possible within the Hebrew system of writing.

As for the use of *ṣādê* to represent the Greek *sigma,* we must remember three things. First, *ṣādê* was not pronounced as *ts,* as is commonly done today, but as the characteristically Semitic 'emphatic' sibilant, which survives in the Arabic *ṣād.* To an untrained European ear, its sound is indistinguishable from the standard phoneme /s/. Second, Hebrew has three letters representing unvoiced sibilants (*sāmek, ṣādê, śîn/śîn*), as compared to the single letter of Greek. In the rabbinic transliteration of Greek words, all three (as well as the voiced *zayîn*) were used to represent *sigma.*[39] *Ṣādê* is often used in this capacity; in fact, it never represents any Greek letter but *sigma.*[40] (Conversely, Hebrew *ṣādê* is regularly represented by *sigma* in the LXX and the Hexapla.[41]) And third, of course, the demands of the alphabetic acrostic precluded the use of any letter but *ṣādê* at the beginning of verse 27.

Consequently, on the question of the accuracy of the transliteration, it is fair to conclude that, given the resources of the traditional consonantal Hebrew alphabet, no more faithful representation of the Greek word *sophia* could be given than the form *ṣôpiyyâ* as found in Proverbs 31:27. It certainly compares favorably with the Aramaic representation of *symphōnia* as *sûmpōnyâ* or *sîpōnyâ* in Daniel 3:5,10,15.

---

[39] S. Krauss, *Griechische und Lateinische Lehnwörter im Talmud, Midrasch und Targum,* 2 vols. (Berlin, 1898; reprinted Hildesheim: G. Olms, 1964), 1. 7–10.

[40] Krauss, *Griechische,* 2. 497.

[41] See A. Sperber, *A Historical Grammar of Biblical Hebrew* (Leiden: Brill, 1966), 105–8, 155–57,177.

III. Conclusion and Some Implications

As the overall conclusion of our discussion, we may state with some confidence that *ṣôpiyyâ* in Proverbs 31:27 represents a hymnic participle, used
in this form because of a deliberate play on the Greek word *sophia*.

What are the implications of this conclusion? I venture to suggest
three.

1. The Song of the Valiant Woman 'probably belongs to the Greek
period'.[42] This late dating of the song, first put forward by F. Hitzig in
1858, has not been widely followed.[43] However, since the play on *sophia*
presupposes a certain knowledge of Greek (however limited) on the part
of both the author and the intended audience, it seems reasonable to
assume that the song was probably composed some time after Alexander's
conquest, presumably in the third century BC.[44]

2. This dating provides us with an approximate but relatively secure
terminus post quem for the final redaction of Proverbs. Since the *terminus
ante quem* seems to be about 200 BC,[45] we are left with quite a narrow
chronological window (the third century) for dating the final form of
Proverbs. Consequently, the song was added to the canonical book shortly
after being composed, which accounts for its position as the last of a
number of appendices to the work.

---

[42] E.G. King, *Early Religious Poetry of the Hebrews* (Cambridge University Press,
1911), 72.

[43] See F. Hitzig, *Die Sprüche Salomo's* (Zurich: O. Füssli, 1858), 334–44. According to Delitzsch (*Spruchbuch*, 527), Hitzig put the date: 'in die Zeiten nach Alexander.' However, the final redaction of Proverbs is commonly put in the fifth or
fourth century BC, though a preexilic dating is not unusual.

[44] On the knowledge of Greek in Palestine, see M. Hengel, *Judaism and Hellenism:
Studies in Their Encounter in Palestine during the Early Hellenistic Period* (Philadelphia:
Fortress, 1974), 58–65, and the summarizing statement on 108: 'It can be demonstrated from the Zeno papyri that the Greek language was known in aristocratic
and military circles of Judaism between 260 and 250 BC in Palestine.' An earlier
date (even before Alexander) is less likely, but not impossible, if we accept the
view that: 'the process of Hellenization was well under way at the end of the
fourth and early in the third centuries B.C.E., and started to some extent, even
before Alexander the Great' (M.E. Stone, *Scriptures, Sects and Visions: A Profile of
Judaism from Ezra to the Jewish Revolts* [Philadelphia: Fortress, 1980], 28).

[45] Ecclesiasticus, dated in the early second century BC, already seems to presuppose the canonical shape and status of Proverbs, and the LXX translation of Proverbs was probably done by at least the mid-second century (see G. Gerleman,
Studies in the Septuagint, III. Proverbs [Lund: Gleerup, 1956], 60).

3. Given the play on *sophia*, but also the artful literary composition of the song as a whole, both the author and the intended audience must have belonged to a sophisticated and highly literate milieu.

Finally, we may propose an interpretative hypothesis. In the light of the date and the milieu indicated, it is particularly striking that the song presents a very practical and down-to-earth ideal of God-fearing wisdom which, as was hinted at in chapter 1, stands in vivid contrast to the intellectual ideal of wisdom favored by Hellenism. If we keep this in mind, the allusion to Greek *sophia* can be interpreted as a cleverly veiled barb in a religious polemic.[46] So well was the barb veiled (it would probably have been obvious only in a skilled recitation) that it appears to have become lost to view almost from the very beginning.[47]

---

[46] On the clash between Hellenism and the religion of the Jews in the third and second century BC, see A. Tcherikover, *Hellenistic Civilization and the Jews* (Philadelphia: Jewish Publication Society, 1959), 117–51, as well as the commentaries on Ecclesiasticus. J. Marböck deals specifically with the two different ideals of wisdom, as background to the notion of wisdom in Ecclesiasticus (*Weisheit im Wandel: Untersuchungen zur Weisheitstheologie bei Ben Sira* [Bonn: Hanstein, 1971]). See also Hengel, *Judaism and Hellenism*, 153–75.

[47] There is no indication that the LXX translators caught the pun. This is probably not only because of the inherent difficulty of translating a pun, but also because they simply did not understand the Hebrew (as suggested above). Note that even the acrostic structure of the song seems to have escaped the translators (witness their construal of *šnym* as the beginning of v. 22, rather than the end of v. 21).

4

The Meaning of *Kîšôr* (Prov. 31:19)

The noun *kîšôr* in Proverbs 31:19 is a *hapax legomenon* of unknown meaning. Today it is usually translated 'distaff' (following Luther), but this is only one of many guesses that have been made in the history of interpretation. Similar uncertainty prevails with respect to the etymology of the word. Previous discussions have failed to take into account two relevant factors which help to delimit the meaning of *kîšôr*: the extremely tightly-knit literary structure of its immediate context, and the history of spinning. The artful construction of Proverbs 31:19–20, which functions as the literary pivot of the Song of the Valiant Woman, shows that *kîšôr* must be a virtual synonym of *pelek* 'spindle'. The history of spinning shows that the distaff was not used in the ancient Near East, and that the *kîšôr*, which is grasped with two hands, was most probably a doubling spindle (like Arabic *mubram*). The technique used in handling the *kîšôr* can be plausibly reconstructed on the basis of Egyptian and Palestinian archeological evidence. Finally, the etymology of the word can be most plausibly traced to Canaanite *ktr*.

In the middle of the Song of the Valiant Woman which concludes the book of Proverbs we find the following verses:

> 31:19 She puts her hands to the distaff (*kîšôr*),
> and her hands hold the spindle (*pelek*).
> 31:20 She opens her hand to the poor,
> and reaches out her hands to the needy. (NRSV)

The word *kîšôr*, which is here translated 'distaff', is a *hapax legomenon* of disputed meaning. Although the rendering 'distaff' is now quite common, it is only one of a number of guesses that have been made about the meaning of this obscure word. Just as the previous chapter explored the ambiguity surrounding *ṣôpiyyâ*, here I propose to give a brief sketch of the history of these guesses, and to suggest a new interpretation of the word, based on the literary structure of its context, and on some forgotten aspects of the history of handspinning.

In a rough and ready way, it is possible to discern four major traditions of interpretation with respect to *kîśôr,* all of which go back to at least the sixteenth century. Tradition 1 is represented by the ancient versions, and interprets *kîśôr* as an abstract concept, for example, 'useful things,'[1] valiant deeds,[2] skill,[3] or success'.[4] However, since all the ancient versions agree that the parallel word *pelek* meant 'spindle', later exegetes came to favor the meaning 'distaff' for *kîśôr,* since the spindle and distaff were the twin spinning implements with which most scholars were familiar. This interpretation represents Tradition 2 and was given wide currency through Luther's German version of the Bible.[5] Tradition 3, which seems to have originated with Sebastian Münster in the sixteenth century, and which is represented in the King James Version, reverses the meanings which Luther assigned to the parallel Hebrew terms, so that *kîśôr* is now translated as 'spindle'.[6] Finally, Tradition 4, which goes back to medieval Jewish exegetes, and is also represented in Christian versions of the sixteenth century, takes *kîśôr* to mean 'spindle-whorl', the small round flyweight attached to a spindle to steady its spinning motion.[7]

---

[1] So the LXX (*ta sympheronta*).

[2] So the minor Greek versions (*ta andreia*), and the Vulgate (*fortia*; cf. *Oxford Latin Dictionary* s.v. 'fortis', 8).

[3] So the Peshitta (*kaššîrûtā'*) and Targum (*kûnšrā'/kûnšěrā'*).

[4] So Saadia's Arabic version, according to G. Dalman, *Arbeit und Sitte in Palästina. V: Webstoff, Spinnen, Weben, Kleidung* (Gütersloh: Bertelsmann, 1937), 50 (*nagāh*).

[5] *D. Martin Luthers Werke. Kritische Gesamtausgabe. Die Deutsche Bibel. Bd. 10.2* (Weimar: Böhlaus, 1957), 102–103. There is some evidence that Luther was dependent in his rendering of *kîśôr* on his co-worker Melanchthon; see chapter 5, Part III. A number of other sixteenth-century Bible versions followed Luther's lead, including the Zürcher Bibel (1531), the standard Protestant translations into Swedish (1541) and Danish (1550), and Castellio's Latin version (1551).

[6] See S. Münster, *Dictionarium Hebraicum* (Basel: Frobenius, 1525) s.v. '*kāśēr*': 'Secundo *kîśôr,* ut Kabvenaki exponit, est lignum parvum cum quo netur, id est, fusum [read: fusus]: Proverb. 31'. Münster's lead is followed by a number of Protestant versions in the sixteenth and seventeenth centuries, including those of Tyndale and Coverdale in English (1531 and 1533), Casiodoro de Reina in Spanish (1569), Diodati in Italian (1603), the *Statenvertaling* in Dutch (1637), and d'Almeida in Portuguese (1753).

[7] This tradition is first documented in the Hebrew-Arabic lexicon of the eleventh-century Jewish philologist Ibn Janâḥ; see A. Neubauer, *The Book of Hebrew Roots by Abu'l-Walîd Marwân Ibn Janâḥ, Otherwise Called Rabbi Yonah* (Oxford: Clarendon, 1875), 334, 792. Ibn Janâḥ is followed by Rashi on Prov. 31:19, and by David Kimḥi; see *Rabbi Davidis Kimchi Radicum Liber sive Hebraeum Bibliorum Lexicon cum Animadversionibus Eliae Levitae,* J.H.R. Biesenthal and F. Lebrecht

Although Tradition 2, which equates *kîšôr* with 'distaff', is reflected in the overwhelming majority of contemporary versions and in many commentaries,[8] the other traditions are far from dead. Tradition 1 was revived by Albright, who argued on the basis of the ancient versions that *kîšôr* means 'skill',[9] and he has recently been followed by Lichtenstein and Lettinga.[10] Tradition 3 has been adopted by Alonso Schökel in his Spanish translation of Proverbs,[11] while Tradition 4 keeps cropping up in the lexicographical tradition which runs from Gesenius to Koehler-Baumgartner.[12] In fact, 'spindle-whorl' is the meaning given in the current edition of *HALAT*, although the secondary literature cited there does not support this conclusion.[13] Rendsburg has recently put forward a proposal which combines Traditions 1 and 3.[14] We see, therefore, that all four major exegetical traditions with respect to *kîšôr* have reputable defenders to this day.

But there have also been scholarly guesses which do not fall under these four major traditions. For example, there is a minor tradition which

---

[7] (*Continued*) (eds.), (Berlin: Bethge, 1847), 172. See also the Latin version of Pagnini (1523), the English Geneva Bible (1560), and the Spanish version in *La Perfecta Casada* by Luis de León (1583).

[8] So, for example, the JPSV, RSV, JB, NEB, NKJV, REB, and NRSV – to mention only English versions. See also the commentaries by Franz Delitzsch (1873) and B. Gemser (1963).

[9] W.F. Albright, *Yahweh and the Gods of Canaan* (Garden City NY: Doubleday, 1968), 136, n. 67.

[10] M.H. Lichtenstein, 'Psalm 68:7 Revisited', *JANESCU* 4 (1972), 108–109; and J.P. Lettinga, 'Een bijbelse vrouwenspiegel', in *Bezield Verband. Opstellen aangeboden aan prof. J. Kamphuis* (Kampen: Van den Berg, 1984), 122–23.

[11] *Nueva Biblia Española. Traducción de los textos originales dirigada por Luis Alonso Schökel y Juan Mateos* (Madrid: Ediciones Cristiandad, 1975), 1321. See also Alonso Schökel, *Diccionario bíblico hebreo–español* (Madrid: Editorial Trotta, 1994) s.v. So too A. Bonora, 'La donna eccellente, la sapienza, il sapiente (*Pr* 31,10–31)', *Rivista Biblica* 36 (1988), 139,148.

[12] The meaning 'spindle-whorl' is given for *kîšôr* in Gesenius' *Thesaurus* (1840), and alternated with the meaning 'distaff' in the various editions and translations of his *Handwörterbuch* throughout the nineteenth century. The seventeenth edition (1918) has 'spindle-whorl', as does KB.

[13] The entry in *HALAT* refers to works by Albright, Dalman, Galling, and Kapelrud, who in the works cited advocate the meanings 'spindle', 'distaff', 'distaff', and 'spinning wheel', respectively.

[14] G.A. Rendsburg, 'Double Polysemy in Proverbs 31:19', in A. Afsaruddin and A.H. Mathias Zahniser (eds.), *Humanism, Culture and the Language in the New East* (Winona Lake: Eisenbrauns, 1997), 267–274. Rendsburg argues that *kîšôr* is deliberately ambiguous, referring to both 'spindle' and 'skill'.

has interpreted *kîšôr* to mean 'spinning wheel'. Although this interpretation is a clear anachronism (spinning wheels were a medieval invention), it has found scholarly defenders from the sixteenth to the twentieth century.[15]

Other guesses have included the proposed meanings 'profit',[16] 'weaver's shuttle',[17] 'the pole of a distaff',[18] 'the mass of spinning material',[19] 'the shaft of the spindle',[20] and 'mending' or 'knitting'.[21] It has even been proposed that *kîšôr* should be emended to *kôš*, a later Hebrew word for 'spindle'.[22] Virtually every scholar who has taken a closer look at this enigmatic *hapax legomenon* has realized that its meaning is difficult to pinpoint, although the context seems to suggest that it has something to do with spinning.

The lexicographical difficulty is compounded by the lack of etymological parallels. It has been said that *kîšôr* stands all by itself in the Semitic languages.[23] It is true that the various proposed meanings have been defended by appeals to cognate roots in Hebrew (*kāšēr, yāšar*),[24] Arabic (*ktr*,

[15] See P. Muffet, *A Commentary on the Whole Book of Proverbs* (1592 and 1594; reprinted in Nichol's Series of Commentaries [Edinburgh: Nichol, 1868]): 'the wheel'; *La Bible. Traduite du texte original par les membres du Rabbinat français, sous la direction de M. Zadoc Kahn, Grand Rabbin*, 2 vols. (Paris: Durlacher, 1930–31): 'le rouet'; the Dutch *Canisiusvertaling* (1939): 'het spinnewiel'; and A. Kapelrud, 'Spinnen', *BHH* 3. 1835: 'ein Spinnrad'.

[16] J.D. Michaelis, *Deutsche Übersetzung des Alten Testaments, mit Anmerkungen für Ungelehrte, VII* (Göttingen: Dieterich, 1778), *ad loc.*, 'Gewinnst'.

[17] A. Calmet, *Commentarius Literalis in Omnes Libros Veteris Testamenti, Tomus Septimus: In Psalmos et Proverbia Salomonis* (Wirceburgi: Rienner, 1792): 755 'radius textorius'.

[18] M. Lemans and S.I. Mulder, *Hebreeuws-Nederduitsch Handwoordenboek* (Amsterdam: Van Embden, 1831), 310: '*de spil* [van een spinrok]'.

[19] A.B. Ehrlich, *Randglossen zur Hebräischen Bibel, V* (Leipzig: Hinrichs, 1912), 177: 'die Masse des Spinnstoffs'.

[20] A.G. Barrois, *Manuel d'archéologie biblique*, 2 vols. (Paris: Picard, 1939–1953), 1.462: 'la tige du fuseau'.

[21] G.R. Driver, 'Notes on Hebrew Lexicography', *JTS* 23 (1922), 407.

[22] W. Frankenberg, *Die Sprüche* (HKAT; Göttingen, 1898), 167: 'Doch ist mir nicht zweifelhaft, dass für das unerklärl. *kîšôr* zu lesen ist *kôš*, im späteren Hebr. (und Syr.) der Name der Spindel'.

[23] See S. Landersdorfer, *Sumerisches Sprachgut im Alten Testament. Eine biblisch–lexikalische Studie* (Beiträge zur Wissenschaft vom Alten Testament 21; Leipzig: Hinrichs, 1916), 45. The isolation of *kîšôr* is not complete if we accept Epstein's emendation *kwš<r>yn* 'spindles', at *y. Yebam.* 12d (see Rendsburg, 'Double Polysemy', 271).

[24] So BDB s.v. *kāšēr*, and D. Kimḥi *yāšar*. For Kimḥi's view, see his *Radicum Liber*, 172.

ktr),[25] Canaanite (*ktr*),[26] and Akkadian (*kašāru, kašurītu*),[27] but none of these has proved convincing to a majority of scholars. In fact, etymological derivation from a postulated Sumerian form *ki-sur, kid-sur*, or *giš-sur* presently seems to enjoy the greatest favor.[28] Given this confused situation, it will be helpful to bring to bear some new evidence on the meaning of *kîšôr*. In what follows I will argue that literary considerations rule out Tradition 1, and that historically attested techniques of spinning rule out Traditions 2 and 4. Instead, the evidence seems to favor a modified version of Tradition 3, in which *kîšôr* is seen to represent a special kind of spindle.

Traditions 2, 3 and 4 are all based on the fact that *kîšôr* is parallel to *pelek*, and therefore probably represents some concrete object used in spinning, whether distaff, spindle, or spindle-whorl. But the literary relationship between *kîšôr* and *pelek* is much closer than at first appears. In order to appreciate this point, we need to take note of the overall artistry of which they are a part.

Verses 19 and 20 have the following structure:

	1	2	3	1	2	3
19a	*ydyh*	*šlhh*	*bkyšwr*	her-HANDS	she-REACHES	to-the-*kîšôr*
b	*wkpyh*	*tmkw*	*plk*	and-her-PALMS	GRASP	SPINDLE
20a	*kph*	*pršh*	*lʿny*	her-PALM	she-SPREADS	to-POOR
b	*wydyh*	*šlhh*	*lʾbywn*	and-her-HANDS	she-REACHES	to-the-NEEDY

It is clear from this that there is a chiastic pattern both in Column 1 and in Column 2.[29] All members of Column 2 also express the actions of *hands*,

[25] A. Schultens, *Proverbia Salomonis* (Leiden: Luzac, 1748), 515. Cf. F. Delitzsch, *Das Salomonische Spruchbuch* (Leipzig: Dorffling und Franke, 1873), 532, n. 1.

[26] Albright, *Yahweh and the Gods*, 136; and W.A.Van Der Weiden, *Le livre des Proverbes. Notes philologiques* (Rome: Biblical Institute Press, 1970), 153.

[27] Driver, 'Hebrew Lexicography', 407.

[28] For *ki-sur*, see A. Boissier, 'A Sumerian Word in the Bible', *Proceedings of the Society of Biblical Archaeology*, 35 (1913), 159–60; for *kid-sur*, Landersdorfer, *Sumerisches Sprachgut*, 45,103,110; for *giš-sur*, the suggestion of F. Cornelius incorporated in W.F. Albright, *Die Religion Israels im Lichte der archäologischen Ausgrabungen. Autorisierte Übersetzung mit Nachträgen des Verfassers von Friedrich Cornelius* (Munich/Basel: Reinhardt, 1956), 242, n. 68. This suggestion, which does not appear in the English edition of Albright's work (*Archaeology and the Religion of Israel* [Baltimore: Johns Hopkins Press, 1946²], 216, n. 63), is adopted in *HALAT* s.v. *kîšôr*. It is also defended by G.A. Rendsburg, 'Double Polysemy', 268–270, 274.

[29] See M.H. Lichtenstein, 'Chiasm and Symmetry in Proverbs 31', *CBQ* 44 (1982), 206–207. See also Bonora, 'La donna eccellente', 148.

and the verbs 'grasp' and 'spreads', though parallel members within the chiasmus, at the same time represent a neat antithesis of closing and opening actions. Add to this that each box in the scheme corresponds to a single stress accent in the Hebrew, and that verse 19 as a whole stands in contrast to verse 20 as earning to giving, as production to distribution. Moreover, the whole fits into the overall acrostic pattern of the poem: verse 19 begins with the letter *yod* (with a play on the noun *yād*, 'hand'), and verse 20 begins with the subsequent letter *kap* (with a play on the noun *kap*, 'palm' or 'hand'). If we consider that the poem as a whole, apart from the coda of verses 30–31, is structured around an *inclusio* marked by the noun *ḥayil* and the theme 'her worth to husband and household', it also becomes clear that verses 19–20 are at the exact center of this struc- ture. The tightly-knit structure of these two pivotal verses lends support to Dahood's suggestion that *kappāh* (v. 20a in the MT) be revocalized to *kappehā*, written defectively, thus corresponding to *kappehā* in verse 19b.[30] If he is right, a further feature of the poet's artistry emerges: all members of Column 1 now rhyme with each other: *yādehā, wĕkappehā, kappehā, wĕyādehā*.

In view of this intricate piece of literary craftsmanship (which seems to have gone unnoticed in the commentaries), it is virtually certain that Column 3 also displays a symmetrical pattern: the pair *kîšôr*/'spindle' balances the synonymous pair 'poor/needy'. The literary structure there- fore indicates that *kîšôr* is in some sense a synonym of *pelek*, 'spindle', and that Tradition 1 is to be rejected.

Before turning to the history of spinning for further light, we need to establish the philological point that *pelek* does indeed mean 'spindle', and not 'spindle-whorl', *pace* Koehler-Baumgartner.[31] The fact is that all the ancient versions agree that *pelek* means 'spindle', and their testimony has been dramatically confirmed by the epigraphic evidence that has come to light in the last century. The word for 'spindle' turns out to be a cognate of Hebrew *pelek* not only in Aramaic,[32] but also in Akkadian,[33] Ugaritic,[34]

---

[30] M. Dahood, *Psalms 101–150* (AB 17A; Garden City NY: Doubleday, 1970), 288; also in L.R. Fisher (ed.), *Ras Shamra Parallels. The Texts from Ugarit and the Hebrew Bible*, vol. 1 (Rome: Pontificium Institutum Biblicum, 1972), 237, n. 305. Dahood's proposed revocalization is also adopted by A.R. Ceresko, 'The A:B::B:A Word Pattern in Hebrew and North-west Semitic', *UF* 7 (1975), 81.

[31] See KB and *HALAT* s.v. ('Spinnwirtel').

[32] See G.H. Dalman, *Aramäisch-Neuhebräisches Wörterbuch zu Targum, Talmud und Midrasch*, 2 vols. (Frankfurt/Main: Kauffmann, 1897–1901), s.v. *pilkā'* 2 ('Spindel').

[33] See *AHW* s.v. *pilakk/qqu(m)*.

[34] See C.H. Gordon, *Ugaritic Textbook* (AnOr 38; Rome: Pontificium Institutum

Phoenician,[35] and Eblaite.[36] Any doubts about its meaning are removed by the bilingual Phoenician-Hittite inscription of Karatepe, in which the hieroglyphic sign of the Hittite text corresponding to *plkm* in the Phoenician text consists of a pictogram clearly representing a spindle.[37] In the light of this strong epigraphic evidence, it is surprising that Koehler–Baumgartner give 'spindle-whorl' as the meaning for Hebrew *pelek*. The reason for this is undoubtedly a postulated semantic affinity with Classical and Modern Arabic, since the Arabic cognate *falaka* and variants does mean 'spindle-whorl'.[38] But this is an unsafe guide to the meaning of Hebrew *pelek*, not only because Classical Arabic is far removed from biblical Hebrew in time and space, but also because there is an identifiable reason why the root *plk* developed this specialized meaning in Arabic, in contrast to the earlier Semitic languages of the Fertile Crescent.[39] Consequently, we can be quite certain that Hebrew *pelek* does mean 'spindle'.

---

[34] (*Continued*) Biblicum, 1965), 468 (no. 2050). Ugaritic *plk* is to be vocalized *pilakku*; see J. Nougayrol, 'Textes suméro–accadiens des archives et bibliothèques privées d'Ugarit', *Ugaritica V* (Paris, 1968), 242–43 (137 II 22).

[35] See S. Segert, *A Grammar of Phoenician and Punic* (Munich: Beck, 1976), 271, Glossary s.v. *plk*.

[36] See G. Conti, *Il sillabario della quarta fonte della lista lessicale bilingue eblaita* (Miscellanea Eblaitica 3; Firenze: Dipartimento di linguistica, Università di Firenze, 1990), 39, 133–34.

[37] See H.T. Bossert, 'Die phönizisch–hethitischen Bilinguen von Karatepe. 3. Fortsetzung,' *Jahrbuch für die kleinasiatische Forschung* 1 (1951), 280 (no. 186). The sign in question is no. 305 of the Liste des signes in E. Laroche, *Les hiéroglyphes hittites* (Paris: Editions du CNRS, 1960), 157, and no. 301a in Piero Meriggi, *Hieroglyphisch-Hethitisches Glossar. Zweite Auflage* (Wiesbaden: Harrassowitz, 1962), 226. This hieroglyphic sign makes it improbable that the corresponding *plkm* of the Phoenician text means 'pathways', *pace* N. Heltzer, '*Plkm* in the Karatepe Inscription II, 6', *Anuario de Filologia* 8 (1984), 171–75.

[38] Among the attested forms are *falaka* (Delitzsch, *Spruchbuch*, 532), *felake* (Dalman, *Arbeit und Sitte*, 5.42, 49), *filka* (Dalman, 5.51), *filkatum* (R.S. Tomback, *A Comparative Semitic Lexicon of the Phoenician and Punic Languages* [Missoula: Scholars Press, 1978], s.v. *plk*), and *falakat* (*HALAT*, s.v. *pelek*).

[39] The word for 'spindle' is formed from the root *plk* in Akkadian, Ugaritic, Phoenician and Aramaic. The root *ǧzl*, 'spin', is not used for this purpose in these earlier Semitic languages, although it is attested as a verb in Ugaritic. However, in Syriac and Arabic the standard word for 'spindle' is derived from this root, yielding the forms *muʿzělâ* in Syriac, and *maǧzal/muǧzal/miǧzal* in Arabic. As a result, the Arabic derivatives of *plk* acquired a more specialized sense, namely 'spindle-whorl'. Note that in later Aramaic there is also evidence of a narrowing of the meaning of *plk*'; see J. Naveh, 'Varia Epigraphica Judaica', *Israel Oriental Studies* 9 (1979), 28–30 (epigraphic *plk'* = 'spinning vessel').

Having established that *kîšôr* must be something roughly synonymous with 'spindle', and therefore in all likelihood some kind of spinning implement, we turn now to the history of spinning to help us decide what specific implement it was. Handspinning seems to have been an almost universally practised technique before the introduction of the spinning wheel in the late Middle Ages. This is not to say, however, that all spinning before modern times was done in precisely the same way. It is thoroughly unwarranted, for example, to assume that in Israel 'the spinning was done, as all the world over, by means of the *distaff* and *spindle*'.[40] The fact is that some six different types of handspinning have been distinguished by historians of technology, and the distaff plays a role in only one of them – and even there it is optional. Grace M. Crowfoot, who is the leading authority in this area, designates these six types with the following labels: 'hand spinning' (here used in a restricted sense of the term, denoting the absence of any tools), 'spinning by twisting a hooked stick', 'rotation of spindle in hand', 'grasped spindle', 'supported hand spindle', and 'suspended spindle'.[41] The most sophisticated and best-known method is that of the 'suspended spindle' (or 'drop spindle') which has traditionally been associated with the distaff, at least in Europe. But even for this method the distaff is far from indispensable:

> A distaff is any tool that holds the supply of raw fibres for the spinner during spinning. *It is a convenient tool but usually not necessary.* It is most often used for flax, because flax fibres can be long and difficult to manage. In Europe, where it is most widely used, the distaff is usually 10 to 40" long and is held under the left arm or with the end stuck in the spinner's belt.[42]

---

[40] J. Hastings, *Dictionary of the Bible. Second Edition* (New York: Scribner, 1963), 933.

[41] G.M. Crowfoot, *Methods of Hand Spinning in Egypt and the Sudan* (Bankfield Museum Notes, Second Series, No. 12; Halifax: King & Sons, 1931), reprinted in G.M. Crowfoot and H. Ling Roth, *Hand Spinning and Woolcombing* (McMinnville, OR: Robin and Russ Handweavers, 1974). See also her contribution in C. Singer (ed.), *A History of Technology*, vol. 1 (Oxford: Clarendon, 1954), 424–25. A different classification and terminology is used by H.T. Horwitz, 'Die Entwicklung des Spinnens', *Ciba–Rundschau* 5 (1941–43), 1795–1808, but Crowfoot is followed by R.J. Forbes, *Studies in Ancient Technology*, vol. 4 (Leiden: Brill, 1964²), 153–57.

[42] C. Crockett, *The Complete Spinning Book* (New York: Watson–Guptill Publications, 1977), 35 (my emphasis).

The distaff in this sense does seem to have been a standard spinning tool in classical antiquity,[43] and this circumstance probably accounts for the widespread scholarly assumption (ever since Luther) that it must have been standard in the ancient Near East as well.[44] But even in the west, where suspended spindle spinning has been widespread, and in some areas persists to this day, the use of the distaff is not universal.[45]

As far as I can tell, the evidence for the use of the distaff in the ancient Near East (at least until the impact of Greco-Roman culture in Hellenistic times) is non-existent. This is a point explicitly made with reference to ancient Egypt by Crowfoot,[46] and is reaffirmed by Dalman, Forbes, and Barber in their studies of ancient textile technology.[47] As for ancient Mesopotamia, an authoritative study of the relevant spinning implements is marked by the conspicuous absence of any reference to the distaff.[48] This is confirmed by the iconographic evidence with respect to ancient Near Eastern spinning. A much-reproduced bas-relief found at Susa portrays a spinning woman using a spindle but no distaff.[49] (Ironically, this picture is reproduced in the article 'Distaff' of the *Interpreter's Dictionary of the Bible*.[50]) The distaff is also conspicuous by its absence in surviving representations of

[43] See H. Blümner, *Technologie und Terminologie der Gewerbe und Künste bei Griechen und Römern. 2. Auflage*, 4 vols. (Leipzig: Teubner, 1912), 1.122–23; and E.J.W. Barber, *Prehistoric Textiles. The Development of Cloth in the Neolithic and Bronze Ages* (Princeton: Princeton University Press, 1991), 69–70.
[44] European scholars assumed that the conjunction of spindle and distaff was rooted in the nature of things. See Schultens, *Proverbia*, 515: '*Colus & fusus naturalem habent ordinem, atque hac in materia semper conjungi solent.*'
[45] See e.g., P. Scheuermeier, *Bauernwerk in Italien, der italienischen und rätoromanischen Schweiz. Band II: Eine sprach-und sachkundliche Darstellung häuslichen Lebens und ländlicher Geräte* (Bern: Stämpfli, 1956), 261–62.
[46] Crowfoot, *Methods of Hand Spinning*, 29,31,35–37.
[47] Dalman, *Arbeit und Sitte*, 52; Forbes, *Ancient Technology*, 4.161; Barber, *Prehistoric Textiles*, 50,70.
[48] A. Salonen, *Die Hausgeräte der alten Mesopotamier nach sumerisch–akkadischen Quellen. Eine lexikalische und kulturgeschichtliche Untersuchung*, 2 vols. (Helsinki: Suomalainen Tiedeakatemia, 1965–66), 147–54. See also H. Waetzoldt, *Untersuchungen zur neusumerischen Textilindustrie* (Rome: Centro per le Antichità e la Storia dell' Arte del Vicino Oriente, 1972), 120–22, where the distaff is again absent from a discussion of spinning implements. I do not know the basis of the claim in Forbes, *Ancient Technology*, 4.171, n. 4, that Akkadian [gis]SU-KIN/*šuru* means 'distaff'. The meaning of this word is given as '(Schilf-)Rohr' in *AHW*.
[49] See, e.g., *ANEP*, 43 (no. 144), *ISBE*, 4.599; Barber, *Prehistoric Textiles*, 58. Cf. Boissier, 'A Sumerian Word', 160, n. 8: 'Note the absence of the distaff.'
[50] *IDB*, 1.856.

spinning women from Mari and Maraş.[51] As for pre-Roman Syria and Palestine, we come to similar results: we find the word *plk* in Eblaite, Ugaritic, Phoenician and Hebrew, but we find no mention of the distaff. The case for the use of the distaff in the Palestine of Bible times seems to rest exclusively on Luther's influential guess about *kîšôr*.[52]

The evidence from the practice of Near Eastern handspinning in the twentieth century leads to a similar conclusion: the distaff is rarely used in Egypt,[53] and never in Palestine.[54] In this respect the culture of the ancient Near East is like that of the South American Indians, among whom the use of the distaff is largely unknown.[55] All of this seems to warrant the conclusion that *kîšôr* in all likelihood does not mean 'distaff'. In the words of the French archeologist A.G. Barrois: 'The valiant woman of Proverbs puts her hands to the *kîšôr*, which is not the distaff, since the spinning women of the East do not use it at all'.[56]

Perhaps it might be argued that the Song of the Valiant Woman, since it seems to reflect an influence of Greek culture in its clever bilingual pun

---

[51] For the Mari picture, see Barber, *Prehistoric Textiles*, 57; and H. Crawford, *Sumer and the Sumerians* (Cambridge: Cambridge University Press, 1991), 125; for the representation from Maraş, see H.T. Bossert, *Altanatolien – Kunst und Handwerk in Kleinasien von den Anfängen bis zum völligen Aufgehen in der griechischen Kultur* (Berlin: Wasmuth, 1942), 198 (Fig. 814); and Barber, 59. The ambiguous iconographic and archeological evidence from Iran and Mesopotamia which Barber (56–57,63) interprets as possibly indicating the presence of distaffs is quite inconclusive.

[52] E.g., the claim by Forbes in *Ancient Technology*, 4.164 that the distaff was used in ancient Palestine is based on the assumption that *kîšôr* in Prov. 31:19 (and its Syriac translation *kaššîrûtaʾ* in the Peshitta) refers to the distaff.

[53] Crowfoot, *Methods of Hand Spinning*, 33,34,37,38,43.

[54] See S. Weir, *Spinning and Weaving in Palestine* (London: British Museum, 1970), 8, and *The Bedouin. Aspects of the material culture of the Bedouin of Jordan* (n. p.: World of Islam Festival Publishing Company, 1976), 34.

[55] See O. Frödin and E. Nordenskiöld, *Über Zwirnen und Spinnen bei den Indianern Südamerikas* (Göteborg: Zachrisson, 1918), 37–38 (no distaff); L.M. O'Neale, *Textiles of Highland Guatemala* (Washington: Carnegie Institution of Washington, 1945), 8 (no distaff); and 'Weaving' in J.H. Steward (ed.), *Handbook of South American Indians, Vol. 5: The Comparative Ethnology of South American Indians* (New York: Cooper Square Publishers, 1963), 98,103 (distaff only among the Quechua Indians).

[56] Barrois, *Manuel*, 1.462: 'La femme forte des Proverbes met la main au *kîšôr*, qui n'est pas la quenouille, dont les fileuses orientales ne se servent point'. Cf. the article 'Huso' by C. Wau in *Enciclopedia de la Biblia* (Barcelona: Garriga, 1963), 50: 'en la antigüedad oriental, las hacendosas mujeres de casa (desde las reinas y princesas hasta las esclavas) no conocieron la rueca [= distaff].'

on *sophia*,[57] may also reflect another aspect of Greek culture, namely the use of the distaff. But this is very improbable, since cultural influence on the level of domestic crafts would normally lag far behind intellectual influence.[58] In any case, if *kîšôr* did reflect a Greek cultural innovation, we would expect it to be a Greek loanword, and we would not expect the translators of all the Greek versions to have misunderstood it.

But the *coup de grâce* for Tradition 2 (*kîšôr* = 'distaff') is delivered by the wording of Proverbs 31:19 itself. The Hebrew text states that the Valiant Woman 'puts her *hands* (Hebrew *yādehā*) to the *kîšôr*. The English plural, here reflecting a Hebrew dual, indicates that the *kîšôr* is an implement that is manipulated with *both hands*. But this cannot be the distaff, since we have seen that the distaff is normally 'held under the left arm or with the end stuck into the spinner's belt'.[59] In other words, the distaff is normally not manipulated by hand at all, and certainly not by both of them.[60] Suspended spindle spinning requires at least one hand to be free to twirl the spindle, while the other normally draws out the prepared fibres, which may or may not be attached to a distaff. Spinning cannot be done if both hands are occupied with the distaff. Luther, followed by the NEB and NIV, evades this difficulty by translating *yādehā* as a singular, 'ihre Hand', but this not only disturbs the intricate chiastic structure which we noted above, but also obscures the practical objections to equating *kîšôr* with the 'distaff'.

We conclude, therefore, that what we have called Tradition 2, which has enjoyed its widespread popularity due to the influence of Luther, cannot be maintained. By the same token, it is clear that Tradition 4 must be rejected as well. In no form of spinning do the hands manipulate the spindle-whorl, either singly or together. Spindle-whorls, many of which have turned up in archeological excavations in Palestine, are rarely more than a few centimeters in diameter,[61] and it is difficult to imagine how

---

[57] See chapter 3.

[58] Barber, *Prehistoric Textiles*, 78, speaks of the 'powerful conservatism' that is evident in the history of handspinning.

[59] See note 42.

[60] The article 'Distaff' in *ISBE* suggests that: ' "She puts her hands to the distaff" could mean that she was reaching to pull the prepared fibers from the stick on which they were held.' However, in spinning with suspended spindle (the only method for which a distaff is used), the activity of pulling the prepared fibers from the distaff is normally done by the left hand alone, while the right hand twirls the spindle. It should also be noted that the freestanding distaff (which could be dressed or 'dizened' by both hands) seems to be unknown before the thirteenth or fourteenth century CE; see W. Endrei, *L'évolution des techniques de filage et du tissage du Moyen Age à la révolution industrielle* (The Hague: Mouton, 1968), 7–18.

[61] According to D. Irvin, *ISBE*, 4.597, excavated spindle-whorls vary in size from

such small objects, especially when attached to a spindle, could be manipulated by two hands in spinning. In any case, the action of putting two
hands to a spindle-whorl has no correlate in any attested mode of spinning. Both Tradition 2 and Tradition 4 betray ignorance of the way
spinning would actually have been done in ancient Palestine.

The same might be said of Tradition 3 (*kîšôr* = 'spindle'), if it were not
for the fact that different types of spinning require different types of
spindle. It is certainly true that the two-handed action described in verse
19a does not fit the familiar 'suspended spindle' type of spinning which
was most common in Greco-Roman antiquity, and in western Europe
thereafter. In this type of spinning, as we have noted, the spindle is twirled
with the right hand, leaving the left hand free to draw out the fibres. It is
clear that *kîšôr* cannot mean this kind of drop spindle. However, there is
another kind of spindle which does fit the description in our verse. This is
the spindle used in the so-called 'grasped spindle' method of spinning.
Crowfoot describes it as follows:

> In this method of spinning, a prepared rove [a thread drawn out but only
> slightly twisted] is passed through a ring or over a forked stick or other support,
> and is spun on *a large spindle grasped in both hands.*[62]

It would seem that the *kîšôr* is this kind of spindle, and that we now have
a perfect match between verse 19a and a known form of spinning.
This type of spinning, often associated with so-called 'spinning bowls',[63]
is in fact attested in the ancient Near East. There is abundant iconographic evidence that spinning was done in this way in ancient Egypt.[64]
But there is no reason to believe that it was restricted to Egypt; in fact
the same type of spinning has been documented in modern times
among North American aboriginals,[65] as well as in Spain,[66] and in

---

[61] (*Continued*) 1.3 to 8–10 cm in diameter. See also Dalman, *Arbeit und Sitte*, 5.51
(2.2 to 4.3 cm) and the illustration in K. Galling (ed.), *Biblisches Reallexikon. 2.
Auflage* (Tübingen: Mohr–Siebeck, 1977), 312.

[62] Crowfoot, *Methods of Hand Spinning*, 14 (my emphasis).

[63] See T. Dothan, 'Spinning Bowls', *IEJ* 13 (1963), 97–112. What Dothan calls a
'spinning bowl' is named a 'plying bowl' by Irvin (*ISBE*, 4.598; cf. *Biblisches
Reallexikon. 2. Aufl.*, 313) and a 'fiber-wetting bowl' by Barber (*Prehistoric
Textiles*, 73).

[64] Crowfoot, *Methods of Hand Spinning*, 14–17.

[65] See M.L. Kissell, 'A New Type of Spinning in North America', *American
Anthropologist*, 18 (1916), 264–70; eadem, *Yarn and Cloth Making: An Economic
Study* (New York: Macmillan, 1918), 21–24; and Crowfoot, *Methods of Hand
Spinning*, 14.

[66] Crowfoot, *Methods of Hand Spinning*, 14,45.

Romania.[67] That it was practised in ancient Palestine is indicated, not only by Proverbs 31:19, but also by the discovery of the characteristic spinning bowls in Palestinian excavations.[68]

There is also a philological point which supports our proposal that *kîšôr* is the kind of spindle used in grasped spindle spinning. The idiom *šlḥ yd* does not really fit with other kinds of spinning implements. This was pointed out by both Ehrlich and Humbert with respect to the distaff.[69] Humbert, in the course of his extensive study of this idiom, writes: 'With *bĕ* the expression *šālaḥ yād* always has a grasping or aggressive meaning, *except in Prov 31:19* (to lay hold of the distaff)'.[70] But this apparent exception disappears if the spinning tool in question is indeed *grasped* with both hands. In that case the verbal idiom has exactly the same force as it has elsewhere. In other words, *ydyh šlḥh bkyšwr* in verse 19a is synonymous with *kpyh tmkw plk* in verse 19b. In both cases the woman *grasps* a spindle in both hands.

On the basis of the available evidence, it seems that the grasped spindle method of spinning was used either for respinning or for doubling, that is, for making two-ply or three-ply yarn out of previously spun threads.[71] In other words, the *kîšôr* was likely a *doubling spindle* and was kept terminologically distinct from *pelek*, the generic term for spindle. We find this same kind of terminological differentiation in some other languages. In

---

[67] M. von Kimakowicz-Winnicki, *Spinn- und Webewerkzeuge. Entwicklung und Anwendung in vorgeschichtlicher Zeit* (Würzburg: Kabitzsch, 1910), 58–60, which deals with spinning techniques practised in Siebenbürgen, a district of Romania, at the beginning of the twentieth century.

[68] See Dothan, 'Spinning-Bowls'. For a more popular treatment, and an artist's reconstruction of the use of spinning bowls in the 'grasped spindle' method of spinning, see Dothan's article 'Gaza Sands Yield Lost Outpost of the Egyptian Empire', *National Geographic* 162.6 (Dec. 1982), 739–69, esp. 757,762–63. The spinning bowls found at Deir el-Balah in the Gaza strip (and in other parts of Palestine) indicate that grasped spindle spinning was in fact practised in ancient Palestine. The artist's reconstruction (762) is misleading in that the spindle depicted is far too small for this kind of spinning, and thus obscures the fact that the spindle was literally 'grasped' by both hands.

[69] Ehrlich, *Randglossen V*, 177; P. Humbert, ' "Etendre la main" (Note de lexicographie hébraïque)', *VT* 12 (1962), 387.

[70] Humbert, ' "Etendre la main",' 387: 'Or, avec *bĕ* la tournure *šālaḥ yād* a toujours un sens préhensif ou agressif, sauf dans Prov. xxxi 19 (se saisir de sa quenouille)' (my emphasis).

[71] Crowfoot, *Methods of Hand Spinning*, 14–17; Von Kimakowicz-Winnicki, *Spinn- und Webewerkzeuge*, 58–60; Irvin, *ISBE*, 4.598; and Barber, *Prehistoric Textiles*, 71–72.

the Arabic of the Sudan, for example, the generic word for 'spindle' is *muġzal*, but a doubling spindle is called *mubram*.[72] A similar distinction is made in Finnish between *värttinnä* and *taina*,[73] and in German between *Spindel* and *Zwirnspindel*.[74] It is my proposal that an analogous distinction holds between *pelek* and *kîsôr* in biblical Hebrew. It is a distinction which runs parallel to that between the Hebrew verbs *ṭāwâ*, 'spin' and *šāzar*, 'twine, twist, ply'.[75]

My overall conclusion is therefore that *kîsôr* refers to a special kind of spindle, specifically the large kind of spindle used in 'grasped spindle' spinning. It was held and rotated by both hands, and used especially for doubling already spun single-ply yarn. In the context of Proverbs 31:19, this interpretation fits both the phraseology of verse 19a, and the tightly-knit literary structure of verses 19–20. It also fits what we know about the technology of spinning in the ancient Near East, and the prevalence of plyed thread in the surviving bits of ancient textile that have been found in Palestine.[76]

Having arrived at this conclusion, it remains for me to make a few comments about the etymology of *kîsôr*. Although the Sumerian word *ki-sur* (which was previously only a hypothetical form) is now attested in the recently discovered tablets of Ebla,[77] it is unclear what it means, and I doubt whether we need to go as far afield as Sumerian to explain the Hebrew word. It is much more plausible, in my judgment, to derive *kîsôr* from a postulated Phoenician **kōšār*, and to relate it to the well-known Ugaritic epithet *ktr* and the god Kothar. Not only has Aron Dotan shown that such a derivation follows regular phonetic laws,[78] but it seems very

---

[72] Crowfoot, *Methods of Hand Spinning*, 11,43,47. Among the Bedouin of Jordan the doubling spindle is called the *mabram*; see Weir, *The Bedouin*, 34.

[73] K. Vilkuna, 'Spinning (Finland)', *Kulturhistorisk Leksikon for Nordisk Middelalder* (Copenhagen: Rosenkilde og Bagger, 1971), 16.500–501. See the Modern Finnish dictionary *Nykysuomen Sanakirja*, 3 vols. (Helsinki: Söderström, 1973), s.v. 'taina'.

[74] Von Kimakowicz-Winnicki, *Spinn- und Webewerkzeuge*, 58–60. Note that a larger spindle used for doubling is also found among certain tribes of South American Indians; see O'Neale, 'Weaving', 101.

[75] See KB and *HALAT* s.vv.; Barber, *Prehistoric Textiles*, 50,72.

[76] See D. Irvin in *Biblisches Reallexikon*, 2. Aufl., 146, and in *ISBE*, 4.598: 'Fabric woven of plyed thread is found among the earliest textile remains in Palestine (in the Jericho tombs) and among the latest (the Qumran scroll wrappings).'

[77] G. Pettinato, *Testi Lessicali Bilingui della Biblioteca L. 2769* (MEE 4; Napoli: Istituto Universitario Orientale di Napoli, 1982), 213, n. 141.

[78] A. Dotan, 'Phoenician A > O Shift in Some Greek Transcriptions', *UF* 3 (1971), 293–97, esp. 295. Dotan is followed by Lettinga, 'Vrouwenspiegel', 122.

appropriate that an instrument of the spinner's craft should be associated with a Canaanite god of technical skill.[79] We find a curious parallel in the Swedish word *herkul*, derived from the name of the Roman god Hercules, which also designates a specific type of spinning implement, in this case a special kind of distaff.[80]

---

[79] This derivation was already suggested in Albright, *Yahweh and the Gods*, 136. On the association of *kîšôr* and Kothar see also A. Cooper, 'Divine Names and Epithets in the Ugaritic Texts', in S. Rummel (ed.), *Ras Shamra Parallels: The Texts from Ugarit and the Hebrew Bible*, vol. 3 (Rome: Pontificium Institutum Biblicum, 1981), 385–87 (no. 18). It can be objected against this derivation that in Aramaic the apparent cognates of Hebrew *kšr* (see, e.g., n. 3) also have the meaning 'skill', while their middle radical is *shin*, not *taw* (as we would expect from an Aramaic reflex of Canaanite *ṯ*). The solution to this difficulty is probably that the Aramaic words in question are themselves derived from Canaanite or Akkadian (so E.Y.Kutscher in *HALAT*, s.v. *kšr*).

[80] Cf. N. Lithberg, *Den korta herkuln eller handrocken* (Fataburen, 1930), cited in M. Stenberger (ed.), *Vallhagar. A Migration Period Settlement on Gotland/Sweden*, 2 vols. (Copenhagen: Munkgaard, 1955), 2.861, n. 70.

Part Two

5

A Pattern in the History of Interpretation (to 1600)

I. Introduction

My goal in this chapter is to demonstrate that there is a pattern in the history of interpretation of 'the Song of the Valiant Woman' (Prov. 31:10–31). This pattern reveals itself not only in the parallel development of the Jewish and Christian traditions of interpretation, but also in the close connection between broader hermeneutical and theological epochs and the specific interpretation of Proverbs 31:10–31. The year 1600 is an appropriate cut-off point because it can be said to mark the end of the Reformation period, and thus the beginning of the modern concern with literal (grammatical–historical) interpretation. That concern, which eventually developed into historical-critical scholarship, will be the focus of our attention in the following chapter. But for now we will concentrate upon earlier interpretation of the Song.

To my knowledge, there is virtually no secondary literature on the topic I have chosen, so that my research is 'original' at least in the sense that no one has gone over the exegetical material with this specific passage in mind. It is also original in the sense that I have unearthed texts which are virtually forgotten, and that aspects of the history of the text and translation of Proverbs 31:10–31 have come to light which have not been noticed before.

I am restricting myself to interpretations of the Song which are not part of the tradition of the biblical text itself, including the ancient versions. This means that I will leave out of account the suggestion that the MT contains (in 31:30) a trace of a scribal interpretation,[1] or the

---

[1] As suggested, e.g., in the notes to the Jerusalem Bible.

evidence that the LXX translators betray a certain hermeneutical bias in their version.[2]

Instead, I will begin my story with the first allusions to and comments on the Song that are found in the Talmud and early patristic writers, drawing on the relevant indices of biblical passages which modern editions conveniently provide, as well as the very useful reference work entitled *Biblia Patristica*, the first three volumes of which (plus a supplement on Philo) have now appeared.[3]

By way of preliminary orientation, it may be useful to articulate a broad overall thesis which, though it will have to be qualified and modified in what follows, can nevertheless serve as a rough and ready description of the historical lay of the land. Generally speaking, the following thesis can be defended: from the time of the earliest extant records of biblical interpretation up to the Protestant Reformation of sixteenth-century Europe, the Song of the Valiant Woman was overwhelmingly understood in allegorical terms. Since then, it has usually been interpreted 'literally' as the portrait of an exemplary woman. In other words, for more than a millennium the Valiant Woman was understood by the vast majority of interpreters as an allegory of some spiritual reality (e.g. the Torah or the Church), but this long tradition was decisively broken by the Reformers of the sixteenth century.

It would carry us too far afield to enter into the broader question of the origin of allegorical interpretation in general and its application to biblical exegesis in particular. Suffice it to say that the method of allegory (to be distinguished from typology) became dominant in the Greek philosophical school of Stoicism in order to give a philosophically acceptable sense to the myths of Greek popular religion,[4] and that this same method, for analogous reasons, was popularized in biblical studies by Philo of Alexandria,[5] the Jewish philosopher who was to prove so influential in patristic interpretation. Philo himself, who restricted his commentaries almost exclusively to the five books of Moses, appears not

[2] See B. Gemser, *Sprüche Salomos*. Zweite Auflage (HAT; Tübingen: Mohr, 1963), 9–10.

[3] *Biblia Patristica. Index des citations et allusions bibliques dans la littérature patristique*, 3 vols. (Paris: Editions du Centre National de la Recherche Scientifique, 1975–1980).

[4] See J. Pépin, *Mythe et Allégorie: Les origines grecques et les contestations judéo–chrétiennes*. Nouvelle édition, revue et augmentée (Paris: Etudes Augustiniennes, 1976).

[5] Pépin, *Mythe et Allégorie*, 231–242.

to have commented on the Song,[6] but his allegorical method was applied to it by many subsequent students of the Bible.

II. Talmudic and Patristic Interpretations

It took some time before full-scale commentaries on the book of Proverbs came to be written, so we must content ourselves, for the first centuries of our era, with the evidence of incidental allusions to and quotations from Proverbs 31:10–31 in order to acquire a picture of how the Song was read in this period.

Rabbinic exegesis

For evidence of rabbinic exegesis I will limit myself to the Talmud, specifically the Babylonian Talmud, where the Song is quoted on six different occasions.

The most significant point to note about these occasions is that most of them reflect an allegorical interpretation, and that the one which was to become standard in later Jewish exegesis (the Valiant Woman as allegory of the Torah) is already represented. In one of the stories concerning Rabbi Eleazar ben Simeon, he applies to himself verse 14 of the Song: 'She is like the merchant ships; she brings her food from afar'.[7] The editorial note in Epstein's edition comments, ' *"She"* is referred to the Torah; for the sake of his learning ... his *"food"* – i.e. wealth – had been brought to him from afar.'[8] In another place we read of Rabbi Eleazar again in connection with the Song:

> R. Eleazar further stated, What is the purport of what was written, *She openeth her mouth with wisdom, and the Torah of lovingkindness is on her tongue?* [Prov. 31:26] Is there then a Torah of lovingkindness and a Torah which is not of lovingkindness? But the fact is that Torah [which is studied] for its own sake is a *'Torah of lovingkindness'*, whereas Torah [which is studied] for an ulterior motive is a Torah which is not of lovingkindness.[9]

---

[6] The *Supplément* to the *Biblia Patristica*, which records the biblical references in Philo, indicates one place where Prov. 31:10–31 may be alluded to (*Quaestiones in Genesim* I,26), but this turns out to be only a general statement about the place of women, not a direct reference to the Song.

[7] *B. Meṣ.* 84b. I am quoting from the English translation found in Epstein's edition.

[8] I. Epstein (ed.), *The Babylonian Talmud*, Part 4, *Nezikin*, vol. 1, ad loc. (London: Soncino, 1938–1948).

[9] Epstein, *Babylonian Talmud, Sukkah,* 49b.

Here the expression *tôrat ḥesed* of Proverbs 31:26, which when applied to a literal understanding of the Valiant Woman means something like 'kind teaching', is understood of the Torah as a basic religious category of Judaism. The Valiant Woman herself represents Torah, and therefore what she speaks, what 'is on her tongue', is *tôrat ḥesed*.

The equation of the Valiant Woman with Torah is not the only allegorical interpretation which we find in the Talmud. In two other passages, for example, we find that particular verses of the Song are correlated with the actions of individuals in biblical history. In *Sanhedrin* 20a we find the following discussion concerning Proverbs 31:29 and 30:

> R. Joḥanan said: what is meant by the verse, *Many daughters have done valiantly, but thou excellest them all?* – '*Many daughters*', refers to Joseph and Boaz: '*and thou excellest them all*', to Palti son of Layish.
>
> R. Samuel b. Naḥmani said in R. Jonathan's name: What is meant by the verse, *Grace is deceitful, and beauty is vain, but a woman that feareth the Lord, she shall be praised?* – '*Grace is deceitful*' refers to [the trial of] Joseph; '*and beauty is vain*', to Boaz; while '*and a woman that feareth the Lord, she shall be praised*', to the case of Palti son of Layish. Another interpretation is: '*Grace is deceitful*', refers to the generation of Moses; '*and beauty is vain*' to that of Joshua; '*and she that feareth the Lord, shall be praised*', to that of Hezekiah. Others say '*Grace is deceitful*', refers to the generation of Moses and Joshua; '*and beauty is vain*' to the generation of Hezekiah; while '*and she that feareth the Lord, shall be praised*', refers to the generation of R. Judah son of R. Ila'i, of whose time it was said that [though the poverty was so great that] six of his disciples had to cover themselves with one garment between them, yet they studied the Torah.

In another place (*Ber.* 10a) we read the following:

> R. Joḥanan said in the name of R. Simeon b. Yoḥai: What is the meaning of the verse, *She openeth her mouth with wisdom, and the law of kindness is on her tongue* [Prov. 31:26]? To whom was Solomon alluding in this verse? He was alluding only to his father David who dwelt in five worlds and composed a psalm [for each of them].

There are two points to be noted about this last quotation, apart from its obviously allegorical reading of a verse in the Song. The sentiment here expressed, though spoken by R. Joḥanan, is attributed to R. Simeon ben Yoḥai, who was the father of R. Eleazar ben Simeon,[10] the *tanna* who, as we have seen, interpreted the Valiant Woman as the Torah. Father and son espoused two quite different allegorical interpretations of the Song, specifically of the *tôrat ḥesed* of verse 26. Secondly, R. Simeon clearly

---

[10] See Shmuel Safrai, 'Eleazar ben Simeon' in *EncJud*, 6.599.

assigns the authorship to Solomon, which possibly means that he equated the 'Lemuel' of 31:1 with Solomon, an opinion which we shall meet again in our inquiry.

Apart from the four passages we have mentioned which read the Song allegorically, there are also two places in the Talmud where it appears to be taken in a straightforward literal sense. In *Pesaḥ* 50b we read:

> Our Rabbis taught: He who looks to the earnings of his wife or of a mill will never see a sign of blessing. 'The earning of his wife' means [when she goes around selling wool] by weight. '[The earnings of] a mill' means its hire. But if she makes [e.g., woollen garments] and sells them, Scripture indeed praises her, for it is written, *she maketh linen garments and selleth them* [Prov. 31:24].

And in *Ta'anit* 26b we find a statement attributed to R. Simeon ben Gamaliel, which includes these words:

> The daughters of Jerusalem came out and danced in the vineyards exclaiming at the same time, 'Young man, lift up thine eyes and see what thou choosest for thyself. Do not set thine eyes on beauty but set thine eyes on [good] family. "Grace is deceitful, and beauty is vain; but a woman that feareth the Lord, she shall be praised"' [Prov. 31:30]. And it further says, 'Give her of the fruit of her hands; and let her works praise her in the gates' [Prov. 31:31].

This last passage, again, is noteworthy for a number of reasons. First of all, whereas all our earlier quotes were from the Gemara, this one is from the Mishna. Secondly, in connection with this, it is clear that this use of Proverbs 31 is chronologically early: not only did R. Simeon ben Gamaliel live in the first century AD,[11] but he is describing a Jewish custom which traditionally took place on 'the fifteenth of Ab and the day of Atonement', and therefore had presumably been going on some time before R. Simeon's own day. Thirdly, it appears that, within the context of this traditional folk custom, that is, outside the formal tradition of rabbinic learning, the Song was quoted in a straightforward literal sense, being applied to the courtship of young men and women. Finally, the concluding quotation has the look of a later addition, and probably does not belong to R. Simeon's words – at any rate, not to the traditional words of the folk custom being described.

The upshot of our survey of quotations of the Song in the Talmud is the following. There is some evidence of an early literal interpretation, probably going back to pre-Christian times. This was supplanted, or at least supplemented, by a later allegorical reading, either referring the

---

[11] See Israel Burgansky, 'Simeon ben Gamaliel I' in *EncJud*, 14.1555.

Song to different events and persons of biblical history, or else to the
Torah. The latter interpretation is first attested in the late second century
AD with R. Eleazar ben Simeon, whose allegorical interpretation of the
Song breaks with that of his father.

A final word needs to be said about a place in the Talmud where the
Song is not quoted, but clearly alluded to. In *Yoma* 47a we find the statement: 'All women are valiant, but the valour [*grp*] of my mother exceeded
them all.' This is evidently an allusion to Proverbs 31:29, not least because
the expression ʿālâ ʿal in the sense 'exceed' or 'surpass' is rare, and found in
the Bible only in that text.[12] We learn from this allusion that the idiom ʿāśâ
ḥayil, which can mean both 'to do valiantly' and 'to gain riches',[13] was
taken in rabbinic times to mean the former in Proverbs 31:29, at least if
Jastrow is right in giving 'valour' as the meaning of *grp*.[14]

Literal interpretations in the Church Fathers

Turning now to early Christian interpretation, we observe that the same
pattern emerges: an early literal reading, which is followed by one or two
church fathers, is soon overwhelmed by allegorical interpretation. By the
end of the patristic period all Christian interpreters take the Song to be an
allegory, though there is no general consensus as to what it is precisely that
the Valiant Woman is supposed to symbolize.

The earliest record of a Christian interpretation of the Song is found
in the second-century church father Clement of Alexandria. In the third
book of his *Paidagogos* he quotes the Song a number of times as a model
for God-fearing women. In a discussion of the legitimacy of manual
labour, for example, he writes that the 'Pedagogue' (that is, the word of
God) approves the kind of woman who 'will stretch out her arms to the
useful things (*ta chrēsima*) and extends her hands to a spindle; opens her
hands to the poor, and stretches out her palm to the indigent', thus giving
a direct application of the literal meaning of Proverbs 31:19–20.[15] A little
later, speaking in lofty terms of the work of a wife and mother in her

[12] See the lexica, s.v. ʿālâ.
[13] See the lexica, s.v. ḥayil.
[14] See Leo Jung's note *ad loc.* in *The Babylonian Talmud. Seder Moʿed III* (ed. I.
Epstein; London: Soncino Press, 1938), 222.
[15] *Paid.* 3,49,5 (my translation). He appears to be quoting the LXX from memory
since he has the future *ektenei*, 'will stretch out' instead of the present *ekteinei*, and
the synonym *chrēsima* instead of *sympheronta*, but for the rest follows the LXX
word for word.

household, he describes her with phrases drawn from the Song of the Valiant Woman.[16]

We find a very similar use of the Song in the third-century *Didascalia Apostolorum*, the third chapter of which contains a complete translation of Proverbs 31:10–31. The heading of the chapter, which sets the context for the interpretation of the Song here given, begins: 'An instruction to women, that they should please and honor their husbands alone, caring assiduously and wisely for the work of their houses with diligence'.[17] The quotation of the Song itself is introduced with these words: 'O woman, fear your husband and reverence him, and please him alone, and be ready for his service. And your hand shall be for the wool, and your mind upon the spindle, as He has said in Wisdom: Who can find a valiant woman'.[18]

The textual history of the Song as quoted in the *Didascalia Apostolorum* is a study in itself, which we cannot pursue in this context. It is enough to say that this part of the *Didascalia* is extant only in a Syriac translation of the Greek original, and that the Song in the Greek was quoted in a version which betrays the influence of the LXX but is not identical with it. This produces a number of distinctive renderings, such as verse 29, which reads (in Vööbus's English translation of the Syriac) 'and her many daughters have become rich. And she did many great things and she was exalted above all other women'.

The *Biblia patristica* at present covers only the first three centuries of the Christian era, so that I cannot be sure whether I have missed significant references to the Song in the patristic literature after the third century. As far as I know, the literal interpretation is found in only two other church fathers: Gregory of Nazianze in the fourth century, and Paulinus of Nola in the fifth.

Gregory, in the context of the funeral oration on his father, also devotes a few paragraphs to his mother, Nonna. Among other things, he writes:

> I have heard sacred Scripture saying: 'Who shall find a valiant woman?' and also that she is a gift of God ... It is impossible to mention anyone who was more fortunate than my father in this respect.[19]

---

[16] *Paid.* 3,67,2–3.

[17] A. Vööbus (ed.), *The Didascalia Apostolorum in Syriac* (Louvain, 1979), 20.

[18] *Didascalia Apostolorum*, 20-21.

[19] Gregory of Nazianze, *Oratio XVIII*, 7 (*PG* 35, 993A). I am quoting the English translation by L.P. McCauley in *Funeral Orations by Saint Gregory Nazianzen and Saint Ambrose* (*FC* 22; Washington: Catholic University of America Press, 1953), 124.

A little later he adds:

> While some women excel in the management of their households and others in piety – for it is difficult to achieve both – she nevertheless surpassed all in both, because she was pre-eminent in each and because she alone combined the two. She increased the resources of her household by her care and practical foresight *according to the standards and norms laid down by Solomon for the valiant woman.*[20]

This last phrase (*kata tous Solomōntos peri tēs andreias gynaikos horous kai nomous*) again clearly alludes to the Song of the Valiant Woman (which begins with the words *gynaika andreian* in the LXX), and is significant not only because it again appears to equate Lemuel and Solomon, but also because it clearly takes the literal sense of the Song to be normative for the practical domestic life of the Christian woman.

In the letters of Paulinus of Nola (353–431) we twice find a similar application of the Song, once with reference to Paulina, the late wife of his friend Pammachius, and once with reference to his friend Aper's wife, Amanda. The first letter, addressed to Pammachius, contains the following passage:

> But she, as she always was, so shall she forever be *a crown for her husband* [Prov. 12:4], and *her lamp shall not go out* [Prov. 31:18]. For, as it is written, *she has stretched out her arms to useful deeds* [Prov. 31:19], *she opened her mouth with wisdom* [Prov. 31:26], *she did good things for her husband* [Prov. 31:12], she crowned you with glory and honour, in order that she might *rejoice* with you *in the last days* [Prov. 31:25].[21]

The second passage is too long to quote in full, but again applies many phrases from the Song to the exemplary life of Amanda. For example, we read:

> She is the kind of person in whom *the heart of her husband trusteth* [Prov. 31:11]. As Scripture says, *she renders her husband good and not evil all the days of her life*

---

[20] *Oratio XVIII*, 8 (my emphasis).

[21] Paulinus of Nola, *Epistola* 13,5 (*PL* 61,210): 'Verum illa, ut fuit semper, ita et erit in perpetuum corona viro suo, et non extinguetur lucerna eius: extendit enim, ut scriptum est, brachia sua ad opera utilia, os suum aperuit prudenter, operata est viro suo bona; gloria et honore coronavit te, ut iucundaretur tecum in diebus novissimis' (my translation). The English translation by P.G. Walsh in *Letters of St. Paulinus of Nola*, 2 vols. (*ACW* 35; London: Longmans, Green and Co., 1966), I, 122, makes a number of mistakes and fails to recognize the allusion to Prov. 31:25.

[Prov. 31:12], so you have no worry about the secular matters of your house ...[22]

Paulinus is the first author we have quoted who wrote in Latin, and the Bible version which he uses is the Vetus Latina, the Latin translation of the LXX which was in common use before it was superseded by Jerome's Vulgate. It is the Vetus Latina which accounts for Paulinus' use of phrases like *circumspectus in foribus*, reflecting LXX's *peribleptos ... en pylais* (Prov. 31:23), and *duplicia pallia*, reflecting LXX's *dissas chlainas* (Prov. 31:22).[23]

To my knowledge, Paulinus is the last patristic writer to espouse a literal interpretation of the Song. Apart from the church fathers we have mentioned, all others seem to have adopted an allegorical reading, beginning with Origen in the third century.

Allegorical interpretations in the Church Fathers

Origen

Origen (c. 185–254) is the first person who is known to have written a complete commentary on the book of Proverbs. Only fragments of this commentary have survived,[24] but fortunately the section on the Valiant Woman appears to have been preserved complete.[25] We learn from this section that Origen took the Valiant Woman, in his philosophical way, to be an allegorical symbol of *psyche*, the human soul. A representative passage is his comment on verse 15:

> Also, the sun of righteousness as a bridegroom finds the soul getting up at night and awake, and certainly also praying that she might not fall into temptation, quoting the text 'I was awake and became like a single sparrow on a roof' [Ps. 101:8]. Now the *broma* ('food') of the soul is the study of the divine words, its *erga* ('works') are the virtues, its *therapainides* ('servant-girls') are the senses. These then are the things which the soul, 'more valuable than precious stones', supplies to its bodily home.[26]

---

[22] Paulinus of Nola, *Epistola* 44, 4 (*PL* 61, 388–389): 'Quae talis est, *fidit in ea cor mariti ejus. Operatur enim*, ut scriptum est, *viro suo bona tota vita sua, et non mala*: et ideo non sollicitus agis quae in domo tua terrena aguntur' (Walsh's translation). Note, again, that Walsh fails to catch all the allusions to the Song in Paulinus' text, e.g. *pretiosior lapidibus pretiosis* (cf. Prov. 31:10).

[23] *PL* 61,389.

[24] *Expositio in Proverbia*, PG 17, 149–252.

[25] PG 17, 249–252.

[26] PG 17, 249–252: ἢ καὶ τὴν ἐκ νυκτὸς ἀνισταμένην ψυχὴν γρηγοροῦσαν εὑρίσκει ὁ τῆς δικαιοσύνης ἥλιος νύμφιος, πάντως δὲ χαὶ προσευχομένην

It is to be noted that Origen is commenting on the LXX text of the Song, and it is to this text that the words *brōma, erga* and *therapainides*[27] refer. We notice how Origen characteristically mingles concepts derived from Scripture (the Psalms quote) and Platonic philosophy (the soul in its relation to body).

Origen is significant both because he was the first author of a commentary on Proverbs and because he is the first in the Christian tradition to propose an allegorical interpretation of the Song. With one significant exception, the remaining patristic authors who refer to our passage do so incidentally or very briefly. The exception is Augustine, who devoted one of his sermons to it. All of these authors agree in treating the Valiant Woman as an allegory, though they do not agree on what spiritual reality she represents. In what follows we shall simply list, in a roughly chronological order, the remaining patristic allusions, reserving for Augustine's sermon a more extended treatment. As the concluding figure of patristic exegesis we shall deal briefly with Gregory the Great.

Hilary of Poitiers to Andrew of Crete

(1) Hilary of Poitiers (d.367). In his commentary on the book of Psalms, *Tractatus Super Psalmos,* Hilary makes the following comment on the phrase, 'Your wife will be like a fruitful vine' (Ps. 128:3):

> However, in order that we may now know what ought to be understood under the designation "wife", we must observe what is dealt with under the same name of wife elsewhere as well.[28]

He then quotes a number of biblical passages where the word *uxor,* 'wife' is mentioned, including Proverbs 31:10 in the Vetus Latina: *Uxorem virilem quis inveniet?* This he explains as follows:

> Therefore, we must understand the valiant wife according to the manner of

---

[26] *(Continued)* τοῦ μὴ ἐμπεσεῖν εἰς πειρασμόν, λέγουσαν τὸ Ἠγρύπνησα καὶ ἐγενόμην ὡς στρουθίον μονάζον ἐπὶ δώματος. Βρῶμα δέ ἐστι ψυχῆς, ἡ μελέτη τῶν θείων λόγων, ἔργα δέ, αἱ ἀρεταί, θεραπαινίδες δέ, αἱ αἰσθήσεις.Ταῦτ' οὖν παρέχει ἡ τιμιωτέρα λίθων πολυτελῶν ψυχὴ τῷ σωματικῷ αὐτῆς οἴκῳ. (my translation).

[27] *Therapainides* here presupposes *therapainisi* in the LXX of Prov. 31:15. This seems to be a textual variant of the *therapaisi* found in the printed editions.

[28] PL 9, 708: 'Ut autem nunc cognoscamus quid sub uxoris nuncupatione intellegi oporteat, contuendum est quid et alibi sub eodem uxoris nomine tractetur' (my translation).

proverbs, namely as the one whom Solomon desired to take as bride [Wisdom 8:2] … This woman, therefore, which is taken as his wife, is valiant wisdom, who accomplishes all things and subjects them to herself, and who is mighty in the work of useful deeds.[29]

For Hilary, the Valiant Woman is an allegory of *sapientia* (wisdom).

(2) Didymus of Alexandria (c.313–398). Among the *Fragmenta in Proverbia* attributed to this Didymus (also known as Didymus the Blind), we find the following comment on the phrase 'her clothing is fine linen and purple' (Prov. 31:22):

> It says that the contemplation of things that have come to be, and the contemplation of the Holy Trinity, are the garment of a pure mind, consisting of fine linen and purple.[30]

Here, apparently, the Valiant Woman is an allegory of *nous* (mind).

(3) Epiphanius of Salamis (c.315–403). In a passing reference in Epiphanius' work *Ancoratus* (chapter 101) we find the statement:

> But understand the valiant woman to be the church of God, your mother.[31]

(4) Jerome (342–420). In his commentary on Ezekiel, Jerome has the following comment on the phrase 'I swathed you with *byssus* (fine linen)' (Ez. 16:10):

> Jerusalem … is also swathed with *byssus*, from which the finest threads in the high priest's garment are woven. And the wife in Proverbs who wove two cloaks for her husband, both of the present and of the future world, is said to have made for herself garments of *byssus* and purple.[32]

---

[29] PL 9, 708: 'Ergo secundum proverbiorum rationem uxorem virilem nosse debemus, eam nempe quam sibi Solomon sponsam optarit assumere . . . Haec igitur tamquam uxor assumpta sapientia virilis est, perficiens omnia, et sibi subdens, et in labore utilium operum valida' (my translation).

[30] PG 39, 1645–46: τὴν θεωρίαν τῶν γεγονότων καὶ τὴν θεωρίαν τῆς ἁγίας Τριάδος, ἔνδυμα εἶναι λέγει νοῦ καθαροῦ, ἐκ βύσσου καὶ πορφύρας (my translation)

[31] PG 43, 200: Ἀνδρείαν δὲ γυναῖκα νοεῖτε μοι τὴν Ἐκκλησίαν τοῦ θεοῦ τὴν ἡμῶν μητέρα (my translation)

[32] PL 25, 132–133: 'Hierusalem . . . et bysso accingitur, de qua tenuissima in veste pontificis fila texuntur; et uxor, in Proverbiis, quae viro suo duas texuit chlamydes, et presentis saeculi et futuri, sibi de bysso et purpura fecisse dicitur vestimenta' (my translation).

This passage refers to the LXX of Proverbs 31:22, which begins (erroneously[33]) with *dissas chlainas*, here rendered by Jerome as *duas chlamydes*, 'two cloaks'. It is not clear how he interprets the Valiant Woman, but the reference to 'the present and future world' shows that he takes the two cloaks in an allegorical sense, and presumably therefore also the heroine herself.

As an exegetical curiosity it may be pointed out that Jerome here follows the mistaken construal of *šnym* and *mrbdym* in the LXX of Proverbs 31:21–22 (see note 33), while his own translation in the Vulgate corrects this error.[34] This would not be so surprising if it were not for the fact that this part of the Ezekiel commentary was completed in 412, some seven years after Jerome finished the Old Testament part of the Vulgate (405). It is further noteworthy that Jerome renders the relevant phrase from the LXX as *duas chlamydes*, whereas the Vetus Latina had *duplicia pallia* (see the comments about Paulinus of Nola above).

For the history of interpretation it is also of interest that Jerome comments elsewhere on both the alphabetic pattern and the metre of the Song. In one of his letters to Paula he discusses alphabetic acrostics in Scripture, and observes:

> A final alphabetic acrostic also concludes the Proverbs of Solomon, which is scanned in iambic tetrameter, beginning from the place in which it says 'A valiant woman who shall find?'[35]

The recognition of the alphabetic acrostic probably enabled Jerome to correct the LXX at Proverbs 31:21–22, but he makes a mistake of his own by describing the metre of the Song as iambic tetrameter.

(5) Johannes Cassianus (c.360–c.433). Like Epiphanius of Salamis, Cassianus took the Valiant Woman to represent the church. He makes this clear in a famous section of his *Collationes* which deals with two kinds of theoretical (as opposed to practical) *scientia*:

---

[33] The LXX construes *šnym* at the end of v. 21 with *mrbdym* at the beginning of v. 22. We know this is a mistake because, in the context of the alphabetic acrostic, *mrbdym* is required to be at the beginning of the *mem*-line.

[34] The Vulgate has 'omnes enim domestici eius vestiti sunt duplicibus (*šnym*). Stragul[at]am vestem (*mrbdym*) fecit sibi.'

[35] Epistola XXX, *PL* 32,445: 'Proverbia quoque Salomonis extremum claudit alphabetum quod tetrametro iambico supputatur, ab eo loco in quo ait: *Mulierem fortem quis inveniet?*' (my translation).

Now theoretical *scientia* is divided into two parts, that is, into historical interpretation and spiritual understanding. That is also why Solomon, when he had listed the varied grace of the Church, added: "For all in her house are doubly clothed" [Prov. 31:21].[36]

This section in Cassianus is famous, not because it illustrates the allegorical interpretation of our Song, but because it contains the classic statement of the twofold interpretation of Scripture which was to dominate the Christian Middle Ages.[37] We here see that the influential distinction between historical (i.e. literal) and spiritual interpretation was initially justified by an appeal to the word *dupliciter* in verse 21 of the Song.

It is further noteworthy that this use of the Song was only possible because of a distinctive rendering of the verse in question, which takes *šnym* as the last word of verse 21 (*dupliciter*), not as the first word of verse 22, following the LXX (*duplicia pallia* or *duas chlamydes*). Interestingly, Cassianus quotes the relevant line in a distinctive rendering; the wording *Omnes enim qui apud eam sunt, vestiti sunt dupliciter* conforms to neither the Vetus Latina (*Omnes enim qui apud eam sunt. Duplicia pallia ...*, attested in Augustine[38]) nor the Vulgate (*Omnes enim domestici eius vestiti sunt duplicibus.*)

(6) Opus Imperfectum in Matthaeum (fifth century). This work, which was long attributed to John Chrysostom, was in fact written by an unknown Arian author of the fifth century.[39] In the context of a commentary on the words 'when Jesus got into the boat' (Mt. 8:23), the author writes:

> we must inquire how this boat must be understood on the spiritual level ... There is no doubt that this boat symbolized the Church, in accordance with what the Holy Spirit says about her through Solomon, in the words: "she has become like a ship of distant trade" [Prov. 31:14]. This is the church, which by the word of preaching travels in every direction, with the apostles as sailors, the Lord as helmsman, and the Holy Spirit as wind, carrying with her a great

---

[36] *PL* 49, 962: 'Theoretice vero in duas dividitur partes, id est, in historicam interpretationem, et intelligentiam spiritalem. Unde etiam Salomon cum Ecclesiae multiformem gratiam enumerasset, adjecit: *Omnes enim quid* [*sic*] *apud eam sunt, vestiti sunt dupliciter*' (my translation). Note that *quid* must here be a misprint for *qui*.
[37] See H. de Lubac, *Exégèse médiévale. Les quatre sens de l'Ecriture*, 3 vols. (Paris: Aubier, 1959–1961), 1.190–193.
[38] *CCSL* 41,461.
[39] J. Quasten, *Patrologia*, 3 vols. (Westminster MD: Newman, 1963), 3.471.

and precious ransom, with which it has purchased every race of men – or rather, the entire world – by the blood of Christ.[40]

Clearly, the Valiant Woman is again understood as an allegory of the church.

From a textual point of view it is worth noting that Proverbs 31:14 is here quoted in a somewhat unusual form. *Facta est tamquam navis mercaturā longinquā* may be a free citation from memory of the Vetus Latina wording, *Facta est tamquam navis quae negotiatur a longe.*[41] Alternatively, it may be a free rendering directly from the Greek of the LXX (*naus emporeuomenē makrothen*), since the *Opus Imperfectum* is possibly a translation from a Greek original.[42]

(7) Pseudo-Procopius of Gaza (sixth century). This unknown author of a commentary on the complete book of Proverbs again interprets the Valiant Woman as an allegory of wisdom, understood in terms of Neoplatonic philosophy. Suffice it to quote his explanation of the words 'But you surpass them all' (Prov. 31:29b):

> This wisdom, as the science of sciences, stands above all the sciences of human things as their cause, and it has transcended them all by the activities of knowledge and virtue, being a science of divine things.[43]

In this highly theoretical account of wisdom, the husband in the Song is repeatedly equated with mind (*nous*).

(8) Andrew of Crete (c. 660–740). In his Fourth Oration, on the Nativity of the Virgin Mary, Andrew lists a whole series of scriptural epithets which apply to Mary, including 'daughter'. In that context he quotes the LXX of Proverbs 31:27 as applying to Mary:

---

[40] *PG* 56,755: 'Quaerendum enim est, quid haec navis juxta spiritualem rationem intelligi debeat … Et non dubium est navem istam Ecclesiam figurasse, secundum quod per Salomonem de ea Spiritus sanctus loquitur, dicens, *Facta est tamquam navis mercatura longinqua*, id est Ecclesia, quae navigantibus apostolis, gubernante domino, flante Spiritu sancto, praedicationis verbo ubique discurrit, portans secum magnum et inaestimabile pretium, quo omne genus hominum, vel potius totum mundum sanguine Christi mercata est' (my translation).

[41] *CCSL* 41,453.

[42] Quasten, *Patrologia*, 3.471.

[43] *PG* 87.1, 1544: Αὕτη δὲ ἡ σοφία, οἷα ἐπιστήμη ἐπιστημῶν ὑπὲρ πάσας τὰς τῶν ἀνθρωπίνων πραγμάτων ἐπιστήμας ὑπάρχει, ὡς τούτων αἰτία, καὶ ταῖς κατὰ γνῶσιν καὶ ἀρετὴν ἐνεργείαις ὑπερβέβηκε πάσας, θείων πραγμάτων ἐπιστήμη ὑπάρχουσα. (my translation).

'Many daughters have gained riches, many have done mighty deeds, but you transcend and have surpassed them all'.[44]

To my knowledge, this is the first place where the Valiant Woman is related to the Virgin Mary. It was not, as we shall see, to be the last.

At this point we could make reference also to the commentary on Proverbs attributed to Salonius, the fifth-century bishop of Geneva, in which the Valiant Woman is taken as an allegory of the church. It has recently been shown, however, that this commentary is actually the work of a much later medieval author. Accordingly, we will deal with it later under the heading Pseudo-Salonius.

It is clear from the patristic authors we have surveyed so far that the allegorical interpretation of the Song was widespread in the early Christian centuries, but also that it was inconsistent. The Valiant Woman is taken to refer to soul (Origen), wisdom (Hilary of Poitiers and Pseudo-Procopius of Gaza), mind (Didymus of Alexandria), the church (Epiphanius of Salamis, Johannes Cassianus and the author of the *Opus Imperfectum*) and the Virgin Mary (Andrew of Crete). However, it was especially the equation of the Valiant Woman with the church which was to prove influential. This was due very largely to the authority of Augustine and Gregory the Great.

The authoritative interpretations of Augustine and Gregory
Augustine (354–430) devoted one of his sermons (number 37 in modern editions) to the Song. This sermon was taken down in shorthand while it was being delivered, and later published. It is the longest treatment of the Song which has come down to us from antiquity, and it is also the most informal and the most influential. It is tempting to dwell on the many interesting features of this sermon (it contains evidence, for example, of colloquial Latin pronunciation, of lively interaction between Augustine and his audience and of popular theological polemics; it also seems to have been preserved in two textual traditions, going back to *two* stenographers in Augustine's audience[45]), but we shall restrict ourselves to its allegorical hermeneutics and its value as witness to the Vetus Latina.

Apparently the Song had been read to the audience before the sermon began. Augustine refers to this at the beginning of the sermon proper (after requesting his hearers to be quiet as they listen, since his voice is not strong):

---

[44] *Homiliai*, PG 97,872.
[45] C. Lambot (ed.), *Sancti Aurelii Augustini Sermones de Vetere Testamento* (*CCSL* 41; Turnholt: Brepols, 1961), 444–445; and idem 'Le sermon de Saint Augustin sur la femme forte du livre des Proverbes', *Revue Bénédictine* 65 (1955), 208–217.

What we are holding in our hands, namely the Scripture which you see, urges us to study and extol a certain woman, of whom you heard a moment ago in the reading, a woman of high standing who has a husband of high standing, a husband who found her when she was lost and adorned her when she was found. About this woman I will say a few things as time allows – the things which the Lord suggests, following the course of the text which you see me holding. After all, it is the day of the martyrs,[46] and therefore we must give the more praise to the mother of the martyrs. Now that I have said this by way of introduction, you have understood who this woman is. See also whether you recognize her as I go through the reading. To judge from your attitude, every-one in the audience is now saying to himself: "She must be the Church". I confirm that thought. For what else could be the mother of the martyrs? That's right: your understanding is the right one. The woman about whom we want to say a few words is the Church.[47]

Augustine goes on in this vein, continually interacting with his audience, and dealing with each verse of the Song in succession. Each detail of the Valiant Woman's description is related to some biblical image connected with the church – the 'precious stones' of verse 10 to the New Testament image of living stones, the 'night' of verse 15 to the tribulations of the church, the 'lamp' of verse 18 to Christian hope, the *duplicia pallia* of verse 22 to the two natures of Christ, and so on. As an example of his general approach, here is Augustine's commentary on the words 'She also strengthens her arms for the spindle [*in fusum*]' in 31:19b:

[46] The sermon was given on July 17, 'on the anniversary of the Sicilian martyrs', according to the title. See Lambot's introduction to his edition of the Sermon, 445.

[47] *Sermo* 37, 1 as found in Lambot's edition, *CCSL* 41, 446–447. My rendering is a bit free, to capture the informal and colloquial character of the original, which was clearly delivered 'off the cuff'. The original reads: 'Et hoc quod gestamus in manibus, scriptura scilicet quam uidetis, commendat nobis inquirendam et laudandam mulierem quamdam, de qua paulo ante cum legeretur audistis, magnam, habentem magnum uirum, eum uirum qui inuenit perditam, ornauit inuentam. De hac secundum lectionis tenorem, quam me portare conspicitis, pauca pro tempore quae dominus suggerit dicam. Dies est enim martyrum, et ideo magis laudanda est mater martyrum. Iam quae sit ista mulier me proloquente accepistis. Videte etiam utrum me legente agnoscatis. Omnis nunc auditor, quantum ex affectu uestro satis apparet, dicit in corde suo: 'Ecclesia debet esse'. Confirmo istam cogitationem. Nam quae potuit esse altera martyrum mater? Ita est. Quod intellexistis, hoc est. De qua muliere uolumus aliquid dicere, ecclesia est.'

In fusum: not from *infundere* [i.e. *infusum*], but "for that spinning implement called *fusus*". About that spindle I will give the explanation which the Lord gives me. For this kind of spinning applies to both men and women. Listen to the meaning of the words: *She strengthens her arms for the spindle.* He could have said: "for the distaff", but he said "spindle", perhaps for good reasons. To be sure, it might seem that it is not absurd to take "spindle" to refer to spinning, and "spinning" to refer to good work, as of a virtuous woman and a hard-working, thrifty wife. However, I will not withhold from you, beloved, what I personally understand by this spindle. Everyone who lives a life of good works in the holy Church, who effects rather than neglects God's command-ments, does not know what he is doing tomorrow, but does know what he did today. He is fearful about his future deed, but glad about his past deed. And he is careful to persevere in good deeds, for fear of losing the past through neglect of the future. But in praying to the Lord, in his every petition, he does not have a sure knowledge of his future deed, but of his past deed, based on what he has done, not on what he is going to do. Now then, if you agree with me that this is true, consider the two implements involved in spinning: the distaff and the spindle. It is the wool wrapped on the distaff which passes over to the spindle; it must be drawn out and spun into thread. That which is wrapped on the distaff is future; that which has been collected on the spindle is already past. Therefore your deed is on the spindle, not on the distaff. For on the distaff is that which you are going to do; on the spindle what you have done. There-fore, look and see if you have something on the spindle: there let your arms be strengthened. There your conscience will be strong; there you will be secure and say to God: "Give, because I have given; forgive, because I have forgiven; act, because I have acted." After all, you do not claim a reward except for a deed that is done, not a deed that is to be done. Therefore, whatever you are engaged in, let your whole attention be fixed on the spindle, but that which has been collected on the spindle does not have to be brought back to the distaff. Therefore be careful what you do, so that you may have it on the spindle, that you may strengthen your arms for the spindle, that your whole effort may be directed to the spindle, that the spindle may have something which may console you, which may give you the confidence to pray and hope for the things that have been promised.

Perhaps you say, "And what shall I do, what do you bid me have on my spindle?" Listen to what follows: *But she opened her hands to the poor* [Prov. 31:20a]. No indeed, we are not ashamed to teach you the holy art of spinning! Take note, if anyone has a full wallet, a full barn, a full cellar, all these things are on the distaff – let them pass over to the spindle! Look at the way she spins (*neat*), in fact look at the way she "spin" (*neiat*)[48] – as long as all are instructed, never mind the grammarians![49]

---

[48] Augustine here deliberately uses the colloquial pronunciation *neiat* with which his audience is familiar. See Lambot, 'Sur la femme forte', 215–217.

[49] *Sermo* 30, 13–14 as found in Lambot's edition, *CCSL* 41, 457–459: 'In FVSVM, non ab "infundendo", sed in illud instrumentum lanificii, quod uocatur

It is worth observing that Augustine does briefly acknowledge that a
literal meaning of the spindle is possible, making the Valiant Woman
represent simply 'a virtuous woman and a hard-working, thrifty wife', but
he dismisses this in favour of his own much more fanciful interpretation
of the spindle, which is clearly reminiscent of the classical Greco–Roman
conception of the *Moirai* or *Parcae* (i.e. the Fates) who spin humanity's
destiny.[50]

We turn now to the text of the Song which Augustine uses. As we
have noted, this is the Vetus Latina, which is a translation of the LXX. In a
few places, Augustine's text reflects an interesting variant reading in the

---

[49] (*Continued*) fusum. De fuso isto, quod dominus donat dicam. Neque enim ista
lanificia sunt a uiris aliena. Audite quid sit: BRACHIA SVA FIRMAVIT IN
FVSVM. Potuit dicere: In colum. Fusum dixit, forte non frustra. Quamuis possit
uideri nec absurde intellegi de fuso lanificium significatum, de lanificio bonum
opus, tamquam castae mulieris et matronae impigrae et diligentis. Tamen ego,
carissimi, in isto fuso, quod intellego, non tacebo. Omnis qui uiuit in bonis
operibus in sancta ecclesia, non neglector sed effector praeceptorum dei, quid
faciat cras nescit, quid fecerit hodie scit. De futuro opere timet, de praeterito
gaudet. Et ut perseueret in bonis operibus uigilat, ne forte negligens futurorum
perdat praeteritum. In orando tamen domino, in omni deprecatione sua, non
habet firmam conscientiam de opere futuro sed de praeterito, ex eo quod fecit,
non ex eo quod facturus est. Iam ergo si hoc uerum esse mecum uidetis, attendite
in lanificio duo instrumenta ista: colum et fusum. In colo lana inuoluta est, quae
filo ducenda et nenda transeat in fusum. Quod in colo inuolutum est, futurum est;
quod fuso collectum est, iam praeteritum. Opus ergo tuum in fuso est, non in
colo. In colo enim est quod facturus es; in fuso quod fecisti. Vide ergo si aliquid
habes in fuso, ibi firmentur brachia tua. Ibi erit fortis conscientia tua, ibi securus
deo dices: "Da, quia dedi; dimitte, quia dimisi; fac, quia feci". Non enim petis
praemium, nisi opere gesto, non opere gerendo. Quidquid ergo operaris, totus
animus ad fusum sit. Quia et quod pendet in colo, ad fusum traiciendum est, non
autem illud quod collectum est in fuso ad colum reuocandum est. Ergo uide quid
agas, ut habeas in fuso, ut brachia tua firmes in fusum, ut totum conetur ad fusum,
ut habeat aliquid fusum quod te consoletur, quod te confirmet, quod tibi det
fiduciam deprecandi et sperandi promissa. "Et quid agam?" forte dicis 'quid me
iubes habere in fuso?' Audi quod sequitur: MANVS AVTEM SVAS APERVIT
PAVPERI. Eia, non nos pudet lanificium sanctum docere uos. Videte, si quis
habet plenum saccellum, plenum horreum, plenam apothecam, omnia ista in
colo sunt, transeant in fusum. Videte quemadmodum neat, immo uidete
quemadmodum neiat – dum omnes instruantur, grammatici non timeantur' (my
translation).
[50] See S. Eitrem, 'Moira', *RE XV*, 2449–2497, esp. 2479–2484. Augustine seems
to be dependent here on the version of the myth found in Apuleius, *De mundo*
38,373 where the spindle and distaff are also correlated with past and future.

LXX. For example, the beginning of verse 13 is quoted by Augustine as *Inveniens lanas et linum*, 'Finding wool and flax.' This reflects the LXX variant reading *heuramenē*, which probably arose because the correct reading *mēryomenē* (which is printed in all modern editions of the LXX) is a rare verb which here probably means 'drawing out' or 'spinning'. Similarly, the beginning of verse 27 is quoted by Augustine as *Severae conversationes domorum eius*, 'The occupations of her households are strict'. The LXX has two different readings for the adjective in this sentence, both of which are quite well-attested: *stegnai*, 'watertight', 'strict', and *stenai*, 'narrow'. The Vetus Latina, as quoted by Augustine, would seem to reflect the first of these readings. A third example of a noteworthy LXX reading underlying Augustine's text is found in verse 31, quoted by Augustine as *Date illi de fructibus manuum suarum*, 'Give her of the fruits of her hands'. What is remarkable about this is that the best-attested LXX text here has *Dote autę apo karpōn cheileōn autēs*, 'Give her of the fruit of her lips'. The Vetus Latina here reflects a textual variant in the Greek (*cheirōn*) which (though faithful to the MT) does not have the manuscript authority to replace the reading of the printed LXX editions (*cheileōn*).

There is also one case where the Vetus Latina is guilty of a serious, though understandable, mistranslation. The LXX of verse 20 reads *Cheiras de autēs diēnoixen penēti, karpon de exeteine ptōchō*, 'She opened her hands to the poor, and she extended her *karpos* to the needy'. It is clear from the parallelism of *cheiras* and *karpon*, as well as from the MT (which has *kappāh* and *yādehā*) that *karpos* is here to be taken as a synonym of 'hand', in other words, that it here means 'wrist'.[51] In the Vetus Latina, however, it is translated 'fruit', the much more common meaning of *karpos: Fructum autem porrexit inopi*. Needless to say, this gives Augustine occasion to hold forth on the importance of fruitbearing, but has little to do with the original text, either in Hebrew or Greek.

Before leaving Augustine, we should note that the textual tradition of his *Sermo* 37 also includes what Lambot calls an 'interpolated text' of this sermon, which was at one time attributed to Ambrose, and printed among his works.[52] Apart from a few short interpolations which expand on Augustine's exposition, this text is of interest because it corrects the Vetus Latina on a few points. In verse 13, for example, it has *Filans* rather than *Inveniens*, reflecting *mēryomenē* instead of *heuramenē* in the LXX text. In verse 27 it has *angustae* rather than *severae*, reflecting an original *stenai*

---

[51] See the Greek lexica s.v.
[52] Lambot, *CCSL* 41, 444–445. It was published in the Roman edition of Ambrose's works (1581) and later in the Paris edition of 1603, col. 1097–1106.

instead of *stegnai*. In these and a few other places a hand has obviously retouched the sermon in order to make it conform more closely to another text of the LXX.

Augustine's *Sermo* 37 was to prove quite popular and influential, witness the fact that eleven medieval manuscripts of it have survived.[53] It is undoubtedly because of this popularity and influence that the equation of the Valiant Woman with the church gradually became dominant in the Christian West, replacing competing interpretations. We see this illustrated in the writings of Gregory the Great (c.540–604), the man who is often said to be the last Latin Church father, and whose authority, together with that of Augustine, was very great in the Latin West of the subsequent Middle Ages.

Gregory did not write a commentary on Proverbs, nor did he deliver a sermon on the Song of the Valiant Woman, but he frequently refers to the Song in his extant writings. The following is a sampling of his references to it:

(1)   'Therefore Solomon speaks of the Church in these words: *Her husband is noble in the gates, when he sits with the senators of the land*' [Prov. 31:23].[54]
(2)   '[M]indful that it is written about the Church universal: *She does not eat bread in idleness*' [Prov. 31:27b].[55]
(3)   '[A]s it is written about the holy Church: *She made linen clothing and sold it* [Prov. 31:24]; about which it also is said a little later [*sic*] in that passage: *She saw that her trading is good*' [Prov. 31:18].[56]
(4)   'About these gates Solomon says again: *Give her of the fruit of her hands, and let her works praise her in the gates*' [Prov. 31:18]. For then the holy Church receives from the fruit of her hands, when the

[53] Lambot, *CCSL* 41, 445. Note also that *Sermo* 139 of Caesarius of Arles (c.470–542) is largely an abridgement of Augustine's sermon (*CCSL* 103; Turnholt: Brepols, 1953, 571–576).
[54] M. Adriaen (ed.), *Sancti Gregorii Magni Homiliae in Hiezechihelem Prophetam* (*CCSL* 142; Turnholt: Brepols, 1971), 28: 'Hinc Salomon de Ecclesia loquitur, dicens: *Nobilis in portis vir eius cum sederit cum senatoribus terrae*' (my translation).
[55] D. Norberg (ed.), *Sancti Gregorii Magni Registrum Epistularum Libri I–VII* (*CCSL* 140; Turnholt: Brepols, 1982), 278: 'memor quod de ecclesia uniuersali scriptum est: *panem otiosa non comedit*' (my translation).
[56] M. Adriaen (ed.), *Sancti Gregorii Magni Moralia in Job, Libri XI–XXII* (*CCSL* 43A; Turnholt: Brepols, 1979), 922: 'sicut de sancta Ecclesia scriptum est: *Sindonem fecit et vendidit*; de qua et paulo post illic dicitur: *Vidit quod bona est negotiatio eius*' (my translation).

recompense of her labour raises her up to partake of the things of heaven'.[57]

It would be easy to multiply these examples, especially from Gregory's widely-read *Moralia in Job* (the index to M. Adriaen's critical edition of this work lists thirteen references to the Song), but the point is clear: Gregory consistently takes the Valiant Woman to be an allegory of the church. The most noteworthy difference between his treatment and Augustine's is that Gregory now uses the Vulgate instead of the Vetus Latina. In the case of Proverbs, the Vulgate represents a very considerable improvement in terms of fidelity to the MT.

III. Medieval Interpretations

There is of course no invisible line or precise date which divides the Middle Ages from the period of rabbinic and patristic interpretation which we have been discussing. It could be argued that Andrew of Crete, whom we briefly mentioned above (seventh–eighth centuries), already belongs to the medieval era. However, since our discussion will henceforth focus (mainly through lack of relevant sources from Byzantine literature) on the Latin West, we shall somewhat arbitrarily draw the line which marks the threshold of the Middle Ages between Gregory the Great (sixth century) and the Venerable Bede (seventh–eighth centuries).

Medieval Jewish interpretations

Our discussion of Jewish interpretations of the Song in medieval times must needs be very brief. This is mainly because my own command of medieval Hebrew is virtually non-existent, and because Jewish commentaries from this time period are in any case hard to come by. Moreover, there seems to be some reason to believe that medieval Jewish interpretation of the Song, at least in its popular form, was quite uniform. Although the tradition of Jewish midrash did not normally settle on a standard allegorical interpretation of a given passage of Scripture, the Song of the Valiant Woman was an exception. Alexander Altmann, an authority in these matters, tells us:

---

[57] M. Adriaen (ed.), *Sancti Gregorii Magni Moralia in Job, Libri I-X* (*CCSL* 43; Turnholt: Brepols, 1979), 290: 'De his portis Salomon iterum dicit: *Date ei de fructu manuum suarum et laudent eam in portis opera eius.* Tunc quippe sancta Ecclesia de fructu manuum suarum accipit, cum eam ad percipienda caelestia laboris sui retributio attollit' (my translation).

Rabbinic *aggadah* and Midrash employed the allegorical method in an uninhibited homiletic rather than in a systematic manner … The only exceptions are the allegorical interpretations of Proverbs 31:10–31 (the "woman of valor" being understood as the Torah) and of the Song of Songs.[58]

As we have seen, this interpretation of the Song is already found in the Talmud. That it was widely held in medieval Jewish interpretation, also outside of the homiletic context of the *midrashim*, is shown by the authoritative commentary on Proverbs by Rashi, i.e. Rabbi Solomon ben Isaac (1040–1105), who also interprets the Valiant Woman as representing Torah.[59]

Alongside this interpretation, which can be said to represent the mainstream of medieval Jewish exegesis, there are a number of others, mainly of a more philosophical character. It is to be noted that these other interpretations, though departing from the mainstream, nevertheless agree with it in giving an *allegorical* interpretation. Two representatives of this philosophical approach may be mentioned: Maimonides and Ralbag.

Maimonides (1135–1204) has a passing reference to the Song in his famous *Guide for the Perplexed*. He writes:

> As regards the portion beginning, "Who can find a virtuous woman?" it is clear what is meant by the figurative expression, "a virtuous woman". When man possesses a good sound body that does not overpower him nor disturb the equilibrium in him, he possesses a divine gift.[60]

It is clear from the context (a discussion of the control of bodily passions) that Maimonides here equates the Valiant Woman with a healthy body which does not upset a person's equilibrium. Note his use of the phrase 'figurative expression'.

Ralbag, i.e. Rabbi Levi ben Gershon (1288–1344), understood the Song in a similar way. He took the Valiant Woman to symbolize 'matter' in the Neoplatonic sense. In the words of the sixteenth-century French commentator Mercerus, 'Rabbi Levi takes this passage to refer to matter, that is, the sensitive soul which yields and subjects itself to reason and intellect'.[61] Ralbag's interpretation seems to be a refinement of Maimonides'.

---

[58] A. Altmann, 'Allegorical Interpretation', s.v. 'Bible', *EncJud*, 4.895–96.
[59] See the standard editions of the *Biblia Rabbinica*, which contain Rashi's commentary in the margin of the text of Proverbs.
[60] M. Maimonides, *The Guide for the Perplexed*, M. Friedländer (tr.) (New York: Dover, 1956²), 262.
[61] J. Mercerus, *Commentarii in Iobum et Salomonis Proverbia* (Lugduni, 1651), on Prov. 31:10–31.

Although both Jews and Christians consistently gave an allegorical interpretation of the Valiant Woman in the Middle Ages, there seems to have been very little contact between the two exegetical traditions. It is not until the fourteenth century, as we shall see, that there is evidence of one tradition influencing the other. Until then the Christian tradition appears to be virtually untouched by the Jewish interpretation, and vice versa.

The Venerable Bede

The Venerable Bede (672–735) is the author of an extensive commentary on the Song which is remarkable for its soberness and independence. It has come down to us both as the last part of his commentary on the book of Proverbs[62] and as an independent composition entitled *De muliere forti libellus*.[63] There is good reason to assume that it was originally a separate work, because the comments on the verses of the Song are almost four times as extensive as those on the rest of Proverbs.[64]

The independence of Bede's commentary on the Song has only recently become evident. Since there are many verbal correspondences with the Proverbs commentary that was long attributed to Salonius of Geneva (fifth century), Bede seemed to be heavily dependent on Salonius. As we shall see shortly, however, the commentary ascribed to Salonius is in fact dependent on Bede, not the other way around. Viewed in this light, it becomes apparent that Bede drew very little on his predecessors.

In his Proverbs commentary, Bede marks the transition from 'the words of Lemuel' (Prov. 31:1–9) to the acrostic Song as follows:

> So far the words of Lemuel. From this point on, Solomon, the wisest of Kings, sings the praises of the holy Church in just a few verses but with a fullness of truth. For the song in question consists of twenty-two verses, according to the sequence and number of the Hebrew letters, so that the verses each begin with a different letter. The altogether perfect sequence of this alphabet symbolically indicates the altogether complete description here given of the virtues and rewards of either the individual believing soul or the entire holy Church, which is constituted one catholic church out of all the elect souls.[65]

---

[62] *PL* 91, 937–1040.

[63] *PL* 91, 1039–52.

[64] A simple calculation shows that Bede's comments on the rest of Proverbs average 6.6 verses a page (in Hurst's critical edition of the Proverbs commentary: *CCSL* 119B) compared to an average of 1.7 verses for the Song.

[65] *In Proverbia Salomonis* III, xxxi, 9, in *Bedae Venerabilis Opera, Pars II: Opera*

It is to be noticed in this introduction, not only that Bede accepts the now-standard interpretation of the Valiant Woman as the church, but also that he pays attention to the literary features of the Song as a distinct unit of composition. He clearly distinguishes it from the 'words of Lemuel', although the Vulgate (like the MT) does not clearly mark a break between the two. (The problem did not arise for those commentators whose text was the LXX or Vetus Latina, since there the 'words of Lemuel' occur much earlier, preceding 25:1.) He points out that this distinct literary unit is a song (*carmen*), and that it conforms to the pattern of an alphabetic acrostic. This attention to the literary form of the Song (probably based on information gleaned from Jerome) is very remarkable when we compare Bede with his predecessors.

Furthermore, Bede is the first commentator in our survey who assigns a literary function to the use of the alphabetic acrostic: in his view it serves to convey the notion of completeness or perfection. This explanation of the function of the alphabetic acrostic (which will often be repeated in modern commentaries) is of particular interest in the case of Bede, since he himself wrote poetry using this device.[66]

Although Bede follows the allegorical interpretation of the Song made popular by Augustine and Gregory the Great, he is not without originality in this regard. We must read his exposition in the light of his approach to the book of Proverbs as a whole. His commentary on Proverbs begins with the words:

> *Parabolae* [i.e. Proverbs] in Greek are called *similitudines* in Latin. The reason Solomon gave this title to the present book was to teach us to understand what he says in depth, and not according to the letter ...[67]

---

[65] (*Continued*) *Exegetica*, 2B (*CCSL* 119B; Turnholt: Brepols, 1983), 149: 'Hucusque uerba Lamuhel. Hinc sapientissimus regum Salomon laudes sanctae ecclesiae uersibus paucis sed plenissima ueritate decantat. Constat namque idem carmen uersibus uiginti et duobus iuxta ordinem uidelicet Hebraearum ac numerum litterarum ita ut singuli uersus a singulis litteris incipiant. Cuius ordine perfectissimo alphabeti typice innuitur quam plenissime hic uel animae cuiusque fidelis uel totius sanctae ecclesiae quae ex omnibus electis animabus una perficitur catholica uirtutes ac praemia describantur' (my translation).
[66] E.g., the hymn in honour of St. Aethelthryth inserted in Bede's *Historia Ecclesiastica* (IV,20) and the hymn *In Natali SS. Petri et Pauli* edited by J. Fraipont in *Bedae Venerabilis Opera, Pars IV: Opera Rhythmica* (*CCSL* 122; Turnholt: Brepols, 1955), 428–430.
[67] *In Proverbia Salomonis* I, i, 1: 'Parabolae Graece Latine dicuntur similitudines. Quod huic libro uocabulum Salomon ob id imposuit ut sciremus altius et non iuxta litteram intellegere quae dicit ...' (my translation).

According to Bede, it was in the nature of Solomon's Proverbs to be understood allegorically. Notice also that Bede takes the Valiant Woman to be an allegory not only of the church, but also of the individual soul. This is not to be understood in Origen's philosophical sense, but in the theological sense of the individual believer as member of the universal church. In this way Bede makes the Song more directly applicable to the life of the pious Bible-reader. He thus gives a devotional focus to the patristic tradition of interpretation.

Bede's independence is most evident in the details of his exposition. Although he quotes verbatim from Gregory's *Moralia in Job* on three occasions,[68] and once from Augustine,[69] he generally gives his own explanation of the individual verses. By way of illustration we quote Bede's words about the spindle in verse 19, which may be compared to the passage we quoted above from Augustine's *Sermo* 37:

> The text says *And her fingers grasped the spindle.* When women spin they usually hold the spindle in their right hand and the distaff in their left. "It is the wool wrapped on the distaff which passes over to the spindle; it must be drawn out and spun into thread." [Augustine, *Sermo* 37, 13, 287–288]. Now the right hand often signifies everlasting life in the Scriptures, and the left hand signifies God's gifts in the present life, namely material wealth, temporal peace, and bodily health, as well as knowing the Scriptures and receiving the heavenly sacraments. When we receive these and similar blessings from the Lord's bounty, we bear in our left hand, as it were, the wool wrapped on the distaff, but when we begin, out of love for the things of heaven, to cultivate these blessings in a salutary way, we are already transferring the wool of "the Lamb without blemish" from the distaff to the spindle, from the left to the right hand, because we are making for ourselves, from the gifts of our Redeemer, and from the examples of his deeds, a robe of heavenly glory and a "wedding garment" of love. For the fingers with which she is said to *grasp the spindle* suggest the application of the discernment with which everyone does his work, no doubt for the reason that no parts of our body are distinguished by more joints than our fingers, and are as flexible. Therefore, any person who can truthfully say with the apostle: *But our conversation is in heaven, from whence also we look for the Saviour, our Lord Jesus Christ,* that person's righthand fingers have grasped the spindle, because he has learned to work for the benefits of eternity with diligent discernment. And it is well said that the fingers *grasped,* to highlight the more vividly with what zeal and what urgency we ought to strive, amid the uncertainty of this life, for the certain rewards that are found with the Lord.[70]

---

[68] See the notes in Hurst's edition (*CCSL* 119B) on verses 23, 24 and 27.

[69] See lines 313–314 in Hurst's edition (*CCSL* 119B).

[70] *In Proverbia Salomonis* III, xxxi, 19: '*Et digiti*, inquit, *eius adprehenderunt fusum.*

Notice that Bede here borrows the theme of distaff-and-spindle from
Augustine's *Sermo* 37, even inserting verbatim (without attribution) an
entire sentence from Augustine, but gives both this theme and the rest of
the verse an altogether different exposition. This general pattern of independent exegesis holds good throughout his commentary on the Song.

We find a textual curiosity in Bede's commentary on 31:22, the place
where the Vetus Latina had incorrectly referred to *duplicia pallia*. Bede's
text and commentary read:

> *She made for herself a* stragulatam vestem, *fine linen and purple was her clothing*. A
> *stragulata vestis*, which is usually made very stiff by means of varied weaving,
> signifies the valiant [literally 'strong'] deeds of the Church and the various
> ornaments of her virtues, about which the prophet sang in the eulogy of the
> supreme King (who is, of course, this woman's husband): *The queen stood at thy
> right hand, in gilded clothing, arrayed in varied attire* [Ps. 45:10].[71]

What is unusual about this passage is that Bede is giving an explanation of
a 'ghost-word', a word which has arisen as a result of textual corruption –
in this case the adjective *stragulatus*. Although this adjective is listed in all

---

[70] (*Continued*) Solent feminae nentes fusum in dextera, colum tenere in sinistra. In
colo enim lana inuoluta est quae filo ducenda et nenda transeat in fusum. Saepe
autem in scripturis dextera uitam perpetuam, laeua praesentia Dei dona significat,
opulentiam uidelicet rerum, pacem temporum, sospitatem corporum, scientiam
quoque scripturarum, et caelestium perceptionem sacramentorum. Haec et
huiusmodi bona cum domino largiente percipimus quasi lanam colo inuolutam
in laeua gestamus; at cum ea pro amore caelestium salubriter exercere incipimus
iam lanam agni immaculati de colo in fusum, de laeua in dexteram traicimus quia
de donis nostri redemptoris, de exemplis operum eius stolam nobis gloriae
caelestis ac uestem caritatis nuptialem facimus. Digiti namque quibus
apprehendere fusum dicitur ipsam intentionem discretionis qua quisque operatur
insinuant, ea nimirum ratione quia nulla corporis nostri membra pluribus sunt
distincta articulis ac flexibus apta quam digiti. Quicumque ergo ueraciter dicere
cum apostolo potest: *Nostra autem conuersatio in caelis est unde etiam saluatorem
expectamus dominum nostrum Iesum Christum*, huius profecto digiti dextri apprehenderunt fusum quia discretione sedula pro aeternis bonis laborare didicit. Et
bene dicitur, *adprehenderunt*, ut uiuacius commendetur quanto studio, quanta
festinatione in huius uitae incerto pro certis apud dominum praemiis agere
debeamus' (my translation).

[71] *In Proverbia Salomonis* III, xxxi, 22: '*Stragulatam uestem fecit sibi, byssus et purpura
indumentum eius. Stragulata uestis quae uariante textura solet firmissima confici
fortia ecclesiae opera et diuersa uirtutum eius ornamenta signficat de quibus
propheta in summi regis uiri uidelicet illius laude cecinit: *Adstetit regina a dextris
tuis in uestitu deaurato circumamicta uarietate*' (my translation).

major Latin dictionaries, the only place where it is attested is here, in the Vulgate of Proverbs 31:22. Ironically, however, it is here a corruption for the adjective *stragulus.* Jerome had correctly translated the Hebrew *marbad* in this verse as *stragula vestis*, a well-attested expression in classical Latin meaning a 'bedspread' or 'coverlet'.[72] This was corrupted to *stragulata vestis* in the early Middle Ages,[73] so that it is found in most medieval manuscripts of the Vulgate, as well as in the printed editions of modern times. It was finally corrected to *stragula vestis* in the critical edition of the Vulgate Proverbs published in Rome in 1957.[74] Bede's explanation of the corrupt reading *stragulata vestis* was to prove influential in medieval commentaries, though it is not altogether clear what he means by the phrase 'varied weaving' (*variante textura*). In any case, he seems to have taken *stragulata vestis* to refer not to bedclothes, but to some kind of garment made of very stiff (*firmissima*) material, which can therefore be said to represent the *fortia opera* or 'valiant deeds' of the church.[75]

Before leaving Bede we should take note of the fact that the critical edition of his Proverbs commentary by D. Hurst (1983) is sadly deficient. His *apparatus fontium* still lists the commentary of Pseudo-Salonius as one of Bede's sources (though his *Praefatio* acknowledges that this is incorrect), but fails to record the quotation from Augustine's *Sermo* 37 which we noted above, as well as many biblical allusions. A few examples of the latter are *agni immaculati* (line 321; cf. 1 Pet. 1:19), *vestem nuptialem* (line 323; cf. Mt. 22:11–12) and *promissionem habent vitae quae nunc est et futurae* (lines 361–362; cf. 1 Tim. 4:8). Moreover, the marginal reference 'xxxi, 14' was inadvertently omitted at line 180, and the word *manuum* is missing from the biblical text in line 572. Finally, the manuscript evidence on which the text is based fails to include the separate composition *De muliere forti libellus* as well as the Proverbs commentary transmitted under the name of Hrabanus Maurus which is really Bede's commentary,[76] and the *Glossa Ordinaria* on Proverbs, which draws heavily on Bede's commentary.

---

[72] See, e.g., *The Oxford Latin Dictionary*, s.v.

[73] The correct reading *stragula vestis* is still attested in Isidore of Seville (sixth–seventh century); see his *Etymologiae* 19, 26, 4.

[74] *Biblia Sacra iuxta Latinam Vulgatam Versionem Ad Codicum Fidem Iussu Pii PP. XII. Libri Salomonis* (Roma: Vatican Press, 1957).

[75] For this meaning of *fortis* see *Oxford Latin Dictionary*, s.v., 8. See also *fortia* in the Vulgate of Prov. 31:19.

[76] *PL* III, 681–792.

Pseudo-Salonius

In the period from Bede's death (735) until the twelfth century there is little to report with respect to the interpretation of the Song of the Valiant Woman. We can mention the fact that Saint Boniface, the missionary to the German tribes, explicitly asks for Bede's commentary on Proverbs in one of his letters (dated around 750),[77] and repeat the point just made, namely that Bede's commentary later circulated in Germany under the name of Hrabanus Maurus (ninth century).[78] For the rest, the only literary production that is relevant to our survey during these three-and-a-half centuries is the commentary which was until recently attributed to Salonius, the fifth-century bishop of Geneva.

It would carry us too far afield to enter into the scholarly discussion surrounding the true date and author of the work published as *Salonii Commentarii in Parabolas Salomonis et in Ecclesiasten*. Suffice it to point out that the traditional attribution was still defended by C. Curti in his critical edition of these commentaries, but was challenged by the French scholar Jean-Pierre Weiss in a review of this edition.[79] Since then Weiss has elaborated on his critique in two articles, both published in 1970,[80] and come to the conclusion that Pseudo-Salonius was a schoolmaster in Germany, probably of the ninth century. Apparently quite independently of Weiss, the New Zealand scholar Valerie I.J. Flint also challenged the Salonian authorship, in yet another article published in 1970.[81] She concluded that the true author is Honorius Augustodunensis (eleventh–twelfth century), under whose name a version of the commentary was circulated in medieval Germany. We will content ourselves with the conclusion that Pseudo-Salonius lived after Bede and before the early twelfth century.

The commentary on Proverbs by Pseudo-Salonius now turns out to be a thoroughly unoriginal work, composed very largely of excerpts from Bede's commentary, occasionally supplemented with passages drawn from Gregory the Great.[82] Pseudo-Salonius' own contribution consists

---

[77] Quoted in J.-P. Weiss, 'Essai de datation du Commentaire sur les Proverbes attribué abusivement à Salonius', *Sacris Erudiri* 19 (1969/70), 95–96.

[78] See n. 76; cf. *Clavis Patrum Latinorum*, no. 1351; and Weiss, 'Essai de datation', 102–103.

[79] Curti, *Salonii Commentarii in Parabolas Salomonis et in Ecclesiasten* (Catania, 1964); Weiss, *Revue des Etudes Latines* 44 (1966), 482–84.

[80] 'Essai de datation' (n. 77 above) and *Studia Patristica* X (Berlin, 1970), 161–167.

[81] 'The True Author of the Salonii Commentarii in Parabolas Salomonis et in Ecclesiasten', *Recherches de Théologie Ancienne et Médiévale* 37 (1970), 174–186.

[82] Weiss, 'Essai de datation', 87–94.

almost exclusively in the format of the commentary, which is that of a dialogue between teacher and student, no doubt for use in schools. The section on the Valiant Woman begins:

> *Teacher.* Who is that Valiant Woman of whom it says: *Who shall find a valiant woman? Her price is remote and from the farthest regions?*
> *Student.* The holy catholic Church is called a valiant woman. The reason she is called a woman is that she gives birth to spiritual sons for God out of water and the Holy Spirit. She is called valiant because she disdains and despises all the things of this world, whether harmful or advantageous, because of faith and love for her Creator and Redeemer.[83]

Note that in Pseudo-Salonius' commentary the reference to the alphabetic acrostic and its function is omitted, and that the allegorical interpretation is restricted to the church, without reference to the individual soul. For the rest, the content of the commentary is drawn directly from Bede, both here and throughout the section dealing with the Valiant Woman. Though based on Bede throughout, Pseudo-Salonius' comments are very selective, using only a fraction of Bede's work. In fact, he gives extracts of Bede's commentary on only nine of the twenty-two verses, namely 10, 14, 24, 22 (in that order!), 25 and 28–31. The remaining thirteen verses are simply passed over in silence.

Whoever Pseudo-Salonius was, and whenever in the early Middle Ages he lived, it is clear that he was a transmitter of Bede's views of the Song, and thus of the broader allegorical tradition which interprets the Valiant Woman as the church.

Individual interpretations in the twelfth century

It was in the twelfth century that the intellectual culture of the Latin West began the resurgence which was to culminate in the great achievements of the thirteenth century. Around the turn of the twelfth century we meet Bruno of Segni, also known as Bruno of Asti (c.1045–1123), who wrote a short commentary on the Song entitled *Expositio de Muliere*

---

[83] I am quoting from the Migne edition, *PL* 53, 989 (substituting *Magister* and *Discipulus* for *Veranus* and *Salonius*; see Weiss, 'Essai de datation', 98–99): '*Magister.* Quae est mulier illa fortis de qua dicit: *Mulierem fortem quis inveniet? procul et de ultimis finibus pretium ejus? Discipulus.* Mulier fortis appellatur sancta Ecclesia catholica; quae ideo mulier dicitur, quia Deo spirituales generat filios ex aqua et Spiritu sancto. Fortis ideo dicitur, quia cuncta saeculi hujus adversa simul et prospera, propter fidem et amorem sui Conditoris ac Redemptoris contemnit et despicit' (my translation).

Forti.[84] This commentary is of interest because it is not a mere reworking of earlier material, and because its author is known as 'one of the best exegetes of the Middle Ages'.[85] A curious feature is the Latin poem with which Bruno concludes his exposition, the first stanza of which reads:

Certissime cognovimus	'We know most certainly
Quod sermo Salomonicus	that the word of Solomon
Mulierem fortissimam	by the Most Valiant Woman
Significat Ecclesiam.[84]	means the Church'.

Though he is here clearly following the standard allegorical tradition established by the authority of Augustine, Gregory and Bede, he is no slavish epigone of these earlier giants. Consider, for example, his comments on the 'fingers' and 'spindle' of Proverbs 31:19b:

> We understand by her "fingers" all those believers who are small in achievement and position. It is the ones who take care of the lighter tasks and who are equipped only with faith and hope, that grasp the spindle. For any woman can spin, and it is no great chore to believe and hope.[87]

If we compare the above-quoted passages by Augustine and Bede on this same verse, it is clear that Bruno is exercising a great deal of independence. Even when he does rely on his predecessors, he is not reluctant to make modifications, as in his comment on *stragulata vestis* (Prov. 31:22):

> *Stragulata* [*vestis*] is a kind of clothes which is made with great variety. Therefore, the garment of the Church is *stragulata*, because she is depicted with great variety. For in her are resplendent the virtues of humility, peace, perseverance, godliness, meekness and so on.[88]

Bruno picks up the idea of *varietas* from Bede, but changes its focus; the cloth designated by the adjective is not stiff, but multicoloured, and

---

[84] *PL* 164, 1229–34.

[85] See the article 'Bruno von Segni' in *Lexikon für Theologie und Kirche*, which concludes with the words 'Darf als einer der besten Exegeten des Mittelalters gelten'.

[86] *PL* 164, 1234.

[87] *PL* 164, 1231: 'Per digitos quoscunque fideles intelligimus, qui minoris meriti et officii sunt. Hi autem fusum apprehendunt, qui leviora negotia procurant, solaque fide et spe muniuntur. Filare namque quaelibet muliercula potest, credere autem et sperare, non magnus labor est' (my translation).

[88] *PL* 164, 1231: 'Stragulata enim genus vestium est, quod multa varietate fit. Stragulata est igitur vestis Ecclesiae, quoniam multa varietate depingitur. Ibi enim humilitas, pax, patientia, pietas, mansuetudo, caeteraeque virtutes refulgent' (my translation).

therefore denotes not the valiant deeds, but the many virtues of the church. Nevertheless, it is still the church which the Valiant Woman represents.

So common has the equation of the Valiant Woman with the church become in the twelfth century, that preachers quote verses from it in their sermons to make a point about the life of the church, or of the individual believer, without bothering to explain the allegorical interpretation which makes this possible. We find such incidental allusions repeatedly, for example, in the sermons of Guerric of Igny (c.1075–1157):

> Therefore it is written in the praise of the Valiant Woman, who "arose at night" [Prov. 31:15], and who by working day and night with her hands "ate not her bread in idleness" [Prov. 31:27]: "Her lamp will not go out at night" [Prov. 31:18], that is, her faith will not fail in temptation.[89]

There are at least three other places in Guerric's sermons where we find a similar unexplained application to the life of the Church.[90] Apparently his audience could be trusted to make the appropriate allegorical connection.

However, the twelfth century also gives some evidence of exegetical innovation. With the rise of Mariology we also find the first examples in the west of an interpretation of the Valiant Woman as the Virgin Mary. Around the middle of the century we discover, in one of the sermons of Julien de Vézelay (c.1085–c.1162), the application of two verses in the Song (24 and 27) to Mary.[91] And near the end of the century we meet with a sermon which attempts to synthesize the Mariological interpretation with the traditional view:

> We can therefore undoubtedly understand the Valiant Woman as the wisdom of God, or the mother of wisdom himself: Mary, or the mother of the wise: the Church, or indeed the seat of wisdom: the soul.[92]

---

[89] J. Morson and H. Costello (eds.), Guerric d'Igny, *Sermons* (*Sources Chrétiennes* 166; Paris: Editions du Cerf, 1970–73), I, 278: 'Inde scriptum est in laude mulieris fortis, quae *de nocte surrexit*, et de die ac nocte operans manibus suis *panem otiosa non comedit*: *Non extinguetur*, inquit, *in nocte lucerna eius*' (my translation).

[90] *Sermons*, I, 212, 214; II, 508.

[91] Julien de Vézelay, *Sermons* (*Sources Chrétiennes* 192–193; Paris: Editions du Cerf, 1972), I, 90.

[92] Adam of Perseigne, *Mariale*, *Sermo* 5, *PL* 211, 734: 'Mulierem itaque fortem sane possumus intelligere Dei sapientiam, aut matrem ipsius sapientiae Mariam, aut sapientium matrem Ecclesiam, aut certe sedem sapientiae animam' (my translation).

These words were written by Adam of Perseigne, a mystic of the school of Bernard of Clairvaux, who flourished around 1190.[93] He is obviously using wisdom as a category which can integrate the interpretation of Bede (church and soul) with the exegetical innovation (Mary). It is not clear whether he had any knowledge of the fathers Hilary of Poitiers and Pseudo-Procopius of Gaza, who had earlier seen wisdom as the reality symbolized by the Valiant Woman.

The *Glossa Ordinaria*

These twelfth-century variations of the standard allegorical interpretation were not destined to become very influential. They were, after all, only passing comments in popular sermons delivered by relatively obscure preachers. They could not compete with the interpretation embodied in another work of the twelfth century which was soon to achieve almost canonical status in Latin Christendom: the *Glossa Ordinaria*.

Apparently initiated by Anselm of Laon (c.1050–1117), first compiled by Anselm himself and a number of associates, and later expanded by others, the *Glossa Ordinaria* was a series of short exegetical notes (*glossae*) on the complete Bible, drawn almost entirely from patristic and early medieval authorities. By the end of the twelfth century it had achieved its definitive form, as well as its definitive place in the scribal layout of the biblical text. That is, it was positioned in the margin and between the lines of the portion of Scripture to which it applied. As Beryl Smalley, the great authority on the *Glossa*, wrote shortly before her death:

> The Gloss became the standard aid to the study of Scripture, the "tongue" of the biblical text, and an essential part of the *pagina sacra* itself. The text and the Gloss were studied together. Biblical lectures dealt with the glossed text. Numerous biblical allusions can only be understood by referring back to the Gloss.[94]

---

[93] See the article on 'Adam of Perseigne' in *The New Catholic Encyclopedia*, vol. 1 (1967).

[94] B. Smalley, 'Glossa Ordinaria' in *Theologische Realenzyklopädie. Band XIII* (1984), 452: 'Die Glosse wurde zur massgeblichen Handreichung für das Schriftstudium, zur "Zunge" des biblischen Textes, und zu einem wesentlichen Teil der *pagina sacra* selbst. Man studierte Text und Glosse miteinander. Biblische Vorlesungen behandelten den glossierten Text. Zahlreiche biblische Anspielungen werden nur unter Rückgriff auf die Glosse verständlich' (my translation).

The author–compiler (*glossator*) of some parts of the *Glossa Ordinaria* is known, but we do not know who was responsible for the glossing of Proverbs and thus of the Song of the Valiant Woman. He was almost certainly a twelfth–century member of Anselm's famous school in Laon, northern France, but may have originated from almost any region of Latin Christendom.

Whoever the author was, the glosses on Proverbs 31:10–31 are taken almost exclusively from Bede's commentary. With the exception of a number of interlinear comments dealing with the supposed meaning of the names of the Hebrew letters with which each verse begins, the *Glossa* on the Song is a compendium of Bede's commentary. Unlike the work of Pseudo-Salonius, however, the abridgement here is intelligently and consistently done. Bede's important opening comment on the alphabetic acrostic and on the Valiant Woman as church or soul is reproduced almost in its entirety, though the wording has been slightly simplified. Here are the Latin texts of both versions:

Bede	*Glossa Ordinaria*
Hucusque verba Lamuhel. Hinc sapientissimus regum Salomon laudes sanctae ecclesiae versibus paucis sed plenissima veritate decantat.	Hucusque verba Lamuelis regis; hinc Salomon paucis versibus, sed plenissima veritate decantat laudes ecclesiae.
Constat namque idem carmen versibus viginti et duobus iuxta ordinem videlicet Hebraearum ac numerum litterarum ita ut singuli versus a singulis litteris incipiant. Cuius ordine perfectissimo alphabeti	Constat enim hoc carmen versibus xxij per ordinem Hebraei alphabeti: & singuli versus singulis incipiunt litteris, ubi
typice innuitur quam plenissime hic vel animae	innuitur quam plene hic vel animae
cuiusque fidelis vel	uniuscuiusque fidelis vel
totius sanctae ecclesiae,	totius ecclesiae sanctae,
quae ex omnibus electis	quae ex omnibus electis
animabus una perficitur	una perficitur
catholica virtutes ac	catholica virtutes
praemia describantur.[95]	describantur ac praemia.[96]

---

[95] See n. 65.

[96] I am quoting from *Biblia sacra cum glossa ordinaria* (Paris, 1590), ad loc.

It is clear from this comparison that Bede's overall interpretation is faithfully incorporated in the *Glossa Ordinaria*. This is true not only of this introductory section, but of the entire commentary on the Song, although the abridgement is usually more thoroughgoing. Throughout, the glossator is concerned not only to abbreviate, but also to clarify. The rather awkward sentence which Bede quotes from Augustine, '*In colo enim lana involuta est quae filo ducenda et nenda transeat in fusum*',[97] becomes simply *de colo lana filo transit in fusum*, which is both shorter and clearer. When Bede uses the verb *insinuant* in the unusual sense of 'suggest' or 'indicate' in that same passage, the glossator changes this to the more straightforward *significat*. The correspondence between the two verses of the commentary is often so close that the *Glossa* can sometimes serve as an independent witness to Bede's text, as when it reads (again in the same passage) *intentionem discretionis QUAM quisque operatur*, 'the application of the discernment which everyone exercises' instead of *QUA quisque operatur*, 'with which everyone does his work' (which is the reading found in the direct textual tradition of Bede's commentary).

The effect of this wholesale incorporation of a shortened version of Bede's commentary into the *Glossa Ordinaria* on the Song was that his interpretation achieved an even higher degree of authority than it already had for the Christians of medieval Europe. The Valiant Woman as allegory of the church was now *de rigueur* in all the schools of Latin Christendom.

The thirteenth century

A striking example of the weight of this authority is provided by an important commentator of the thirteenth century, Hugh of St. Cher, or Hugo a Sancto Caro (c.1200–1263). Hugo was a leading Dominican (the first to be made cardinal) and is remembered as a biblical scholar for his correction of the Vulgate text, his concordance on the Vulgate, and his extensive commentary on the Bible entitled *Postilla super totam Bibliam* (c.1232).[98] The latter was reprinted many times up to the seventeenth century; we will refer to the edition of 1504.

---

[97] See n. 70.

[98] We are assuming that Hugo was indeed the author of this entire work, despite the argument of some that a team of scholars produced the postills published under his name. E.g., R.E. Lerner, 'Poverty, Preaching, and Eschatology in the Revelation Commentaries of "Hugh of St. Cher" ' in K. Walsh and D. Wood (eds.), *The Bible in the Medieval World. Essays in Memory of Beryl Smalley* (Oxford: Blackwell, 1985), 157–190, esp. 181–183.

His commentary on the Song begins with the now familiar words of Bede about the alphabetic acrostic and the Song's reference to the church or the soul. He then continues:

> *A valiant woman who will find* etc. Although this could be expounded literally in some way, according to the text in Ecclesiastes 7: "One man among a thousand have I found; a woman among all these I have not discovered;" yet, because the Glossators make no mention of a literal exposition, we shall proceed with the mystical exposition, not wishing to play the prophet at this point.[99]

In the rest of his *Postilla*, Hugo regularly gives both a literal and a 'mystical' interpretation of each passage. Here, however, he is prevented from pursuing a literal reading (though he acknowledges that it would be possible) because of the authority of the exegetical tradition represented by the *Glossatores* (he is probably thinking in the first place of the compilers of the *Glossa Ordinaria*). It is also noteworthy that he gives an additional reason for restricting himself to a non-literal exposition: he does not want to 'prophesy' or 'play the prophet' (*vaticinari*). This somewhat obscure usage seems to suggest that an interpreter who breaks with the authoritative exegetical tradition must conceive of himself as a prophet, someone endowed with a divine inspiration which overrides human wisdom. Hugo is not prepared to cast himself in that role, at least with respect to this passage.

The rest of his comments on the Song indeed follow the traditional pattern set by Bede. They do, however, bring to bear the text-critical expertise which Hugo had acquired in preparing a corrected text of the Vulgate. On *stragulatam* (verse 22) he first has this comment:

> That is, "reaching to the ankles", or "embroidered", or "firmly woven by means of a variety of weaving" ... *Stragos* is taken to mean "ankle" or "various".[100]

This incorporates the explanations given by both Bede and Bruno, and adds a speculative etymology connecting this puzzling word with 'ankle'.

---

[99] Hugo de Sancto Caro, *Postilla super totam Bibliam*, 6 vols. (Basel, 1504), III, 59 verso, col. 2: '*Mulierem fortem quis inveniet etc.* Quod quamvis ad litteram posset exponi qualitercumque: iuxta illud Eccles. 7 Virum de mille unum repperi: mulierem ex omnibus non inveni: Quia tamen Glossatores nullam de litterali expositione faciunt mentionem, nolentes hic vaticinari: mysticam prosequemus expositionem' (my translation).

[100] *Postilla*, ad loc: 'Id est, talarem vel picturatam vel varietate texturae firmiter textam ... Stragos talus vel varium interpretatur' (my translation).

A little later, however, Hugo notes that:

> some manuscripts have: "She made for herself a *stragulam vestem*." This is the same as a garment made of polymite or hexamite damask cloth, that is, woven with many threads. We read of a *stragula vestis* in 2 Kings 8:15 …[101]

Rather than substituting the correct reading *stragulam* for the corrupt reading *stragulatam*, Hugo assigns different meanings to each (both of them speculative) and retains the ghost-word in the text.

It would seem that the thirteenth century, like the centuries before it, is completely dominated by the standard interpretation of the Song reflected in the *Glossa Ordinaria*. With one exception, I know of no author in the thirteenth century who significantly modifies the basic consensus. The exception is Albertus Magnus.

Albertus Magnus (c.1200–1280) wrote an enormous commentary on the Song entitled *Liber de Muliere Forti*. In the Borgnet edition it runs to almost 200 large pages,[102] and is divided into 22 chapters, corresponding to the 22 verses of the alphabetic acrostic. This mammoth work is not an exception to the general rule which sees the Valiant Woman as an allegory of the church, but rather to the traditional way in which this is worked out. One could say that he radicalizes the tradition by writing an entire theological treatise on ecclesiology on the basis of the Song. The opening words of the book state simply: *Laudes Ecclesiae describit Salomon in figura mulieris fortis*, 'Solomon lists the praises of the Church in the figure of a valiant woman,' and the rest of the work gives a theological elaboration of that assumption, interspersed with philosophy and Aristotelian physics (for example on the formation of snow, in connection with verse 21). The work is so huge, and so far removed from ordinary exegetical concerns, that we will do no more in this context than mention it as a kind of anomaly in the history of interpretation. Later interpreters of the Song, as far as I know, never mention it.[103]

---

[101] *Postilla*, ad loc: 'Aliqui libri habent: *Stragulam vestem fecit sibi*: Et est idem quod vestis polymita sive examita, id est, pluribus filis texta. De veste stragula legitur iiii Regis viii d …' (NB: the adjective *examitus* reflects the Greek *hexamitos*, literally 'of six threads', analogous to *polymitos*, 'of many threads'.)

[102] A. Borgnet (ed.), *Alberti Magni Opera Omnia*, 38 vols. (Paris: Vivès, 1890–99), vol. XVIII, 5-196.

[103] There is one exception to this, namely Cornelius à Lapide in his seventeenth-century commentary, who refers to Albert's *ingens liber* on two occasions.

The fourteenth century

We move now to the fourteenth century, where the exegetical climate is much the same. A single example can illustrate that the standard interpretation is still the one which prevails. In a Latin sermon delivered near the end of his life, John Wycliffe, the well known English religious reformer (c.1328–1384), begins his exposition of the Song:

> It is clear from the plain meaning of this Scripture passage, and from the unanimous witness of holy men, that today's Bible reading speaks of Christ, the bridegroom of the Church, and of the holy mother Church, his bride.[104]

Note again the appeal to the authority of the exegetical tradition. Accordingly, the rest of Wycliffe's sermon on the Song runs along traditional lines.

Although Wycliffe's sermon shows that the standard interpretation of the Song was still taken for granted in the late fourteenth century, there had appeared earlier in the century another series of glosses on the entire Bible which directly challenged the consensus. These were the famous *Postillae* of Nicholas of Lyra (1270–1349), which were to achieve, by the end of the Middle Ages, an authority almost equal to that of the *Glossa Ordinaria*, and to have a significant influence on the sixteenth-century Reformer Martin Luther. What distinguished Lyra from the earlier medieval glossators was above all the fact that he had a knowledge of Hebrew. This meant not only that he was in a position to consult the original text of the Old Testament, but also that he had access to the works of medieval Jewish commentators. His *Postillae* show an especially heavy reliance on the commentaries of 'Rabbi Solomon' (that is, Rashi), the famous eleventh-century French commentator on the Bible and Talmud. Compared to the *Glossa Ordinaria*, which had restricted itself to the Latin text of the Vulgate, and to Christian commentaries on it, Lyra's *Postillae* were therefore a dramatic innovation. At long last there was significant contact between the Jewish and Christian traditions of interpretation.

Lyra begins his notes on the Song:

> In the last part of this book is placed the praise of the valiant woman. It is commonly interpreted by our scholars to refer to the Church, which is

---

[104] I. Loserth (ed.), *Ioannis Wyclif Sermones*, 4 vols. (London, 1887–90), vol. IV, 147–48: 'Constat ex evidencia huius scripture et concordi sanctorum testimonio quod ista epistola loquitur de Christo sponso ecclesie et sancta matre ecclesia sponsa sua' (my translation). Note that *epistola* is here used in the sense of assigned Scripture reading for a particular Sunday in the liturgical calendar.

metaphorically called the valiant woman, and her bridegroom Christ, whereas
her sons and daughters are called the Christian people of both sexes. And they
say that this is the literal sense, the way it says in Judges 9: "The trees went to
the bramble bush, etc." The literal sense does not refer to the physical trees,
but to Abimelech and the Shechemites who anointed him as their king. And
although this exposition is reasonable and commonly accepted, yet I am not
pursuing it, because it is sufficiently widespread in the *Glossae* and common
Postillae. Now Rabbi Solomon agrees with the Catholic scholars with respect
to the fact that we here have a metaphorical way of speaking. But he says that it
is sacred Scripture which is understood by the valiant woman. It is this exposition that I intend to pursue, because it seems to be reasonable, and is not commonly held. On some points, however, I intend to speak differently from him,
according as it is suitable to our faith, especially because they call only the Old
Testament sacred Scripture, but I include both, namely Old and New.[105]

Apart from the interesting argument that the allegorical interpretation in
this case *is* the literal interpretation (to which we shall return later), this
passage is striking in that it deliberately prefers a Jewish authority over the
authority of the Christian *doctores*, although of course Lyra hastens to add
that Rashi's notion of Scripture (actually, the Jewish scholar had written
Torah) will have to be expanded to include the New Testament. The
standard medieval Jewish allegory here replaces (in Christianized form)
the standard medieval Christian allegory.

Further evidence of Rashi's influence is found in the notes on individual words and phrases, for example on *ad fortia* (verse 19) and *a frigoribus
nivis* (verse 21):

---

[105] I am quoting from *Biblia latina cum postillis Nicolai de Lyra* (1481) ad loc.: 'In
ultima parte huius libri ponitur commendatio fortis mulieris. Et exponitur
communiter a doctoribus nostris de ecclesia, quae metaphorice dicitur fortis
mulier, et sponsus eius Christus; filii autem eius et filiae populus Christianus in
utroque sexu. Et dicunt quod iste est sensus litteralis, sicut Iudicum IX dicitur:
Ierant ligna ad rhamnum, etc. Sensus litteralis non est de lignis materialibus, sed de
Abimelech, et Sichimitis eum super se regem inungentibus. Et licet haec
expositio sit rationalis et communis, tamen eam non prosequor, quia satis diffuse
traditur in glossis et communibus postillis. Rabbi Salomon vero convenit cum
doctoribus Catholicis quantum ad hoc quod hic est metaphorica locutio. Sed
dicit quod per mulierem fortem intelligitur Sacra Scriptura. Et hanc
expositionem intendo prosequi quia rationabilis videtur, nec communiter
habetur. In aliquibus tamen intendo aliter dicere quam ipse, prout est consonum
Fidei nostrae; maxime quia Sacram Scripturam vocant solum Vetus
Testamentum, ego autem utrumque, scilicet Vetus et Novum' (my translation).

She stretched out her hand to valiant deeds. In Hebrew it says *to the whorl*, which is a kind of small, somewhat heavy ring, attached to the lower part of the spindle, so that it spins in an upright and controlled manner; this explanation fits with what follows: *And her fingers grasp the spindle.*[106]

... *from the cold of snow.* That is, from the punishment of hell, according to what Rabbi Solomon says here, adducing Job 24:19, *He will pass from the waters of the snows to excessive heat*, and speaks of the condemned man.[107]

Although the comment about the spindle-whorl does not mention Rashi, it is taken verbatim from the latter's commentary. (The Hebrew word referred to here is *kîšôr*, the *hapax legomemon* whose meaning we explored at length in chapter 4.)

Lyra continues to stand in the tradition of Latin Christian exegesis as well. Witness his comment on our ghost-word: '*Stragulatam vestem*. That is, interwoven with diverse colours (*diversis coloribus intextam*)'.

Lyra's *Postillae* gradually achieved considerable authority during the fourteenth and fifteenth centuries. An index of this is the fact that they were printed, together with the biblical text, as early as 1481, and that they were often printed thereafter together with the *Glossa Ordinaria*. Another indication of Lyra's influence is found in the marginal notes which accompanied the so-called Second Wycliffite translation of the Bible into English, which appeared in about 1395. This was an idiomatic translation into Middle English of the Latin Vulgate, done by an unknown follower of Wycliffe. The introductory comment on the Song reads:

> *a strong woman*; Christen doctours expownen comynly this lettre, til to the ende, of hooly chirche, which bi figuratif speche, is seid a strong womman; hir hosebande is Christ, hir sones and dougtris ben Christen men and wymmen; and this is the literal understonding, as thei seyen; and this exposicioun is resonable, and set opinly in the comyn glos. But Rabi Salomon seith, that bi a strong womman is undurstondun hooli Scripture; the hosebonde of this womman, is a studiouse techere in hooly Scripture, both men and wymmen; for in Jeroms tyme summe wymmen weren ful studiouse in hooly Scripture. *Lire here. C.*[108]

---

[106] *Biblia latina cum postillis*, ad loc.: '*Manum suam misit ad fortia*. In Hebraeo habetur, *ad vertebrum*, quod est quidam circulus aliquantulum ponderosus in inferiori parte fusi positus, ut recte et ordinate vertatur: et huic dicto consonat quod subditur: *Et digiti eius apprehenderunt fusum*' (my translation).

[107] *Biblia latina cum postillis*, ad loc.: '... *a frigoribus nivis*. Id est, a poena gehennae, secundum quod dicit hic Rabbi Salomo allegans illud Job xxiiii c. *Ab aquis nivium transiet ad calorem nimium*, et loquitur de damnato' (my translation).

[108] Quoted from Josiah Forshall and Frederick Madden, (eds.), *The Holy Bible Containing the Old and New Testaments, With the Apocryphal Books in the Earliest English Versions, Made from the Latin Vulgate by John Wycliffe and his Followers* (Oxford: Clarendon, 1850).

This clearly relies heavily on Lyra, as the concluding reference to 'Lire' also indicates, but does not (unlike Lyra) express a preference for Rashi's view.

The note on 'to stronge thingis' (i.e. *ad fortia*) is also dependent on Lyra, though shortened: 'in Ebreu it is, *to the wherne*; and the lettre suynge acordith wel herto. *Lire here.* C'. (*Wherne* is here clearly the Middle English word for 'spindle-whorl',[109] just as *suynge* means 'following'.)

The foregoing completes our survey of medieval Latin Christian interpretations of the Song of the Valiant Woman, since I have found nothing in the fifteenth century. There is undoubtedly a good deal of relevant material that I have passed over, both in printed and manuscript sources. (There is, for example, an exposition of the Song by the fourteenth-century British monk Richard Rolle which has never been published.[110]) But the overall picture is clear enough: a universal adherence to an allegorical interpretation, almost always with reference to the church.

One final remark needs to be made about this overwhelming allegorical consensus. The persistence of the allegorical interpretation is particularly striking when we consider that there was a strong movement away from the often fanciful and arbitrary excesses of the allegorical tradition during the thirteenth and fourteenth centuries. Among the leaders of this movement were Albertus Magnus and Nicholas of Lyra, who insisted throughout on the importance of the literal sense.[111] As a matter of fact Lyra, in his *Postillae*, self-consciously seeks to restrict himself to the literal sense.[112] Yet both these authors give an allegorical exposition of the Song. Moreover, Hugo of St. Cher, whose *Postilla super totam Bibliam* systematically gives both a literal and a 'mystical' interpretation of the biblical text, deliberately refrains from offering a literal reading of the Song, although he acknowledges that one would be possible. How can we explain this apparent inconsistency in these authors? The answer is, in my opinion, twofold: respect for tradition and a sophisticated understanding of what 'literal' means. First, among the greatest authorities in the late

---

[109] *The Oxford English Dictionary* s.v. 'wherne' needs to be corrected on this point, since this entry states that 'wherne' is a mistake for 'wherve' (also meaning 'spindle-whorl'). The editors were apparently unaware that 'wherne' occurs in this fourteenth-century text as a direct translation of the Latin *vertebrum*.

[110] See N. Marzac, *Richard Rolle de Hampole (1300–1349). Vie et oeuvres, suivies du Tractatus super Apocalypsim* (Paris, 1968), 49, where there is a reference to Rolle's work *Super Mulierem Fortem*, preserved in five British manuscripts.

[111] B. Smalley, *The Study of the Bible in the Middle Ages* (Oxford: Blackwell, 1983³), chapter 6.

[112] The proper title of Lyra's work is *Postilla litteralis*.

Middle Ages were Augustine, Gregory and Bede, all of whom had given an exclusively allegorical interpretation of the Song of the Valiant Woman. It would require an unusual measure of self-confidence (almost a sense of prophetic calling, to judge from Hugo's *nolentes vaticinari*) to depart from such authority in the age of Scholasticism. Secondly, we see in Lyra a hermeneutical justification for equating 'literal' and 'allegorical' in the case of the Song of the Valiant Woman. If 'literal' is defined in terms of authorial intent, and the Song is put on a par with Jotham's parable of the trees in Judges 9:7–15, then it is not unreasonable to argue that the 'literal' meaning of the Valiant Woman is something other than an enterprising Israelite wife and mother. Of course the crucial move in the argument was the hermeneutical identification of the Song as a parable, but once this was made, an emphasis on the literal sense could be reconciled with the traditional interpretation of the Song. Lyra's comment (repeated in the Second Wycliffite version) indicates that this was a common Scholastic view of the literal sense of parables,[113] and something like it may also have been held in the Jewish tradition, since Rashi is also known for his attachment to the literal sense.

Looking back over the roughly fifteen hundred years of interpretation which we have surveyed, it is remarkable how similar the patterns are in both the Jewish and Christian traditions. Both began with a literal understanding, both moved to a variety of allegorical interpretations, and both developed a standard allegorical reading in the Middle Ages which crowded out the others. For the Jews the Valiant Woman represented the Torah; for the Christians she symbolized the church. For more than a thousand years, in both traditions, there was an overwhelming consensus that the Valiant Woman should be understood allegorically. It was this consensus which was challenged by the Reformation.

IV. Interpretations in the Reformation

The sixteenth century saw a great efflorescence of biblical studies in Europe, stimulated by the Renaissance ideal of studying the classics of antiquity in their original languages, and by the Reformation insistence on *sola Scriptura*. The result was a flood of new commentaries, based on a

---

[113] It seems that this definition of the literal sense was developed by Stephen Langton and Thomas Aquinas; see G.A.C. Hadfield's section on 'Medieval Christian' interpretation in the article 'Interpretation, History of' in *The Interpreter's Dictionary of the Bible, Supplementary Volume* (ed. Keith Crim *et al.*; Nashville: Abingdon, 1976), 452–454.

study of the original text, on the various books of the Bible, including Proverbs. A partial list of such sixteenth-century scholarly commentaries on Proverbs includes the following names:[114]

P. Melanchthon (Halle, 1529)
J. Arboreus (Paris, 1533)
P. Melanchthon (Hagenau, 1555)
R. Baynius (Paris, 1555)
V. Strigel (Leipzig, 1565)
C. Jansenius (Louvain, 1568)
H. Osorius (Antwerpen, 1569)
J. Mercerus (Geneva, 1573)
S. Senensis (Lyon, 1575)
L. Lavater (Zurich, 1586)

These commentaries were written by both Protestants and Catholics, and for much of the material covered in the book of Proverbs there were not significant differences in interpretation between the two opposing parties. With respect to the Song of the Valiant Woman, however, there was a decided difference. Whereas the Catholic exegetes continued to defend an allegorical interpretation, the Protestants were unanimous in rejecting allegory and giving an exclusively literal interpretation.

Needless to say, it will not be possible to deal with all the above-mentioned commentaries, not even the Protestant ones, since most sixteenth-century commentaries are available only in a few (usually European) libraries. However, it is possible to pinpoint rather precisely the time and the place in which the new Protestant interpretation took its rise, and to give incidental illustrations of the adoption of the new reading by subsequent Protestants.

Melanchthon and Luther

Luther was the giant who, more than anyone else, precipitated the Reformation. Melanchthon was important mainly as Luther's lieutenant and successor, but for our purposes we must mention Melanchthon first, since he preceded Luther in acquiring a knowledge of Hebrew, in studying the book of Proverbs, and in consistently rejecting allegory in biblical interpretation.

Philip Melanchthon (1497–1560) was taught Hebrew as a child

---

[114] My source for these names and dates is the bibliography of the article 'Sprüchebuch', by G. von Rad in *Religion in Geschichte und Gegenwart*, *Dritte Auflage* (Tübingen: Mohr, 1962), 6.288-89.

by Johannes Reuchlin (1422–1522), the great Christian Hebraist who was the first to write a Hebrew grammar-cum-lexicon in Latin (the *Rudimenta Linguae Hebraicae*, 1506). As it happens, Reuchlin was Melanchthon's great-uncle (the brother of the grandmother who raised him) and personally supervised young Philip's education.[115] When the twenty-one-year-old Melanchthon arrived at the University of Wittenberg as professor of Greek in 1518, he already had a solid grasp of Hebrew. In fact, when the professor of Hebrew, another new appointee at Wittenberg University, left halfway through his first year, Melanchthon was prevailed upon to take over the man's Hebrew lectures.[116] For some years thereafter, Melanchthon would regularly teach a Hebrew reading course at Wittenberg.[117] This was at a time when Luther, his older colleague at Wittenberg, had only an elementary knowledge of Hebrew, and freely acknowledged Melanchthon's superiority in this regard.[118]

Melanchthon had a special interest in the book of Proverbs. When he first arrived in Wittenberg, he planned to publish a trilingual edition (Hebrew, Greek and Latin) of this biblical book,[119] but he never accomplished this, probably because Sebastian Münster published a Hebrew–Latin edition in 1520.[120] He did lecture on the book of Proverbs in the early months of 1524,[121] and these lectures were published (without his permission) later in the same year,[122] under the title *Paroimiae sive Proverbia Solomonis. Cum Adnotationibus Philippi Melanchthonis.*[123] This consisted of theological comments on selected proverbs, not going

---

[115] See W. Maurer, *Der junge Melanchthon zwischen Humanismus und Reformation, Bd. I: Der Humanist* (Göttingen, 1967), chapter 1, 'die Ausbildung in der Obhut Reuchlins'.

[116] H. Volz, 'Melanchthons Anteil an der Lutherbibel', *Archiv für Reformationsgeschichte* 45 (1954), 202.

[117] See the chronological table of Melanchthon's lectures given in P.F. Barton (ed.), *Melanchthons Werke in Auswahl, Bd. IV* (Gütersloh, Gütersloher Verlagshaus, 1963), 10–12. We learn from this that he lectured on Genesis in 1522, Exodus in 1522/23, Proverbs in 1523/24 and again in 1527/28, Lamentations and Daniel in 1524, Psalms in 1527, Micha in 1528, and Jeremiah in an undetermined year.

[118] See Luther's statement in *Luthers Werke, Weimar–Ausgabe, Briefe*, 3.258–59.

[119] Volz, 'Melanchthons Anteil', 201–202.

[120] S. Münster, *Proverbia Salomonis, iam recens iuxta Hebraicam veritatem translata, et annotationibus illustrata* (Basel, 1520).

[121] See n. 117 above.

[122] On the date, see H. Sick, *Melanchthon als Ausleger des Alten Testaments* (Tübingen: Mohr, 1959), 5, n. 16.

[123] Published in Haguenau in 1524 and reprinted there the following year.

beyond chapter 27. Shortly after this unauthorized publication, probably still in 1524,[124] Melanchthon published his own translation, without notes, of the entire book of Proverbs, entitled *Solomonis Sententiae, Versae ad Hebraicam Veritatem a Philippo Melanchthone.*[125] Then in 1529 he published a commentary on Proverbs: *Nova Scholia in Proverbia Salomonis, ad iusti pene commentarii modum conscripti.*[126] Finally, near the end of his life (1555) he published another, more extensive commentary: *Explicatio Proverbiorum Salomonis.*[127] It is clear that Melanchthon had a special and lifelong interest in this book of the Bible, an interest which distinguishes him from his colleague Luther, whose concern with Proverbs was largely limited to what was necessary in connection with his German translation of the Bible.

It was also Melanchthon who took the lead in the resolute rejection, as a matter of principle, of the allegorical interpretation of Scripture. In the words of Hansjörg Sick, who made a special study of Melanchthon's exegetical works on the Old Testament, 'In Melanchthon's interpretation of the Old Testament we observed from the beginning a strong rejection of allegorical interpretation'.[128] It is well known that Luther initially wavered on this point. In some of his earlier works of biblical interpretation he was prepared to make free use of allegory. It was only later, under Melanchthon's influence, that he eschewed allegorical interpretation almost entirely.[129] 'Luther only gradually freed himself from the allegorical method and returned to the literal meaning of the text'.[130]

With this background we turn to Melanchthon's interpretation of the Song of the Valiant Woman. His *Paroimiae* did not include the last chapters of Proverbs, and his *Sententiae* contained only a fresh translation, so we must look to the *Nova Scholia* of 1529 for the first explicit evidence of a non-allegorical reading of the Song. This is what he writes on Proverbs 31:10–31:

[124] *Corpus Reformatorum*, vol. 14, 1; and Sick, *Melanchthon als Ausleger*, 155.
[125] Published in Argentoratus in 1524 and (again) reprinted there the following year.
[126] Halae Suevorum, 1529.
[127] Published in the series *Corpus Reformatorum*, vol. 14, 1–87.
[128] H. Sick, *Melanchthon als Ausleger*, 149: 'Wir beobachteten von Anfang an in der alttestamentlichen Auslegung Melanchthons eine starke Ablehnung der Allegorese'.
[129] Sick, *Melanchthon als Ausleger*, 28–30; and H. Bornkamm, *Luther und das Alte Testament* (Tübingen: Mohr, 1948).
[130] K. Runia, 'The Hermeneutics of the Reformers', *Calvin Theological Journal* 19 (1984), 122, n. 5.

This passage has to do with home management and the duties of a wife and mother. The difference between philosophical and prophetic precepts is that the philosophers lay down nothing concerning the fear of the Lord and faith. Paul very briefly summarized the duties of a wife and mother in the words: "The woman is saved through the bearing of children, if she continues in the faith" [1 Tim. 2:15], that is, a woman will be saved if she has faith and consequently is devoted to her calling. It is a woman's calling to give birth to children and to take care of them. Faith can never be idle, and in male and female does the work proper to each. The work proper to woman is childbearing; she is to know that she pleases God in this work, and to bear whatever befalls her as a burden laid on her by God. For just as Moses, when he led the people out of Egypt, knew that he was doing the right thing because he was leading them out (*educere*) at God's command, so a woman is to know that this ministry of bearing and rearing (*educare*) children is pleasing to God. In another place [1 Tim. 5:14] Paul also assigns to them the administration of household affairs and commands them to be caretakers of the home. Peter enjoins them [1 Pet. 3:4] to be of a modest and gentle spirit, that is, to be chaste and yet not peevish, serious and not irritable. Virtually the same duties are taught in the present passage: to have the fear of God and faith, to be chaste, diligent in taking care of the household, and generous toward the poor.[131]

This remarkable passage could be discussed from many points of view (for example, the prominence given to the bearing and raising of children, when the Song does not mention this at all), but we will restrict ourselves to two comments. The first is that the allegorical interpretation is nowhere in evidence – it is not even polemicized against. The Song is taken in a literal sense as outlining the praiseworthy deeds of a God-fearing woman, just as it was in some early patristic works. The

---

[131] *Melanchthons Werke in Auswahl*, IV, 463: 'Hic locus est oeconomicus de officiis matris familias. Sed hoc interest inter philosophica praecepta et prophetica, quod philosophi nihil de timore Dei et fide praecipiunt. Paulus matris familias officia brevissime complexus est, cum inquit: "Salvatur mulier per filiorum generationem, si in fide manserit", id est: mulier, si habuerit fidem et deinde vocationi suae serviens, salvabitur. Est autem mulieris vocatio gignere et curare subolem. Fides numquam otiosa esse potest, sed in utroque proprium opus exercet. Est autem mulieris proprium opus gignere, et in eo opere sciat se Deo placere, ferat, quidquid accidit, tamquam onus a Deo impositum; ut enim sciebat Moses se recte facere, cum educeret populum ex Aegypto, quia mandato Dei educebat, sic mulier sciat Deo placere hoc ministerium pariendi et educandi. Alio loco etiam committit eis procurationem rei domesticae et iubet esse custodes domus. Petrus iubet, ut sint modesti et mansueti spiritus, hoc est: ut sint pudicae et tamen sine morositate, sine iracundia sint graves. Haec fere officia et hoc loco traduntur, ut habeant timorem Dei ac fidem, ut sint pudicae, sedulae in re familiari custodienda, liberales erga pauperes' (my translation).

second comment is that Melanchthon here explicitly invokes the Reformation doctrine of vocation or calling. This is Luther's famous teaching
concerning every person's *Beruf* before God in their ordinary daily occu-
pation. *Vocatio* was understood as relating, not specifically to God's call to
be a monk or priest, but rather to his call to do an honest day's work as a
carpenter, a cobbler or a housewife. Any legitimate way of earning a living
became a religious calling before the face of God.[132] Melanchthon takes
over this idea from Luther, and applies it to a literal exposition of Proverbs
31:10–31.

We find the same pattern emerging in Melanchthon's second commentary on Proverbs, the *Explicatio* of 1555. This is a new and more
extensive commentary than the *Nova Scholia*, more than an expanded
revision of the latter, but the main points of the interpretation of the Song
remain the same. I will quote only two significant sentences from this new
commentary:

> The third part [of the chapter] is a song about the virtues of an honourable wife
> and mother.
>   Now this whole passage must be understood in a straightforward manner,
> without allegory, as the mirror of an honourable wife.[133]

It is also noteworthy that Melanchthon again makes reference to a
woman's calling; he speaks of the *praecipuae virtutes et officia vocationis* that
apply to a woman. In this second commentary, therefore, Melanchthon
explicitly mentions the two Protestant themes which shaped the new
understanding of the Song: the rejection of allegory and the doctrine of
Beruf or calling.

Melanchthon's Latin translation of Proverbs, first published in 1524
and incorporated into the *Nova Scholia* of 1529, was a linguistic feat in its
own right, the first idiomatic rendering directly from the Hebrew since
Jerome's translation in the Vulgate. Since it was done in close conjunction
with Luther's German translation of the Bible, we will return to
Melanchthon's rendering of the Song in our discussion of Luther's interpretation, to which we now turn.

Although the exegetical writings of Martin Luther (1483–1546) are
voluminous, he never wrote a commentary on the book of Proverbs, or

---

[132] See the article 'Beruf' in *Theologische Realenzyclopädie*, 5, 654–676, esp.
660–666.
[133] *Corpus Reformatorum*, vol. 14, cols. 85–86: Tertia pars carmen est de virtutibus
honestae Matrisfamilias. tota autem haec narratio simpliciter sine allegoria
intelligatur tanquam speculum honestae matronae (my translation).

paid any special attention to it apart from his Bible translation work. The closest he came to commenting on the book was in the jotting of short notes in the margin of his translation of Proverbs. It is from one of these marginal notes that we learn that Luther, like Melanchthon, adopted a literal interpretation of the Song. Alongside Proverbs 31:30 he wrote:

> That is to say, a woman can live with a man honourably and piously and can with good conscience be a housewife, but she must also, in addition and next to this, fear God, have faith and pray.[134]

Since this was written after Melanchthon's commentary, and since Luther's opposition to allegory had needed to be reinforced by Melanchthon, it is safe to say that Luther's non-allegorical interpretation is dependent on Melanchthon, not the other way around.[135]

It can also be shown that Luther's German translation of the Song was dependent on Melanchthon. This can be demonstrated (or at least made very probable) by observing the following sequence of events in the year 1524:

1. Before March 1: Melanchthon lectures on Proverbs.[136]
2. Between Feb. and Sept./Oct.: Luther translates Proverbs.[137]
3. Sept./Oct.: first publication of the 'third part' of Luther's Bible translation (Job through Song of Solomon).[138]
4. Sometime after March 1: Melanchthon's *Paroimiai* are published.[139]
5. After previous item: Melanchthon's *Sententiae* are published.[140]

---

[134] *Luthers Werke, Weimar–Ausgabe, Die Deutsche Bibel*, 10.103: 'Das ist, Eine fraw kan bey einem Manne ehrlich und göttlich wonen, und mit gutem gewissen Hausfraw sein, Sol aber darüber und darneben Gott fürchten, glauben und beten' (my translation). This handwritten note was first printed in the second 1543 edition of Luther's Bible translation. For its earlier history, see op. cit., Bd. 4, xxxiii, 29.

[135] For further passing comments by Luther revealing a literal interpretation of the Song, see *Weimar–Ausgabe* 20,78; 44,659.

[136] Barton, *Melanchthons Werke in Auswahl*, IV, 305.

[137] Luther's translation of the 'third part' of the Old Testament was published in September or October of 1524 (see next note), and in February he was still working on Job (*Weimar–Ausgabe, Deutsche Bibel*, 1, xiii–xiv). Since he was following the traditional order (Job–Psalms–Proverbs) in his work of translation, his version of Proverbs was probably prepared in the summer of 1524.

[138] *Weimar–Ausgabe, Deutsche Bibel*, 1, p.xiv.

[139] See note 122.

[140] See note 124.

In order to appreciate the significance of these dates, we must understand that Melanchthon was working very closely with Luther on his translation, and that he had probably chosen to lecture on Proverbs early in the year in order to be of more effective help to Luther when he came to the translation of this book a few months later.[141]

Luther's procedure in doing his translation work was that he made a first draft of a passage on his own, leaving blanks (or simply transliterating the Hebrew) for words or phrases of which he was uncertain. He then discussed the passage with his two co-workers, Melanchthon and Aurogallus (the then professor of Hebrew at Wittenberg). On the basis of this discussion he revised and completed his translation for publication.[142]

As it happens, Luther's autograph of his original translation (he made revisions continuously throughout his life) has survived into the twentieth century, and has been meticulously edited in the great Weimar edition of his works.[143] Even more strikingly, Luther used a different colour of ink for his own initial draft (dark ink) and for his subsequent revisions after consulting with his colleagues (red ink), and these differences in colour are duly recorded in the Weimar edition. In the words of Hans Volz, the foremost authority in these matters:

> At least in the second and third parts of the Old Testament he used a dark-coloured ink for his first draft, but red ink for the revision which he always carried out with the aid of Melanchthon and Aurogallus. So in these parts Luther's original and the revision carried out with others' assistance are clearly distinguishable.[144]

Turning now to Proverbs 31:10–31, we notice that Luther's initial draft (in dark ink) leaves a blank or writes out the Hebrew in four cases:[145]

---

[141] Melanchthon lectured on Exodus in 1522/23, and on Lamentations and Daniel later in 1524 (see n. 117 above). These lectures, together with those on Proverbs in early 1524, were the first Old Testament lectures he had given since filling in for the absent Hebrew professor in 1518, and coincide with the times Luther was about to translate these parts of the Old Testament. It is a reasonable assumption that this was by design.

[142] See the contribution by H. Volz on 'Deutsche Bibelübersetzungen' in *Die Religion in Geschichte und Gegenwart*. Dritte Auflage, I, 1204.

[143] *Weimar–Ausgabe, Deutsche Bibel*, vols. 1 and 2.

[144] H. Volz, 'Continental Versions to c. 1600: 1. German' in *The Cambridge History of the Bible: The West from the Reformation to the Present Day* (ed. S.L. Greenslade; Cambridge, 1963), 97.

[145] *Weimar–Ausgabe, Deutsche Bibel*, 1, 613.

1. Verse 11: leaves a blank for *yeḥsār*.
2. Verse 19: leaves a blank for *kîśôr*.
3. Verse 22: leaves a blank for *marbadîm*.
4. Verse 24: writes out the Hebrew word *sādîn*.

The revisions which were made on the basis of his discussions with Melanchthon and Aurogallus (clearly indicated by red ink), and which were published in September or October 1524, supply the missing translations as follows:

1. Verse 11: 'und narung *wird ihm nicht mangeln*' (*yeḥsār*).
2. Verse 19: 'Sie streckt yhre hand nach *dem rocken*' (*kîśôr*).
3. Verse 22: 'Sie macht yhr *eyn schmuck*' (*marbadîm*).
4. Verse 24: 'Sie macht *eyn rock*' (*sādîn*).

What is striking about these readings is that each of them disagrees with both the Vulgate and the LXX (Luther's chief aids in interpreting difficult Hebrew words), and agrees with Melanchthon's Latin rendering as published that same year (the *Salomonis Sententiae*). Consider the following comparitive table.

	MT	LXX	Vulgate	Luther 1524	Melanchthon 1524
V. 11	*yeḥsār*	*aporēsei* 'will run short' (subject is *baʿal*)	*indigebit* 'will lack' (subject is *baʿal*)	*wird ihm mangeln* 'will be lacking to him' (subject is *šālāl*)	*deficiet* 'will be lacking' (subject is *šālāl*)
V. 19	*kîśôr*	*ta sympheronta* 'the useful (things)'	*fortia* 'valiant (deeds)'	*rocken* 'distaff'	*colum* 'distaff'
V. 22	*marbadîm*	*chlainas* 'cloaks'	*stragu[la]tam vestem* 'coverlet'	*schmuck* 'ornament'	*ornamenta* 'ornaments'
V. 24	*sādîn*	*sindonas* 'linen garments'	*sindonem* 'linen garment'	*rock* 'coat'	*tunicas* 'coats'

In each case Luther, after consulting with Melanchthon and Aurogallus, chooses a novel rendering which agrees with Melanchthon's Latin translation. Given the fact that Melanchthon had long planned his own translation of the book of Proverbs, and had recently lectured on it, it is probable that these new translations of difficult or ambiguous Hebrew words originated with him, and not with Aurogallus or Luther.

It is of interest to note that the meaning 'distaff' for the obscure word *kîšôr* (a *hapax legomenon*), a meaning which occurs in almost all twentieth-century versions of the Bible, occurs for the first time in Luther's German translation, and thus probably goes back to Melanchthon (see the discussion in chapter 4).

To argue for Luther's dependence on Melanchthon in matters of philological detail is in no way to detract from Luther's magnificent achievement in making the Bible speak idiomatic German. In any case, Luther continually revised his translation, improving it from year to year. For example, he later changed his rendering of *marbadîm* from the mistaken *schmuck*, 'ornament', to the correct *Decke*, 'coverlets'.[146] But it was especially in his feel for the music and idiom of his native German that Luther was a master. A fine example of this is the way he revised his translation of Proverbs 31:12, which reads literally 'She does him good and not evil all the days of her life.' In his initial translation of 1524, Luther rendered this as 'Sie thut yhm guts und keyn böses, seyn lebenlang.' The last phrase is already a considerable improvement over such literal renderings as the Vulgate's *omnibus diebus vitae suae*. But later Luther revised his translation to read 'Sie thut ym liebs und kein leids, sein leben lang,' which he must have done purely for reasons of rhythm and alliteration. Perhaps he is consciously or unconsciously seeking to echo the alliteration found in the Hebrew of the previous verse, *bāṭāḥ bāh lēb baʿĕlāh*, or is influenced by the Vulgate of the next verse, *Quaesivit lanam et linum*. Another example of a felicitous revision is found in Luther's German of verse 30a, which he originally rendered quite literally as 'Gonst ist falsch und schöne ist eytel.' This was later revised to the more idiomatic 'Lieblich und schöne sein ist Nichts.'

Perhaps it could be argued that the very directness of Luther's language and the earthiness of his idiom reflect the renewed appreciation for the literal sense of this passage. In any case, it is to Melanchthon and Luther that we must assign the credit (or blame) for having broken the spell of the allegorical interpretation which had for so long dominated the reading of the Song of the Valiant Woman.

Wolfgang Russ

It is amazing how rapidly and how universally the new non-allegorical interpretation of the Song was adopted by Protestants in

---

[146] *Weimar–Ausgabe, Deutsche Bibel*, 10:2, 103.

sixteenth-century Europe. I am not aware of a single example of the old allegorical interpretation among supporters of the Reformation throughout the sixteenth century. The literal interpretation was espoused by everyone, both in academic commentaries and popular homiletic works.

A good example in the latter category is a German pamphlet entitled *Der Weyber geschefft*, 'The business of women', which was published by an obscure Protestant preacher called Wolfgang Russ in 1533. This was just four years after the publication of Melanchthon's *Nova Scholia*, the first modern commentary to give a literal interpretation of the Song. The twenty-one page pamphlet is written in the Swabian dialect of German, and is reminiscent of Augustine's *Sermo* 37 in that it appears to be the record of an informal sermon which deals with Proverbs 31:10–31 verse by verse. Its full title is *Der Weyber geschefft. Auslegung der ain und dreissigsten Capitels der Spruchen Salomonis, was ein redlich dapffer weib sey, was thon und lassen soll, durch Wolffgang Russ zu Riethen prediger.*[147] ('The Business of Women. Explanation of the thirty-first chapter of the Proverbs of Solomon: what an honest staunch wife is, and how she is to behave, by Wolffgang Russ, preacher in Riethen.') There is not much known about Russ, but he appears to have been a native of Ulm in the southern German region of Swabia, and to have been a Protestant preacher in Riedheim (or Riethen) not far from Ulm.[148]

The first two pages of the pamphlet contain the heading 'These are the words of King Lemuel, the teaching which his mother taught him' (Prov. 31:1), immediately followed by the Song, both in a German translation. The translation turns out to be Luther's original version of 1524 adapted to the Swabian dialect. For example, 'to her maidens' of verse 15 is *yhren dyrnen* in Luther's rendering, but *iren mägten* in Russ's version, probably because *Dirne* in Swabian (as in modern standard German) often means 'prostitute'. Similarly, Luther's word for 'distaff', *rocken*, is changed to *gunckel* (*Kunkel*), the word more commonly used in southern Germany for this spinning implement.[149] In substance, however, the translation offered by Russ is identical to that of Luther. There is no indication that Russ revised Luther's version on the basis of an independent knowledge of Hebrew.

The sermon itself is remarkable for its informal style and colloquial

---

[147] The pamphlet is exceedingly rare. I was fortunate in being allowed to make a photocopy, in 1982, of the copy found in the British Library in London.

[148] See *Huldreich Zwinglis Sämtliche Werke*. Bd. XI (ed. E. Egil and G. Finsler; Leipzig: Heinsius, 1935), 531–532, n. 3.

[149] J. and W. Grimm, *Deutsches Wörterbuch*, vol. 5 (Leipzig: Hirzel, 1873), s.v. 'Kunkel', col. 2653.

speech, spiced with many colourful idioms and pithy proverbial expressions. It has something of the vividness and earthiness of Luther's own language in the *Tischreden*, and is often difficult to translate, not only because of its picturesque expressions, but also because its vocabulary cannot be found in modern dictionaries, not even the great dictionary of the Swabian dialect compiled by H. Fischer.[150]

In his introduction Russ makes no bones about the literal approach which he is taking to the text. He decries the frivolous ways of the young women in his day, who are in need of serious admonition, and then goes on:

> I don't know anything that would serve that purpose better right now than precisely this chapter which we have before us. For the matter is a serious one, as it must be, since a queen teaches it and a king writes it down. It is not something which the majority of our young ladies today find interesting or amusing.
>
> For here one learns home management and piety, not idleness: how one ought to work, how one ought to speak and on what topics – in short, the whole business of running a household is here described.[151]

We have seen how Luther, under Melanchthon's influence, had translated Proverbs 31:12b as *narung wird yhm nicht mangeln*, 'a living will not be lacking to him [i.e. the husband]'. Russ comments on these words as follows:

> Such a competent honourable woman does not let anything spoil or go to waste. She turns to good account everything that comes into the house through hard work and honest Christian business dealings. She can put it all to good use in due time, so that there is something useful to do every day. She is

---

[150] H. Fischer, *Schwäbisches Wörterbuch*. Zu Ende geführt von Wilhelm Pfleiderer. Six volumes in seven (Tübingen: Laupp, 1904–1936).

[151] Russ, *Der Weyber geschefft*, 3: 'ich waiss auch jetzmals nichts das bass darzu thü / und diene / dann eben diss Capitel / das wir hie vor uns haben / Dann es freilich ein ernstlich ding ist / und sein muss / dieweyl es ein Künigin leert / ein Künig auff schreybt / es ist je nicht ding / damit unser jungen frawen der merthail jetz ummgond und kurtzweyl haben.

Dann do lernet man hauss haben / gotsforcht / nit müssig gan / was man arbaiten soll / was und wo von man reden soll / kurtz das gantz hauss geschefft / einer haushalterin ist hie beschriben' (my translation).

In this translation from Russ's sermon, and those which follow, my rendering is occasionally quite free and sometimes speculative. But I have chosen passages where I am confident that I have grasped the general sense of the idioms and the dialectal expressions.

no spendthrift. As the saying goes: 'they suffer no want there'. She does an excellent job of running her household; she knows how to get things done.[152]

Russ has the following to say about Proverbs 31:27, 'She looks to the ways of her household, and does not eat her bread in idleness':

It is not enough that maidservants and menservants (in fact even the children) should carry out and fulfill to our satisfaction their daily tasks and work. A woman must keep an eye on her servants' way of life before God: the company they keep, their gaming companions, and the faith they profess, lest they become a villainous and godless crew who care nothing for God. They must also be brought to the word of God and an honourable life. Any woman who runs her household in the manner described does not eat her bread in idleness. The grass will not grow under her feet, and she will not be spared a good deal of care, trouble and toil.[153]

Finally, I will quote Russ's comments on the climactic verse 30, 'Charm is deceitful, beauty is vain; a woman who fears the Lord must be praised':

How coarse and clumsy the Holy Spirit is, that he dares to say that charm is deceitful, a woman's attractiveness is only skin deep, beauty is vain, unprofitable, superfluous, useless. Our ladies are not going to take kindly to the Holy Spirit, that he dares to tell them the truth in this manner. No wonder that so few people are attached to the word of God; the wonder is that there is still anyone who is attached to it, since the Holy Spirit spares no one, but says the truth straight out, like a town crier, like a fishwife.[154]

---

[152] Russ, *Der weyber geschefft*, 6: 'Ein solch fromm ehren weib / lasst nichts verderben noch zu grundt geen / sie kans als zu eeren pringen / was durch saure arbait / Christlich gewin und gewerb zu hauss kommt / das kan sie als zu seiner zeiten prauchen / das man alle tag etwas her zunemen hab / sie ist kain vil prauch / da ist kayn mangel / wie man sagt / das ist ein feine haushalterin / sie kan wol zuschlagen' (my translation).

[153] Russ, *Der Weyber geschefft* 19: 'Es ist nit gnug / das mägdt und knecht / ja auch die kind jr teglich geschäfft und arbait nach unserm sinn thon und volbringen / Ein weib soll sehen / wie jr gesind ein wandel und leben gegen got füre / was geselschafft / gespilschafft es hab / was glauben es sey / das nit ein verrucht gotloss gesindt sey / das nach got nit frag / das mans auch zum gotswort und erbarkeit ziehe / wölche fraw also hauss helt / wie erzelt / die isst jr brot nit mit faulkait / der wirt wenig grass undern füssenn wachsen / es wirdt on grosse sorg mü und arbait nit zu geen' (my translation).

[154] Russ, *Der Weyber geschefft*, 20: 'Wie ist der gaist gots so grob unnd ungeschickt / das er darff sagenn / Gunst sey falsch / frawenn lieb sey schneyder werck / und schön sey eytel / unnutz upig / vergebens / es solten wol unsere weyber dem hailigen gaist auch nit holtz in die kuchen tragen / das er jn also darff die warheit

Mercerus and Muffet

It would be wearisome to list all the incidental indications throughout the sixteenth century that Protestant exegetes, without exception, gave a literal interpretation of the Song. We could mention, for example, the headings printed at the beginning of Proverbs 31 in the many new Protestant Bible translations. The English 'Great Bible' (1540) has 'Kynges ought to judge justely: The propertye of an honest maryed wife,' in which the second phrase obviously reflects a non-allegorical understanding of the second part of Proverbs 31. Similarly, the great Geneva Bible (1560), the standard English version of the Elizabethan age, has '2 He exhorteth to chastitie and justice, 10 And sheweth the conditions of a wife and worthy woman.' We might also point out that the Reformer John Calvin (1509–1564), although he never wrote a commentary on the book of Proverbs, nevertheless gives evidence of the common Protestant interpretation of the Song when he remarks in his commentary on 1 Samuel that Abigail, the forceful wife of Nabal who later married David, is like the valiant woman of Proverbs 31.[155]

Instead of enumerating such incidental allusions in the sixteenth century, we will conclude our survey by referring briefly to two commentaries on Proverbs published in the latter half of the century, a scholarly one by Johannes Mercerus written in Latin, and a popular one by Peter Muffet written in English.

Johannes Mercerus or Jean Mercier (died 1570) was a French Hebraist of Calvinist persuasion who succeeded his teacher Vatablus at the Collège de France in 1546. It is said of him that 'as exact scholarly exegete he surpasses all other interpreters of the sixteenth century'.[156] Shortly after his death there was published in Geneva a collection of his biblical commentaries, including one on the books of Proverbs.[157] The commentary on Proverbs was long regarded very highly by subsequent

---

[154] (*continued*) sagen / es ist nit wund / das dem gotswort wenig leut hold seind / ein wunder ists / das noch etwar ist / der jhm hold ist / die weyl der hailig gayst niemants verschonet / gerad die warhait herauss sagt / wie ein hörold / wie ein holipper' (my translation).

[155] *Corpus Reformatorum*, vol. 58, col. 546.

[156] H.J. Kraus, *Geschichte der historisch–kritischen Erforschung des Alten Testaments von der Reformation bis zur Gegenwart* (Neukirchen, 1956), 79: 'Johann Mercerus überragt als exakt wissenschaftlicher Exeget alle andern Ausleger des 16. Jahrhunderts'.

[157] Johannes Mercerus, *Commentarii in Jobum, et Salomonis Proverbia, Ecclesiasten, Canticum Canticorum* (Geneva, 1573). I will quote from a later edition published in Leiden in 1651.

interpreters. According to W. Frankenberg, who published a German commentary on Proverbs in 1898, 'Mercerus has made by far the most valuable contribution to the interpretation of Proverbs. The best of what is found in the commentaries on Proverbs goes back, directly or indirectly, to him'.[158]

Mercerus takes the Song to be written by the Lemuel of Proverbs 31:1 (whom he, like many of his predecessors, equates with Solomon), but he regards it as an independent composition:

> Because he has adduced the precepts with which he had been instructed by his mother he has taken the occasion to add the praises of an industrious and godly woman.[159]

He explicitly rejects allegorical interpretation, though he is thoroughly familiar with medieval commentaries, both Jewish and Christian. As we noted above in our discussion of Ralbag, Mercerus knew and used the Proverbs commentary of this eminent Jewish scholar, but he also refers to Rashi, Ibn Ezra, David Kimchi and others.

In his discussion of the term *'ēšet ḥayil* (Prov. 31:10), Mercerus writes that it is the equivalent of the vernacular (that is, French) *une vaillante femme*, the first time (to my knowledge) in the history of the interpretation of the Song that it is explicitly related to heroic categories. The remainder of the commentary is of interest chiefly for its great philological erudition and knowledge of the history of interpretation. For our purposes it is enough to note that this influential scholarly commentary takes a resolutely literal approach to the Song throughout.

The last commentator that we will discuss is Peter Muffet (Moffett), an obscure Englishman who wrote *A Commentary on the Whole Book of Proverbs*, first published in 1592, and reprinted two years later.[160] Apart from this commentary, nothing seems to be known of the author, although we can deduce from the commentary that he was a Protestant clergyman. There is some evidence that he died in 1617.[161]

---

[158] W. Frankenberg, *Die Sprüche* (HKAT; Göttingen, 1898), 16: 'Merc[erus] hat bei weitem das Wertvollste geleistet zur Erklärung der Prov[erbia]. Das Beste was sich in den Komm[entaren] über die Spr[üche] findet, geht auf ihn – mittelbar oder unmittelbar – zurück.'

[159] Mercerus, *Commentarii*, 512: 'Quia precepta attulit quibus a matre eruditus fuerit, per occasionem subjungit laudationem sedulae et piae matronae.'

[160] The work is rare, but is accessible in *Nichol's Series of Commentaries* (Edinburgh, 1868), which contains a reprint of Muffet's commentary. It is from this edition that I quote.

[161] That is the date of death given in one of the entries referring to this commentary (under the name 'Moffett') in the *National Union Catalog*.

The commentary is meant for the lay reader, and is simple, plain, and straightforward. Lemuel is equated with Solomon, which makes Lemuel's mother (Prov. 31:1) Bathsheba, and it is she whom Muffet takes to be the author also of the Song. He comments on verse 10:

> Bathsheba cometh now to describe and commend a good housewife. Her most rare excellency is shewed in this verse. By demanding the question she declareth that many find beautiful and rich women, but few a good or godly wife, who is a special gift of God. By comparing a virtuous woman with pearls, she insinuateth that she is not only a rare, but an excellent blessing of the Lord, for it is well known that precious stones or pearls are in great account among all people.[162]

Muffet's comment on verse 17 is:

> Herein is shewed after what sort the painful wife followeth her business. 'She girdeth her loins with strength,' &c. As one ready to run a race, or to wrestle with a champion, she flieth about her work, and setteth on it with a courage. Her garments hang not loose about her, but she tucketh them up that she may be the more nimble. She is then unlike to many nice dames, who will set their finger to no work, nor scant stir about the house.[163]

We find the same straightforward exposition on the climactic verse 30, ending with a reference (echoing Melanchthon) to the woman's calling:

> 'Favour is deceitful;' comeliness of personage or any outward grace is as a shadow which hath no substance; moreover, it causeth men oftentimes to go astray; finally, under it many vices are hid. For divers that have well-favoured countenances have ill-favoured conditions. 'Beauty is also vain.' A good colour or a good complexion is but a fading flower, which by sickness, sorrow, age, and death, withereth and decayeth. Indeed these two things are of themselves good things, for the which sundry women in the Scripture are praised, but they are but frail good things, and inferior to the fear of God. For this cause it is furthermore said, that 'a woman that feareth the Lord, she shall be praised'. The garland of praise is only to be set on her head who believeth in God, repenteth of her sins, practiseth good works, and walketh faithfully in her calling.[164]

Although Muffet makes no great display of erudition, he does occasionally refer to the Hebrew text (for example, *sādîn* in verse 24), and the

---

[162] *Nichol's Series, Proverbs*, 184.

[163] *Nichol's Series, Proverbs*, 185.

[164] *Nichol's Series, Proverbs*, 188.

English translation on which he bases his text seems to be a modified version of the Geneva Bible. For example, while the Geneva Bible translates *kîšôr* in verse 19 as 'wherne' (that is, 'spindle-whorl', following Rashi and Lyra), Muffet has 'wheel' (that is, 'spinning-wheel'), apparently unaware that this relatively recent invention was unknown in Bible times.

Conclusion

We thus conclude our survey with the commentaries of Mercerus and Muffet, scholarly and popular representatives of the Reformation consensus which decisively broke with the long tradition of interpreting the Song of the Valiant Woman allegorically. The emphasis on the literal sense, together with the historical–grammatical method of elucidating that sense, were to set the stage for the later critical methods which would dominate the interpretation of the Song in modern times. The decisive step away from the old, allegorical and toward the new, 'literal' had been taken in the Reformation.

6

The Song of the Valiant Woman since the Sixteenth Century

This chapter gives an impressionistic account of roughly the last four centuries in the history of interpretation of the Song of the Valiant Woman, supplementing and bringing up to date the survey contained in chapter 5. There is, of course, an enormous amount of repetition, as well as forgettable popular exposition, in what is written on any portion of the Bible. It is thus impossible to give anything approaching an exhaustive survey of the vast body of literature pertinent to this pericope and published since the sixteenth century. But it is possible to provide some representative highlights and incidental illustrations; to convey a sense of the overall hermeneutical and exegetical developments in the last four hundred years. It is only when we get to the last few decades of the twentieth century that I will strive for some measure of bibliographical completeness – although even here it would be impossible (as well as pointless) to list every published discussion, in commentaries or elsewhere, of the remarkable acrostic poem which concludes the book of Proverbs.

Sixteenth Century

The previous discussion concluded with representatives of the Protestant Reformation who broke with the long history of allegorically interpreting the Song. To round out the discussion of the sixteenth century, let me mention two Catholic commentaries published in the latter half of that century: the scholarly treatment by Jansenius (1568), and the popular exposition by Luis de León (1583). What distinguishes these two Catholic discussions of the Song is that they now, perhaps under the influence of the new Protestant reading, make room for the literal interpretation alongside the allegorical one.

Cornelius Jansenius (1510–1576), not to be confused with the later theologian by the same name who became the father of Jansenism, deals with the Song at the end of his Latin commentary on Proverbs.[1] He takes the Song to be part of the words of Lemuel, whom he identifies with Solomon,[2] and explicitly prefers the allegorical interpretation of Bede to that of Lyra, thus taking the Valiant Woman to represent the church (or the individual believer's soul), rather than Scripture.[3] He does not refer to contemporary Protestant exegetes, but does mention the Catholic scholar Cajetan (1469–1534), who had apparently also preferred a literal interpretation.[4] This Jansenius considers less preferable than a traditional allegorical approach.[5] However, the mention of this Catholic authority does apparently embolden him to continue with a literal reading alongside an allegorical one. Consequently, for each of the sixteen units into which he divides the Song, he first gives a literal, and then a 'mystical' interpretation (in which he also finds references to the Virgin Mary[6]).

The commentary is based on the text of the Vulgate, but Jansenius regularly refers to both the Hebrew original, and the Septuagint. Among the noteworthy details of his commentary are the following. On verse 19 he comments that the Hebrew word *kîšôr* which is translated *fortia* in the Vulgate really means a spinning implement, either 'spindle-whorl' or 'distaff'.[7] The latter rendering of course represents the new interpretation of Melanchthon and Luther, although Jansenius does not mention them by name. On the Vulgate's 'she opened her mouth to wisdom' (verse 26), he comments: 'now he shows that she also comports herself well in her speech, and that she is free from the vice of talkativeness and foolishness from which the feminine sex generally suffers'.[8] Unlike many

---

[1] Cornelius Jansenius, *Commentarii in Proverbia* (Lovanii: Ioannes Bogardus, 1568).

[2] Jansenius, *Proverbia*, 535.

[3] Jansenius, *Proverbia*, 539.

[4] Jansenius, *Proverbia*, 539: 'Caietanus etiam carmen quod sequitur putat esse matris Salomonis verba, quibus descripserit officia probae mulieris, ut filius disceret quaerere talem uxorem quae huiusmodi haberet conditiones'. The reference must be to Cajetan's *Parabolae Salomonis ad veritatem hebraicam castigatae* (Roma: Apud Antonium Bladum Asulanum, 1542). I have been unable to consult this work, but it seems that Cajetan, who was known to be unafraid to embrace the literal sense even against the exegetical tradition, followed Melanchthon and Luther in breaking with the allegorical consensus.

[5] Jansenius, *Proverbia*, 539.

[6] Jansenius, *Proverbia*, 540.

[7] Jansenius, *Proverbia*, 545: 'Secundo enim versu [i.e. verse 19] nihil aliud significatur quam nendi opus, quia pro fortia, dictio Hebraica significat verticulum, vel ut alij volunt colum'.

[8] Jansenius, *Proverbia*, 550: 'nunc verò etiam sermone se bene gerere ostendit, eamque liberam esse à vitio loquacitatis & stultitiae quo ferè muliebris sexus laborat'.

commentators, Jansenius conceives of the relationship between the Valiant Woman's exploits and her 'fear of the Lord' in a remarkably integral way. Commenting on the last two verses, he writes that the praiseworthy qualities of the Valiant Woman consist, not in her beauty, 'but only in the things which demonstrate that she fears God. Such are the responsibilities which had been ascribed to her beforehand'.[9] It is her practical activities themselves which manifest her fear of the Lord.

Our second example of Catholic interpretation in the sixteenth century is quite different. It is the booklet by the Spanish priest and poet Luis de León (1528–1595), *La perfecta casada* (1583). This devotional tract has become something of a classic in the Spanish-speaking world, and is still widely read today.[10] The author is best known as a Spanish lyric poet, but he was a Hebraist by profession, and *La perfecta casada* is really his own translation, with popular commentary, of the Song of the Valiant Woman. The well-known nineteenth-century Old Testament scholar Franz Delitzsch called it 'one of the finest expositions of this passage, perhaps the finest'.[11] The Spanish author Marañón could write in 1927 that 'almost all Spanish brides receive, among their wedding gifts, an admirable booklet: *La perfecta casada* of Luis de León'.[12] Its wide appeal is undoubtedly partly due to the fact that the author, while acknowledging the validity of the allegorical interpretation, self-consciously restricts himself to the literal reading.

The first of the work's twenty-one chapters is devoted to a defense of focussing on the literal sense. The author writes:

---

[9] Jansenius, *Proverbia*, 552: 'laudem mulieris non consistere in veritate in huiusmodi re, sed tantum in his quae declarant eam timere Deum, qualia sunt officia prius illi attributa'.

[10] The booklet continues to be in print, in many editions. I will cite from Luis de León, *La perfecta casada. Exposición del Cantar de Cantares de Salomón* (Décima edición; eds. Felix García and Federico Carlos Sainz de Robles; Madrid: Aguilar, 1967). It is also available on the Internet, as part of the Biblioteca Virtual Miguel de Cervantes. An English translation by A.P. Hubbard was published as *The Perfect Wife* (Denton TX: The College Press, Texas State College for Women, 1943), but this is quite unreliable.

[11] Franz Delitzsch, *Das Salomonische Spruchbuch* (Leipzig: Dörffling und Franke, 1873), 527: 'Eine der schönsten Auslegungen dieses Stücks, vielleicht die schönste, ist Luis de León's *La perfecta casada*'.

[12] Cited in the 'Preámbulo' of the Aguilar edition (see n. 10) of *La perfecta casada*, 23: 'casi todas las novias españoles reciben, entre los regalos nupciales, un librito admirable: *La perfecta casada*, del maestro fray Luis de León'.

And as everything in God is good, so in Scripture all the senses which the Holy Spirit put in it are true. With the result that following the one sense is not to reject the other one, and one who in these sacred writings, among the many and true senses which they contain, discovers one of them, and explains it, need not for that reason be taken for a person who rejects the others.[13]

The remaining twenty chapters are each devoted to an exposition, verse by verse, of Luis de León's own Spanish translation of the Hebrew text. (Each chapter deals with one verse, except chapter 9, which treats verses 17–19 together.) It is noteworthy that the Spanish exegete chooses to provide his own vernacular translation of the original, since the Vulgate had been officially declared the authentic version by the Council of Trent (1546). Both his focus on the literal sense and his departure from the Vulgate were dangerous; these same attitudes had earlier contributed to his spending five years in jail under the Spanish Inquisition.[14]

De León's translation of the Hebrew showed considerable philological independence. For one thing, it was quite free. For example, he renders the phrase 'she arises when it is yet night' (verse 15) with the single Spanish verb *madrugó*. The Hebrew word *bayit* is translated in four different ways: *gañanes* (verse 15), *familia* (verse 21), *gente* (verse 21), and *casa* (verse 27). For another, he shows his independence from the Vulgate by rendering *ṭerep* in verse 15 as *raciones*, 'rations' (Vulgate *praeda*), *kîšôr* in verse 19 as *tortera*, 'spindle-whorl' (Vulgate *fortia*), and *ḥesed* in verse 26 as *piedad* (Vulgate *clementia*) – to list only a few examples.

At many places in his commentary de León betrays the social and economic prejudices of his age, especially with reference to appropriate gender roles. When the text says that the Valiant Woman is like a merchant ship, which 'brings her food from afar' (verse 14), he takes this to mean that she never leaves the home: 'Just as the ship travels through various lands looking for profitable goods, so she must make the rounds of all the corners of her house, retrieve from them everything which seems to be worthless, and convert it into something useful and advantageous'.[15]

---

[13] *La perfecta casada*, 43–44: 'Y como en Dios todo lo que hay es bueno, así en la Escritura todos los sentidos que puso en ella el Espíritu Santo son verdaderos. Por manera que el seguir el uno sentido no es desechar el otro, ni menos el que en estas sagradas letras, entre muchos y verdaderos entendimientos que tienen, descubre uno dellos y le declara, no por eso ha de ser tenido por hombre que desecha los otros entendimientos'.

[14] See A.P. Hubbard's 'Biographical Introduction', *The Perfect Wife*, xxii–xxix.

[15] *La perfecta casada*, 80: 'como la nave corre por diversas tierras buscando ganancias, así ella ha de rodear de su casa todos los rincones, y recoger todo lo que pareciere estar perdido en ellos, y convertirlo en utilidad y provecho'.

Although ships may sail far from their home port, this does not apply to the Valiant Woman. She must stay at home. Or again, when the text says that the Valiant Woman 'opens her mouth with wisdom' (verse 26), de León turns this almost into its opposite: 'And to open her mouth with wisdom, as the sage says here, means not to open it except when necessity requires it, which is the same thing as to speak with moderation, and on few occasions, because the occasions are few where necessity requires it'.[16] It is also striking that he has almost nothing to say on verse 24, which speaks of the Valiant Woman as a businesswoman (the entire 'chapter' dealing with this verse consists of 12 lines), but has a long disquisition on breast-feeding and child-rearing in connection with verse 28 – although neither this verse, nor the Song as a whole, mention these traditional topics at all.

La perfecta casada, because of its extraordinary popularity to this day, is probably the most influential commentary on the Song ever written. But it is difficult to agree with Delitzsch that it may well be the finest.

Seventeenth Century

The exclusively literal treatment of the Song in *La perfecta casada* is an exception among Catholic commentators of early modern times. More typical is the interpretation found in the extensive learned commentary on Proverbs produced by Cornelius à Lapide (1567–1637), a Jesuit representative of the Counter-Reformation in the seventeenth century. This exposition of the Song is part of his massive multi-volume work entitled *Commentaria in Sacram Scripturam.*[17] The commentary on Proverbs was completed in 1635, two years before the author's death.

What distinguishes à Lapide's exegetical work, apart from its impressive philological erudition, are two things: the consistent application of the traditional medieval hermeneutic which adopts a fourfold sense of Scripture, and its wealth of citation from the history of interpretation. Apart from the literal sense, which à Lapide also treats extensively, the bulk of the commentary is devoted to the supra-literal senses: the allegorical, the tropological and the anagogical. Unfortunately, his

---

[16] *La perfecta casada*, 153: 'Y el abrir su boca en sabiduría, que el Sabio aqui dice es no la abrir sino cuando la necesidad lo pide, que es lo mismo que abrirla templadamente y pocas veces, porque son pocas las que lo pide la necesidad'.

[17] The work was reprinted many times. I cite the following edition: C. à Lapide, *Commentaria in Sacram Scripturam. Editio Xysto Riario Sfortiae dicata*, 10 vols. (Neapoli: Apud I. Nagar, 1854–59). Volume 3 contains the *Commentaria in Proverbia Salomonis*, with the treatment of the Song on pages 734–766.

terminology is somewhat confusing. He speaks of 'symbolic', 'moral', and 'mystical' senses, and it is not always clear how these correlate with the standard senses. Thus he begins his discussion by saying that allegorically the Valiant Woman represents the church, tropologically she represents the pious soul (as well as the Virgin Mary), and symbolically she represents wisdom (as well as Scripture and heroic power or virtue).[18] It is unclear whether this last 'symbolic' sense is the same as the anagogical, or represents an additional sense. Furthermore, in his commentary on verse 14 ('she searched out wool and flax') he writes that this activity of textile production also applies to the Virgin Mary in each of the four standard senses.[19]

In his voluminous commentary à Lapide cites a wide array of previous commentators, from the church fathers (e.g. Augustine and Gregory the Great), medieval Christian authors (e.g. the Venerable Bede and Nicholas Lyra), and medieval Jewish rabbis (e.g. Ibn Ezra and Rashi), to sixteenth-century Catholic expositors (e.g. Jansenius and Luis de León). Protestant exegetes, however, are never mentioned; the one reference to Luther speaks of him only as a former monk who has become a 'heresiarch'.[20] Because of the doctrine of multiple senses, it is possible for à Lapide to incorporate almost all traditional views with approval, although he seems to have had a personal preference for the Mariological interpretation. (In fact, this may be the first scholarly commentary which consistently defends a Mariological reading, among others, of the Song.)

Despite his emphasis on the non-literal senses, à Lapide gives a very thorough philological treatment of the literal sense, referring constantly to the Hebrew original, and comparing all of the standard ancient versions, including the Peshitta and the minor Greek versions. He even refers to the 'Armena versio apud M. Anton. Abagarum,' which I have not been able to identify.[21]

A notable feature of à Lapide's commentary is also his recognition of the 'heroic' character of the description given of the Valiant Woman. She is said to represent *virtus heroica*, and to be properly called a *heroina*. She does great exploits, described as *actus heroicos*, *opera heroica*, or *heroica facinora*.[22] Nevertheless, à Lapide has no doubt that the Valiant Woman does not venture outside the home. Accordingly, in his comment on verse 15 he writes

---

[18] À Lapide, *Proverbia*, 734b.
[19] À Lapide, *Proverbia*, 740b.
[20] À Lapide, *Proverbia*, 751a.
[21] À Lapide, *Proverbia*, 758b (cf. 752b).
[22] À Lapide, *Proverbia*, 734b, 735a, 746a, 758b, 765a.

Therefore the meaning is as though it said that this vigorous woman, as she works with wool and flax, is like the merchant ships, because, just as those ships bear away garments, textiles, and other commodities to distant parts of the world, in exchange for which they bring back from these same places other commodities, out of which the merchants provide themselves with nourishment and other necessities, so she too gets her 'bread' from afar, that is, the nourishment necessary for her family, since she, in exchange for the products of her hands, also provides herself with goods from far away. Giving to foreigners the clothing which she has made, she receives back from them grain for food. Therefore, although she herself stays at home, and does not travel with the merchants to the remotest Indians, nevertheless, like a kind of ship conveying necessary goods from far away, she herself too 'brings her bread from afar' by giving of her own products to foreigners.[23]

Despite its limitations, the commentary by à Lapide stands as an impressive monument of philological erudition, as well as a *Fundgrube* of information on the history of interpretation. In many ways it has not been surpassed to this day.

A commentary from a quite different theological perspective is that of the well-known Puritan theologian Thomas Cartwright (1535–1603), *Commentaria succincti et dilucidi in Proverbia Salomonis.* This was published posthumously in 1617, one of the first products of the short-lived press established by the Pilgrim Fathers in Leiden, and was to be quite influential in the seventeenth century and beyond (it was reprinted in 1632 and 1638).[24] Although it regularly refers to the original Hebrew, it is chiefly concerned with the practical application of the literal sense of the biblical text. In fact, the commentary makes no mention at all of the traditional 'spiritual' senses of the Song.

At the same time, Cartwright's application of the literal sense is consistently 'spiritual' in the sense of being geared to the religious edification of

---

[23] À Lapide, *Proverbia,* 741a: 'Sensus ergo est, q. d. [= quasi dicat] Mulier haec strenua operando lanam et linum similis est navibus mercatorum, quia sicut illae pannos, telas, aliasque merces in longinquas orbis partes deferunt, pro quibus ex eisdem locis referunt alias merces, unde mercatores sibi victum et necessaria comparant; ita et illa a longe sibi parat panem suum, hoc est victum familiae necessarium, quia pro his quae manibus suis operata est, comparat sibi etiam quae ex longinquo afferuntur, dansque exteris pannum a se confectum, accipit ab eis frumentum in cibum; ipsa ergo cum domi maneat, nec cum mercatoribus extremos currat ad Indos; tamen velut navis quaedam necessaria a longe advehens, etiam ipsa sua exteris communicando portat de longe panem suum'.
[24] See A.F.S. Pearson, *Thomas Cartwright and Elizabethan Puritanism,* 1535–1603 (Cambridge: Cambridge University Press, 1925), 190, 210, 398–399. The edition which I cite is that published in Amsterdam in 1638.

the reader. A case in point is his comment on the words 'she laughs at the coming day' in verse 25:

> By the verb 'laugh' is indicated an exceptional peace of mind. For we generally laugh at those opponents over whom we are confident we will gain a certain and easy victory. Therefore what is here excellently depicted is the blessed state of the godly, and their undoubted assurance concerning their eternal salvation, by virtue of which they are certain of their future, as much as of their present or past condition'.[25]

A few lines later he adds the polemic point that: 'This place provides an excellent refutation of that godless doctrine of the Papists, who torment people's consciences with the continual anguish of doubt and anxiety'.[26]

A point which distinguishes Cartwright's treatment of the Song from that of most others is his concern to apply it to men as well as women. Sometimes this takes the form of an *a fortiori* argument: 'If this is true of women, how much more does it apply to men.' For example, the last quote is followed by the words: 'For if there is as much trust and confidence as here described in a woman, who is by nature more fearful, how much more should men arm themselves against irrational fears.'[27] On other occasions, however, the biblical point being made is simply said to apply equally to men. After commenting, in connection with verse 11, that the Valiant Woman should take care never to appear unchaste, Cartwright adds: 'This same point is also to be applied to the duty of the husband toward the wife.'[28] Or again, after stating in connection with verse 12 that the wife should do good to the husband whatever his age, health or wealth, Cartwright adds: 'These things must be performed also by the husband for the wife.'[29] Along somewhat similar lines, when the

---

[25] Cartwright, *Proverbia*, 1324: 'Singularis haec animi securitas ridendi adject. declaratur. Ridere autem solemus illos antagonistas, de quibus certam nobis ipsis, & facilem pollicemur victoriam. Hic igitur egregiè depingitur beata piorum conditio, & salutis aeternae indubitata certitudo, qua tam de futura, quam praesenti, aut praeterita conditione sua certi sunt'.
[26] Cartwright, *Proverbia*, 1324: 'Egregiè refellitur ex hoc loco impium illud Pontificiorum dogma, qui hominum conscientias perpetua dubitationis, & anxietatis carnificinâ excruciant'.
[27] Cartwright, *Proverbia*, 1324: 'Nam si foeminae naturâ timidiori tantum insit, quantum audivimus, fiduciae, & confidentiae; quantò magis viros decet adversùs panicos terrores seipsos confirmare?'
[28] Cartwright, *Proverbia*, 1308: 'Quod ipsum ad viri etiam erga uxorem officium transferendum est'.
[29] Cartwright, *Proverbia*, 1309: 'Haec etiam uxori à marito praestanda sunt'.

Hebrew says in verse 28 'Her sons rise up and call her blessed,' he writes: 'In *bnyh* (*her sons*) there is a synecdoche of the species, standing for any children at all.'[30] In other words, 'sons' is here used generically to include 'daughters' as well.

Cartwright's Protestant orientation again comes clearly to the fore when he discusses verse 19, which describes the Valiant Woman as engaged in the lowly task of spinning:

> This passage must be given careful attention in order to establish us more firmly in the common duties of this life as duties pleasing to God, against the Anabaptists, who judge them to be too lowly to be engaged in by Christians, and against the Papists, who, although they do not condemn this kind of work, nevertheless, by exalting so highly the tasks which they have dreamt up for nuns, but which have never been approved by the Holy Spirit, slacken the hands of godly women.[31]

Of course the interpretation and influence of the Song of the Valiant Woman was not restricted to academic commentaries on the book of Proverbs. It was widely read and explained in other contexts as well, most notably in the sermons and regular Bible reading of ordinary pastors and laypeople. It also played a crucial role in a new genre of Christian writing which generally went under the title *Oeconomia Christiana*, presenting a Bible-based Christian view of the family. An example is the two-volume work with this title published in 1661 by the Dutch Pietist Petrus Wittewrongel (1609–1662).[32] This Reformed pastor in Amsterdam drew heavily on the Song in his description of the appropriate Christian family.[33]

---

[30] Cartwright, *Proverbia*, 1327: 'In *bnyh* (*filii ejus*) est synec. speciei pro liberis quibuslibet'.

[31] Cartwright, *Proverbia*, 1318: 'Hic locus observandus est ad nos in communibus hujus vitae officiis, tanquam Deo gratis confirmandum, contra Anabaptistas, qui abjectiora esse statuunt, quam ut christiani se in iis exerceant; & Pontificos, qui, tametsi hujusmodi opera non damnent, dum tamen commentitia suarum novarum [nonnarum?] opera nusquam à Sp. Sancto probata tantopere efferunt, manus piarum foeminarum remissiores faciunt'. My current translation presupposes that the *novarum* of the printed text is a misprint for *nonnarum*, and therefore differs from that found in chapter 2 (see n. 29 of that chapter).

[32] P. Wittewrongel, *Oeconomia Christiana. Ofte Christelicke Huyshoudinge*, 2 vols. (Amsterdam: Brandt & Van de Burgh, 1661³).

[33] See L.F. Groenendijk, *De nadere reformatie van het gezin. De visie van Petrus Wittewrongel op de christelijke huishouding* (Dordrecht: J. P. van den Tol, 1984), 115: 'Een grote plaats neemt Spreuk. 31 – de lof der deugdzame huisvrouw – in'.

Eighteenth Century

For this century I will again look at two scholarly commentaries on Proverbs, one Protestant and one Catholic.

The Protestant commentator is the famous Dutch Semitic scholar Albertus Schultens (1686–1750), who is considered by Hans-Joachim Kraus to be one of the forerunners of classical historical criticism. His contribution was especially a philological one, in that he broke with the idea of Hebrew as a special 'sacred language', and treated the language of the Old Testament as just another example of the family of Semitic languages. It is particularly his extensive knowledge of classical Arabic, which he considered the premier Semitic language, which he brought to bear on the study of biblical Hebrew.[34] Consequently, the two learned commentaries which Schultens wrote (on Job and Proverbs), are of interest chiefly from a philological point of view. At the same time, as a Protestant, Schultens had no interest in anything but the literal sense of the Song of the Valiant Woman. However, he paid very little attention to its contemporary relevance.

A good example of Schultens' overall approach is his comment, in *Proverbia Salomonis*, on Proverbs 31:19, which speaks of the two spinning implements used by the Valiant Woman.

> Two terms belonging to *the spinner's art* are here mentioned. It was impossible not to be uncertain about them, because they occur nowhere else (at least in this usage). According to most scholars, *kyšwr* and *plk* mean "spindle-whorl" and "spindle", to others they mean "spindle-whorl" and "distaff", to others finally they mean "distaff" and "spindle". The latter is the more appropriate order. Various suggestions have also been made regarding the etymology. I am not inclined to dwell on these here. I will only propose what the nature of the subject-matter and the force of the words themselves seem to require. "Distaff" and "spindle" have a natural order, and in this connection tend always to occur together. *Kyšwr*, "distaff", derives its meaning from *kšr*, "to be fastened together into a circle", "to be wound up into a ball", which in its origin is Arabic *ktr* and *ktr*. From there we get *kyšwr*, "distaff", around which *the wool is tightly wound*, so that the *threads* can be conveniently *drawn out*.[35]

---

[34] See H.-J. Kraus, *Geschichte der historisch-kritischen Erforschung des Alten Testaments von der Reformation bis zur Gegenwart* (Neukirchen, Kreis Moers: Verlag der Buchhandlung des Erziehungsvereins, 1956), 71–72.

[35] A. Schultens, *Proverbia Salomonis. Versionem integram ad Hebraeum fontem expressit, atque commentarium adjecit* (Leiden, 1748), 515: 'Duo vocabula *artis lanificae* hic adhibita, circa quae, quod nuspiam alibi, isto quidem usu, occurrant, non potuit non fluctuari; *kyšwr & plk verticillum & fusus*, secundum plurimos, aliis *verticillum & colus*; aliis denique *colus & fusus*; qui ordo commodior. Variatur

The rather fanciful etymology from Arabic which Schultens here proposes for *kîšôr* is typical of his approach to Hebrew lexicography, and has
not been followed, to the best of my knowledge, by anyone after him. In
fact, as I argued in chapter 4, *kîšôr* does not mean 'distaff' at all, but a
special kind of spindle. Schultens was misled by his own cultural experience to assume that distaff and spindle were a 'natural' pair, whereas in fact
the distaff appears not to have been used in ancient Near Eastern
spinning.

Another example of Schultens' careful attention to the philological
detail of the literal sense is found in his comment on verse 21, where it is
said that all of the Valiant Woman's household are clothed in *šnym*. This
Hebrew word can be vocalized as either *šěnayim*, 'double clothes' (so
LXX and Vulgate) or *šānîm*, 'scarlet' (so MT and Peshitta). Schultens opts
for the former, and lists five sources from Greek and Roman antiquity to
support it.[36] Furthermore, it is noteworthy that he also departs from the
Masoretic vocalization in verse 16. He reads the verb *nṭʿ*, which the MT
vocalizes as the feminine form *nāṭěʿā*, 'she plants' (spelt without the
expected final *he*), as the masculine form *nāṭaʿ*, 'he plants', and explains:
'that man plants, who is either the husband or even some hired man,
since it is not customary for a woman to plant a vineyard'.[37] He seems to
have overlooked the possibility that a wealthy person (whether male or
female) can be said to 'plant' a vineyard even when a crew of hired
workers do the actual work.

Our second representative commentator in the eighteenth century is
the French Benedictine monk Augustin Calmet (1672–1757), who was
famous for his twenty-two volume *Commentaire littéral sur tous les livres de
l'Ancien et Nouveau Testament* (Paris, 1707–1716). The commentary on
the Old Testament books was later translated in its entirety into Latin, and
it is this version which we will quote.[38] As the title of Calmet's magnum

---

[35] (*continued*) quoque in *Etymo* constituendo. Eis immorari haud lubet. Dabo
tantum, quod natura rei, & vocum ipsarum virtus exigere videtur. *Colus & fusus*
naturalem habent ordinem, atque hac in materia semper conjungi solent. *Kyšwr
colus* dicta a *kšr* necti in orbem, *circumnecti in globum*; quod est *ktr* & *ktr* sua in *Origine*.
Inde *Kyšwr colus*, cui *lana apte circumnectitur*, ut *fila* commode *deduci* queant'.

[36] Schultens, *Proverbia*, 516.

[37] Schultens, *Proverbia*, 514: '*ille plantat*, qui sit vel *maritus*, vel & *mercenarius* aliquis,
quod mos non sit mulierem vineas plantare'.

[38] A. Calmet, *Commentarius Literalis in Omnes Libros Veteris Testamenti, Latinis literis
traditus a Joanne Dominico Mansi*, editio novissima, 11 vols. (Wirceburgi: Apud
Franc. Xaver. Rienner, 1789–1793). From this edition I cite *Tomi Sexti, Pars
Secunda, seu Tomus Septimus: In Psalmos et Proverbia Salomonis* (1792).

opus indicates, he is explicitly concerned with the literal sense, and he applies this literal understanding also to the Song of the Valiant Woman. Accordingly, he begins his exposition:

> Having cited the instructions of his mother, Solomon presents a testimonial to the merit of the distinguished woman – the most extensive and the most beautiful of all those dealing with women in the Old Testament. And since the Spirit of God can neither flatter nor lie, it is permissible to deduce from these magnificent praises what Bathsheba's virtue was like. Furthermore, this distinguished woman has by her penance wiped out the sin which she committed with David, and by the merit of her faithfulness has achieved that she was raised to the highest pitch of virtue and holiness, and was displayed as an example of virtue both to her entire sex and to the souls which strive to form themselves for holiness of life by the exercise of the Christian virtues. The Fathers recognized in her the image of the most holy Virgin (1), and of the Church of Jesus Christ (2), but surely we may discern in Solomon's description of her many things which are very useful for the building up of the moral life of the faithful.[39]

There are two especially striking things in this passage. On the one hand, Calmet (like Luis de León) departs from the Catholic tradition of allegorical interpretation, despite its venerable pedigree, and explicitly favours a literal reading. On the other hand, he clearly applies a traditional Catholic understanding of merit and penance to the Valiant Woman, whom he identifies with Solomon's mother Bathsheba.

In other ways, too, Calmet works with identifiably Catholic theological categories in his exposition of the Song. Consider his comment on verse 30, which mentions the Valiant Woman's 'fear of the Lord':

---

[39] Calmet, *Commentarius* VI, 2, 750–751. The footnotes indicated by the numbers in parentheses refer first to two sermons by Bernard of Clairvaux and the Greek Catena, and second to Augustine, Gregory and Bede, among others. 'Recitatis matris suae institutionibus, Salomon merito illustris foeminae consecrat elogium, omnium, quae in Veteri Testamento de foeminis aguntur, amplissimum & pulcherrimum; cumque nec assentari, nec mentiri possit Spiritus Dei, quae fuerit Bethsabee virtus, e magnificis hisce laudibus arguere licet. Porro illustris haec mulier commissum cum Davide crimen poenitentia diluit, & merito fidelitatis suae obtinuit, ut extolleretur in altissimum virtutis & sanctitatis gradum, ac exhiberetur specimen virtutis tum suo sexui universo, cum animabus, quae Christianarum virtutum exercitio formare se ad vitae sanctimoniam student. Noverunt in illa Patres imaginem sanctissimae Virginis (1), & Ecclesiae Jesu Christi (2): ac sane in iis quae de illa Salomon, plura animadvertere licet aedificandis Fidelium moribus utilissima'.

To this point Solomon had hardly praised anything in his mother but virtues, which, though rare, did not transcend the natural order. He established, as virtually exclusive evidence of her praiseworthy qualities, the diligence, alertness, discipline, and efficient administration of the famous lady; here, however, he teaches that all these qualities, indeed, even her very beauty and her charms, are worthless and of no avail unless the fear of God, piety and true Wisdom are added to them. And this he placed as the epilogue of his testimonial to his mother.[40]

The body of the Song describes 'the natural order', while the addition of the fear of the Lord is an 'epilogue'. The former correlates with 'nature', the latter with 'grace'.

Philologically, Calmet's commentary is competent, referring to both the Hebrew and the ancient versions, but it is generally unoriginal. An exception is his proposal that *kîšôr* in verse 19 refers to a weaver's shuttle, rather than a spinner's distaff or spindle.[41] Oddly enough, he omits to comment on verse 20 – perhaps through simple inadvertence. Furthermore, like many of the commentators on the Song, Calmet reads his own preconceptions into the description of the Valiant Woman. In a concluding paragraph he summarizes her activities as follows: 'She is alert, eager to be active, and hardworking; she keeps to the home, and is busy with supervising her servants and raising her children'.[42] He appears to forget that the Song nowhere makes mention of child-rearing activities, and that verses 14, 16 and 24 suggest that some of her labours take place outside the home.

Nineteenth Century

It is in the nineteenth century that we begin to see the impact of classical historical criticism on the study of Proverbs in general and the concluding acrostic in particular. A representative example is the commentary by

---

[40] Calmet, *Commentarius* VI, 2, 759: 'Hactenus Salomon vix aliud in matre sua laudaverat quam virtutes, raras illas quidem, sed quae naturalem ordinem non superarent. Argumentum laudum suarum ferme unicum constituit industriam, vigilantiam, disciplinam, oeconomiam illustris foeminae: hic autem docet, hasce omnes laudes, quin & pulchritudinem ipsam et lepores, nisi Dei timor, pietas, et vera Sapientia accedant, inanes esse et nihil: atque hunc statuit elogii de matre sua epilogum'.
[41] Calmet, *Commentarius* VI, 2, 755: 'radius textorius'.
[42] Calmet, *Commentarius* VI, 2, 760: 'Vigilans est, agendi studiosa, laboriosa, domi se continens, regendis domesticis & liberis educandis occupata'.

Ferdinand Hitzig, *Die Sprüche Salomo's* (1858). The traditional association of the King Lemuel of 31:1 with King Solomon is now denied, as well as the connection of 31:10–31 with the words of Lemuel's mother. The Song of the Valiant Woman is treated as an independent appendix to the book of Proverbs, and its date is fixed six centuries after Solomon, in the time after Alexander the Great.[43] The Valiant Woman herself is understood literally as the depiction of the ideal Israelite 'housewife'. It is not too much to say that this general picture (with some variation as to the dating) has until recently been the standard critical interpretation of the Song. Another noteworthy feature of this overall approach, which distinguishes it from most previous discussions, is its silence about the Song's contemporary religious or ethical relevance. In the standard critical treatment, the notion of scriptural authority has been methodologically excluded.

Within the framework of this overall new historical-critical attitude to the Song, Hitzig's commentary also evinces a number of specific features which are of interest. To my knowledge, he is the first one to point out that in verse 22 the MT reading *šānîm*, 'scarlet' (or 'crimson', as he prefers to translate it), can be defended by noting the interplay of colours in verses 22 and 23, since the 'fine linen and purple' of verse 22 represent the same basic colours as the snow and crimson of the preceding verse. He writes:

> For the sake of contrast with the white snow the author clothes the family in crimson; it was for that reason that he used 'snow' for winter cold in the A-line ... The white byssus [= fine linen] matches the snow, and the crimson evokes another red colour, purple'.[44]

Hitzig is also one of the few commentators who notes and seeks to explain the unusual participial form represented by *ṣôpiyyâ* in verse 27. He argues that it is to be understood as a participle in apposition to the feminine pronominal suffix of *lĕšônāh*, which concludes the preceding verse. Accordingly, he translates verses 26b and 27a 'and gracious

---

[43] F. Hitzig, *Die Sprüche Salomo's* (Zurich: Verlag von Orell, Füssli und Comp., 1858), 334. An earlier commentary in the new critical mode is that of Ernst Bertheau, *Die Sprüche Salomo's* (Kurzgefasstes exegetisches Handbuch zum Alten Testament, Siebente Lieferung; Leipzig: Weidmann, 1847).

[44] Hitzig, *Sprüche*, 338: 'Des Gegensatzes halber zum weissen Schnee kleidet der Verf. die Familie in Carmesin; aber ebendarum sagte er in *a* "Schnee" für Winterkälte . . . Der weisse Byssus tritt dem Schnee für Winterkälte gegenüber, und das Carmesin zieht den gleichfalls rothen Purpur nach sich'.

instruction is on her tongue, *while she looks to* the order of her house-hold'.[45] Although this is grammatically very forced, it has the virtue of pinpointing a genuine philological anomaly which calls for an explanation.

As a curiosity we may also mention Hitzig's comment on the well-known A-line of verse 30, which declares that beauty is fleeting and deceptive. He writes: 'The thought expressed in the A-line is especially appropriate, since the beauty of a mother will have faded at a time when the judgement of her sons can be considered worthy of mention'.[46] This seems to reflect a prejudice both against the appearance of older women and the judgement of younger men!

Another notable nineteenth-century commentary in the same historical-critical tradition as Hitzig is the ICC commentary by C.H. Toy (1899).[47] It was Toy who introduced a significant text-critical innovation in verse 30, which was to prove popular in many subsequent commentaries. On the basis of the LXX, he emended the text to read, not 'a woman who fears the Lord', but 'a wise woman', thus making the original Song completely 'secular'. The MT is attributed to the work of a 'pious redactor'.[48]

Whereas Hitzig and Toy can be considered typical representatives of the newly dominant historical criticism of the nineteenth century, we can take the work of Rudolf Stier as representing the other end of the ideological spectrum with respect to the Song of the Valiant Woman.[49] Stier was the advocate of a 'pneumatic–symbolic interpretation' of the Old Testament,[50] and applied this to Proverbs 31 by arguing that both Lemuel's mother and the Valiant Woman were allegorical symbols of Wisdom.[51] Somewhat confusingly, he also identifies the latter with the Holy Spirit and the Fear of the Lord.[52] Although his interpretation is rather idiosyncratic, he supports it with great philological erudition, and

---

[45] Hitzig, *Sprüche*, 339 (my emphasis): 'und holdselige Lehre ruht auf ihrer Zunge, indem sie sieht auf die Ordnung ihres Hauses'.

[46] Hitzig, *Sprüche*, 340: 'Der Gedanke in *a* ist um so mehr am Platze, da die Schönheit einer Mutter verblüht sein wird zu einer Zeit, da das Urtheil ihrer Söhne erwähnenswerth dünkt'.

[47] C.H. Toy, *A Critical and Exegetical Commentary on the Book of Proverbs*, International Critical Commentary (Edinburgh: T. & T. Clark, 1899), 548–50.

[48] Toy, *Proverbs*, 550.

[49] R. Stier, *Die Politik der Weisheit in den Worten Agur's und Lemuel's, Sprüchwörter Kap. 30 und 31* (Barmen: Langewiesche, 1850). On Prov. 31:10–31, see 77–100, as well as the 'Anhang für Gelehrte', 133–146.

[50] Kraus, *Geschichte der historisch-kritischen Erforschung*, 198–200.

[51] Stier, *Politik der Weisheit*, 78,139.

[52] Stier, *Politik der Weisheit*, 134 (Holy Spirit); 98,146 (Fear of the Lord).

an extensive knowledge of the exegetical tradition, both Christian and Jewish. Some of his arguments linking the Valiant Woman with Wisdom are worth taking seriously,[53] although he goes beyond plausibility when he claims that verse 26 should be translated 'she opens her mouth *as* Wisdom', taking the preposition as the so-called '*beth essentiae*'.[54] Stier was an isolated figure in the nineteenth century, and has been largely ignored and forgotten, although Han-Joachim Kraus does write some words of appreciation in his survey of modern Old Testament scholarship.[55]

Most confessionally oriented commentators in the nineteenth century positioned themselves between Hitzig and Stier. The pre-eminent example is Franz Delitzsch, the renowned Lutheran Old Testament exegete, whose commentaries are still widely used today. In his commentary on Proverbs, published in 1873, he clearly distantiated himself from Hitzig, not only in rejecting his late dating of the Song,[56] but also in accepting the Song as 'an invaluable part of biblical moral instruction'.[57] Yet he also has little sympathy for Stier, of whom he writes: 'Stier has done what in the present state of biblical interpretation is well-nigh unbelievable, and has interpreted allegorically the matron here commended'.[58] Instead, as we saw above, he refers to *La perfecta casada* by Luis de León as perhaps the finest commentary ever written on the Song.

Perhaps, however, it is Delitzsch himself who has written the finest commentary. It is marked by great philological exactitude, sober exegetical judgement, encyclopedic knowledge of the exegetical tradition, and a sympathetic respect for the nuances of the text. A few of the specific excellences of his treatment of the concluding pericope of Proverbs are the following. He points out (citing Von Hofmann) that the Song, after listing the Valiant Woman's praiseworthy deeds, 'refers all these virtues and accomplishments of hers to the fear of God as their root'.[59] In

---

[53] E.g. Stier, *Politik der Weisheit*, 139.

[54] Stier, *Politik der Weisheit*, 144.

[55] Kraus, *Geschichte der historisch-kritischen Erforschung*, 200.

[56] F. Delitzsch, *Das Salomonische Spruchbuch* (Leipzig: Dorffling und Franke, 1873), 527. See also the English translation (E.T.) of this work, M.G. Easton (tr.), *Biblical Commentary on the Proverbs of Solomon*, 2 vols. (Edinburgh: T. & T. Clark, 1874–75), 2.325.

[57] Delitzsch, *Spruchbuch*, 527: 'ein unschätzbares Stück biblischer Sittenlehre'. (E.T. 2.326).

[58] Delitzsch, *Spruchbuch*, 527: 'Stier hat das bei dem gegenwärtigen Stande der Schriftauslegung schier Unglaubliche geleistet und das hier gepriesene Weib allegorisch gedeutet.' The polemical first clause is omitted in the E.T. (2.326).

[59] Delitzsch, *Spruchbuch*, 527: 'führt alle diese ihre Tugenden und Leistungen auf die Gottesfurcht als ihre Wurzel zurück'. My translation differs from that in E.T. (2.326).

other words, there is no dichotomy between 'secular' and 'spiritual' in the poem. He explains the semantic development of *šālāl* in verse 12 (from 'plunder' to 'gain' in general) by comparing the similar development of German *kriegen* (from 'capture in war [*Krieg*]' to 'acquire' in general).[60] He also explains the comparison with merchant ships in verse 14:

> [I].e. she is like such ships as sail far away and acquire wares from afar, which are equipped, sent out, and guided by an active, enterprising spirit. In the same way the shrewdly calculating eyes of the Valiant Woman, who is concerned for the care and advancement of her household, go far beyond her immediate circle, she also spots faraway opportunities for bargains and good deals, and fetches from afar … the provisions which her household needs, or else the products which these provisions yield when she exploits these sources of income which she has spotted.[61]

Clearly, Delitzsch has here broken with the strained interpretations of earlier commentators, who could not countenance a wife who travelled far from home on business. On the unusual form *ṣôpiyyâ* in verse 27, Delitzsch writes:

> Although there is an inner connection between 27[a] and verse 26, yet 27[a] is hardly to be construed as an apposition to the suffix in *lĕšônāh* (Hitzig). Participles with or without determination often occur in descriptions as predicates of the subject in question, having the same value as abstract present-tense declarative sentences, e.g. Isa 40:22 f., Ps 104:13 f.[62]

Such astute grammatical observation comes close to recognizing this anomalous verbal form as a hymnic participle.

---

[60] Delitzsch, *Spruchbuch*, 528 (E.T. 2.327).
[61] Delitzsch, *Spruchbuch*, 530: 'd.h. sie hat die Art solcher Schiffe, welche weithin segeln und von fernher Waare holen, ausgerüstet, entsendet und gelenkt von betriebsamem Unternehmungsgeiste – ebenso geht der klug berechnende Blick der auf Versorgung und Förderung ihres Hauses bedachten wackeren Frau weit über den nächsten Kreis hinaus, sie erspäht auch ferne Gelegenheiten billiger Einkäufe und vortheilhaften Umsatzes, und bringt den Bedarf ihres Hauses an Nahrungsmitteln oder mittelbar was ihm diesen Bedarf abwirft von ferne herbei …, indem sie jene erspähten Erwerbsquellen ausbeutet.' My translation differs from that in E.T. (2.329).
[62] Delitzsch, *Spruchbuch*, 537: 'Obgleich innerer Zus. zwischen 27[a] und v. 26 besteht, so ist 27[a] doch schwerlich als Appos. zum Suff. in *lĕšônāh* gedacht (Hitz.). Partizipien mit oder ohne Determination kommen in Beschreibungen häufig als Prädicate des in Rede stehenden Subjekts vor, gleichen Werths mit abstract präsentischen Aussagesätzen z.B. Jes. 40, 22 f. Ps. 104, 13 f.' My translation differs from that in E.T. (2.339).

Although Delitzsch was undoubtedly the premier commentator on the Song among theologically orthodox scholars in the nineteenth century, he was certainly not alone. Another influential and often reprinted commentary was that of the British pastor Charles Bridges, *An Exposition of the Book of Proverbs*.[63] Though based on scholarly sources, this is not an academic commentary, but a work for the general public. The following extract gives an impression of this popular work:

> One thing however is most remarkable. The standard of godliness here exhib-
> ited is not that of a religious recluse, shut up from active obligations under the
> pretence of greater sanctity and consecration to God. Here are none of those
> habits of monastic asceticism, that are now extolled as the highest point of
> Christian perfection. One half at least of the picture of *the virtuous woman* is
> occupied with her personal and domestic industry.[64]

Bridges' commentary on Proverbs was so widely and highly regarded in conservative theological circles that a revised version, with modernized English and the biblical text of the New American Standard Bible, was published in 1978.[65]

Practical treatments like that of Bridges were also produced in Jewish circles. An example is the commentary on Proverbs, originally written in twenty-two instalments in the Jewish weekly *Der neue Jeschurun* (1883–1885), by the leader of Orthodox Judaism in Germany, Rabbi Samson Raphael Hirsch (1808–1888). The last of the twenty-two instalments deals with 'The Valiant Wife' as a model for contemporary Jewish women. Like Bridges' work, this volume was also republished in a new linguistic garb (an English translation), more than a century after it first appeared.[66]

Before leaving the nineteenth century, we should take note of a small but significant contribution to the study of the Song contained in an obscure *Festschrift* published in 1884. It consists of two paragraphs in an essay by David Rosin simply entitled 'Beiträge zur Bibelexegese'.[67] In these two paragraphs he argues that the Song describes a woman who

[63] C. Bridges, *An Exposition of the Book of Proverbs* (New York: Carter, 1865).
[64] Bridges, *Proverbs*, 528.
[65] *A Modern Study of the Book of Proverbs. Charles Bridges' Classic Revised for Today's Reader by George F. Santa* (Milford MI: Mott Media, 1978).
[66] S.R. Hirsch, *From the Wisdom of Mishlé* (Jerusalem/New York: Feldheim, 1976), 247–253.
[67] D. Rosin, 'Beiträge zur Bibelexegese', in *Jubelschrift zum neunzigsten Geburtstag des Dr. Leopold Zunz* (Berlin: Louis Gerschel Verlagsbuchhandlung, 1884), 36–78, specifically 73–74.

really existed, and that the description follows, in chronological order, the various stages of the woman's life from her wedding day to her death. The concluding section (verses 28–31) are the actual words of the eulogy spoken at her grave by her husband and sons.

Twentieth Century

A. Before 1980

Hitzig and Delitzsch may be said to have set the pattern for academic treatments of the Song in the twentieth century until the 1980s. Apart from philological details – and even these were few – scholarly commentaries disagreed mainly on the date of this pericope and its contemporary relevance. They generally agreed that a literal interpretation was called for, that the Valiant Woman represented a moral ideal in ancient Israel, and that the Song was an independent appendix to the book of Proverbs, with no connection to the preceding words of Lemuel. Many of those who stood in the historical-critical tradition represented by Hitzig also followed Toy in declaring secondary the reference to 'the fear of the Lord' in verse 30.[68] Consequently, the poem as a whole was considered to be 'a secular song'.[69] Commentators generally repeat each other, and are largely ignorant of the exegetical tradition. Occasionally they make elementary blunders, as when McKane writes that the '(spindle-)whorl' (a common meaning assigned to *kîšôr* in verse 19) was used 'for turning the distaff' (*sic*).[70]

There are four publications which constitute exceptions to this overall pattern of scholarly traditionalism before the 1980s. The first is found in the fifth volume of the *Randglossen* of the Jewish scholar Arnold B. Ehrlich.[71] Apart from a series of original, but often idiosyncratic

---

[68] See, e.g., W.O.E. Oesterley, *The Book of Proverbs* (London: Methuen, 1929), 287; B. Gemser, *Sprüche Salomos* (HAT; Tübingen: J. C. B. Mohr, 1937), 84; R.B.Y. Scott, *Proverbs – Ecclesiastes* (AB; New York: Doubleday, 1965), 187; H.-P. Rüger, 'Zum Text von Prv. 31,30', *Die Welt des Orients* 5 (1969), 96–99; W. McKane, *Proverbs: A New Approach* (Philadelphia: Westminster, 1970), 670; R.N. Whybray, *The Book of Proverbs* (Cambridge: Cambridge University Press, 1972), 186.

[69] C. Kuhl, *Die Entstehung des Alten Testaments* (Bern/Munich: Franke, 1960²), 270: 'ein weltliches Lied'.

[70] McKane, *Proverbs*, 668.

[71] A.B. Ehrlich, *Randglossen zur Hebräischen Bibel. Textkritisches, Sprachliches und Sachliches. Fünfter Band: Ezekiel und die kleinen Propheten* (Leipzig: Hinrichs, 1912), 175–179.

philological notes, Ehrlich argues that the Valiant Woman does all her work in order to make it possible for her husband to study the Torah. Thus he writes on verse 11:

> It would be a great mistake to think that the first colon refers to marital faithfulness, since that goes without saying for the *ʾēšet ḥayil* [Valiant Woman]. The meaning here is simply that the husband relies on his wife for his means of support. The word *šālāl* in the second colon, where this substantive designates gain which accrues to one without lifting a finger, also fits this interpretation. For in this Song the husband does nothing to support himself. The wife labours and toils night and day, and takes care of everything, while her spouse leads a contemplative life, or else – more probably – is studying the first rudiments of the Mishnah; see on verse 23. That is largely the way things were in the time of the Talmud, and that is the way they often still are among the Jews of Poland and Russia. It was in such circumstances that the later custom arose of reciting this Song of the Valiant Woman in the family circle before the first meal of the Sabbath. This is meant to be the husband's tribute to his spouse, who toils for him night and day throughout the week.[72]

A second notable contribution before the 1980s is an early publication by the well-known French Hebraist Paul Joüon. He argues that the verbs which describe the activities of the Valiant Woman should be translated as past tenses. The poem as a whole is a eulogy on an actual historical Israelite woman:

---

[72] Ehrlich, *Randglossen*, 5.175–76: 'Man würde sehr irren, wollte man beim ersten Gliede an die eheliche Treue denken, denn diese versteht sich bei der *ʾēšet ḥayil* von selbst. Hier will nur gesagt sein, dass der Mann hinsichtlich seines Lebensunterhalts auf sein Weib vertraut. Dazu stimmt auch *šālāl* im zweiten Gliede, wo dies Substantiv den Gewinn bezeichnet, den man ohne sein Dazutun erhält. Denn in diesem Liede tut der Mann für seinen Unterhalt nichts. Die Frau arbeitet und plagt sich Tag und Nacht und schafft alles herbei, während ihr Gatte ein beschauliches Leben führt, oder, was wahrscheinlicher ist, die ersten Anfänge der Mischna studiert; vgl. zu V. 23. So waren die Verhältnisse zum grossen Teil zur Zeit des Talmuds, und so sind sie vielfach noch jetzt unter den Juden in Polen und Russland. Unter solchen Verhältnissen entstand später die Sitte, vor dem ersten Sabbatmahle dieses Lied von der wackern Frau im Familienkreise zu rezitieren. Dies soll der Tribut des Mannes an seine Gattin sein, die sich die Woche über Tag und Nacht für ihn plagt.' Along the same line are Ehrlich's comments on verse 23 (178), and on verse 30 (179): 'Our heroine's fear of God consists mainly in the fact that she frees her spouse from all the cares of life, so that he can devote himself to the study of Torah without interruption.' ('Die Gottesfurcht unserer Heldin besteht hauptsächlich darin, dass sie ihren Gatten von allen Sorgen des Lebens freimacht, sodass er ungestört dem Thorastudium obliegen kann.')

Certain expressions in the poem do seem to indicate that the Valiant Woman is described in the past tense. We should note to begin with that the description contains such specific features that they cannot help but make us think of a real person, albeit idealized. Here it is the woman who runs the household: she creates a weaving business, sells the products of her industry to the Canaanites, buys a field and plants a vineyard, while her husband seems to have no other virtue than to have had confidence in her (verse 11) and to let her be, with the result that he acquires wealth (verse 11) and respect (verse 23). These precise and concrete features are much better understood if they apply to a real person. Other features indicate that this person is no longer alive. The praise which her sons and husband give her could hardly be addressed to a woman still living. The words of verse 25, 'she smiled at the last day', must be understood, it would seem, as a reference to her death; similarly, in verse 12, the words 'all the days of her life' presuppose that she has ended her days. But the decisive argument in favour of a translation in the past tense is found in the verbal forms that are used.[73]

Joüon appears not to be aware of David Rosin, who (as we have seen) made a similar suggestion in 1884. He does refer to Ehrlich's proposal that the Valiant Woman frees up her husband for the study of Torah, and is inclined to agree with it.[74] Oddly enough, despite his scrutiny of verbal forms in the Song, he makes no special mention of the anomalous participial form *ṣôpiyyâ* in verse 27.

The third contribution which we will single out is that of Margaret B. Crook. Unlike Joüon, she argues that: '[t]he Woman of Worth is an ideal; there never was any such person'.[75] Instead, the Song should be

---

[73] P. Joüon, 'Les temps dans Proverbes 31, 10–31 (la femme forte)', *Biblica* 3 (1922), 349–350: 'Certaines paroles du poème semblent bien indiquer que la *femme forte* est décrite au passé. Remarquons préalablement que la description contient des traits si particuliers qu'ils font penser invinciblement à un personnage réel bien qu'idéalisé. Ici c'est la femme qui fait marcher la maison: elle crée une entreprise de tissage, vend aux *Cananéens* les produits de son industrie, achète un champ et plante une vigne, tandis que le mari ne semble pas posséder d'autre mérite que d'avoir eu confiance en elle (v. 11) et de la laisser faire; ainsi lui sont venues richesses (v. 11) et considération (v. 23). Ces traits précis et concrets se comprennent beaucoup mieux s'il s'agit d'un personnage réel. D'autres traits indiquent que ce personnage n'est plus vivant. L'éloge que font les fils et le mari (vv. 28–29) ne peut guère s'adresser à une femme encore vivante. Les mots du v. 25 *elle a souri au dernier jour* semblent bien devoir s'entendre de la mort; de même, au v. 12, les mots *tous les jours de sa vie* supposent qu'elle a terminé ses jours. Mais l'argument décisif pour traduire au passé se trouve dans les formes verbales employées.'

[74] Joüon, 'Les temps', 349 n. 3.

[75] M.B. Crook, 'The Marriageable Maiden of Prov. 31:10–31', *Journal of Near Eastern Studies* 13 (1954), 139.

interpreted as 'a memorandum from a first known school of home eco-
nomics'.[76] The list of the Valiant Woman's accomplishments is a program
of study in domestic arts – comparable to a college catalogue![77] – which
details the instruction given at a school for aristocratic girls who would
shortly marry leading citizens of Israelite society. The Song is therefore 'a
memorandum for a girl to take home and keep for future guidance when
she returns home from school'.[78]

Apart from this novel proposal with respect to the *Sitz im Leben* of the
Song (which appears to have been followed by no one else), Crook's
article is of interest chiefly because it proposes an early dating of the Song.
She compares various features of the description of the Valiant Woman to
comparable circumstances in the ancient Near East dated to the second
and early first millennia BC. Although she is not specific in assigning a date
to the Hebrew poem, she does speak of 'the antiquity of the poem',[79] and
argues that the system of land tenure reflected in it 'might be appropriate
to a period in Israel preceding the eighth century'.[80] It would seem that
she would classify the Song among the earliest poetry to have survived
from ancient Israel.

Among the philological details which are worth noting in Crook's
treatment is her observation that the verb *lāqaḥ* in verse 16, which has
been rendered 'buy' since antiquity, may not have this meaning at all. The
Valiant Woman is simply said to 'take' a field; 'the land in question would
probably be held by a woman's husband, or his family'.[81] Although she
does not refer to Toy, she also rejects the reference to the 'fear of the Lord'
in verse 30, since this is 'an obviously late emendation' in a text which was
'nonreligious in origin'.[82]

Fourthly, we turn to an article by the French Old Testament scholar
Edmond Jacob. Jacob proposes two major theses with respect to the Song:
that the Valiant Woman is an allegory of Wisdom, and that each verse of
this alphabetic acrostic is related to the shape of the Hebrew letter with
which it begins. He seems to be unaware that the allegorical interpretation of the Valiant Woman as Wisdom has a long tradition – from Hilary
of Poitiers in the fourth century to Rudolf Stier in the nineteenth – and

---

[76] Crook, 'Marriageable Maiden', 137.
[77] Crook, 'Marriageable Maiden', 140.
[78] Crook, 'Marriageable Maiden', 140.
[79] Crook, 'Marriageable Maiden', 139.
[80] Crook, 'Marriageable Maiden', 138.
[81] Crook, 'Marriageable Maiden', 138.
[82] Crook, 'Marriageable Maiden', 137.

that Stier in particular had anticipated many of the arguments which he adduces.[83]

Jacob's imaginative proposal with respect to the letters of the alphabet does not, however, seem to have had any precedents. Taking as his point of departure the fact that each verse of the Song begins with a different letter of the Hebrew alphabet, he argues that there is a connection between the content of each verse and the shape of its initial letter (assuming that the alphabet in question was written in the Paleo–Hebrew script). An example is verse 15, which begins with the letter *waw* (shaped like a capital Y), and speaks of the Valiant Woman rising early to give food to her household and tasks to her maidservants. Jacob explains: 'The vertical shaft ends in a kind of fork, of which one branch would correspond to the orders given, the other to the food distributed'.[84] In this way Jacob construes a relationship (often quite fanciful) between each of the first twenty verses and the shape of their initial letter.[85] However, Jacob admits that he is stumped when he comes to verses 30 and 31: 'With respect to the last two letters, the *śîn* and the *taw*, it is difficult to find any correspondence between their shape and the content of the verses which they introduce. But no doubt we here have the exception which proves the rule'.[86] Perhaps conscious of the fact that this conclusion is unlikely to carry conviction, he writes in his final paragraph: 'We are keenly aware of having yielded to the temptation of sacrificing scholarship to play'.[87] It is perhaps not surprising that no one has followed Jacob on this point.

B. Feminist studies (1980–2000)

It is in 1980 that we see the beginnings of the flood of new studies of the Song which has continued unabated until the end of the century. Alongside commentaries, there have been many articles in journals, and separate

---

[83] E. Jacob, 'Sagesse et Alphabet. A propos de Proverbes 31.10–31', *Hommages à André Dupont-Sommer* (ed. A Caquot and M. Philonenko; Paris: Adrien-Maisonneuve, 1971), 287–295, especially 290, 294.

[84] Jacob, 'Sagesse et Alphabet', 292: 'La barre verticale se termine par une sorte de fourche, dont une branche correspondrait aux ordres donnés, l'autre à la nourriture distribuée.'

[85] Jacob, 'Sagesse et Alphabet', 291–294.

[86] Jacob, 'Sagesse et Alphabet', 294: 'Quant aux deux dernières lettres, le sin et le taw, il est difficile de trouver quelque correspondance entre leur graphie et le contenu des versets qu'elles introduisent. Mais nous avons sans doute là l'exception qui confirme la règle.'

[87] Jacob, 'Sagesse et Alphabet', 295: 'Nous avon nette conscience d'avoir cédé a la tentation de sacrifier la science au jeu.'

discussions in monographs and *Festschriften*, which represent a break with
the exegetical traditions inherited from the nineteenth century. Ironically,
as in the case of Jacob, the new proposals which are put forward often
constitute an unwitting return to earlier positions in the history of
interpretation.

Especially significant in this period has been the impact of feminism,
which has undoubtedly been the most vigorous ideological force in biblical studies in the closing decades of the twentieth century. To highlight
the importance of this new movement, we will first deal with feminist
studies of the Song, and then turn to a briefer discussion of more traditional treatments in this time period.

The opening salvo, so to speak, is found in an article written in Dutch
by Hanneke van der Sluis-van der Korst and Douwe van der Sluis. The
title of the article can be translated 'The Scandalous Virtuous Housewife:
An Interpretation of Proverbs 31:10–31'.[88] The two authors take aim at
both standard readings of the Song in modern times: the conservative religious interpretation (in the tradition of Delitzsch), and the conventional
historical-critical interpretation (in the tradition of Hitzig). Of the
former they write:

> In this way, then [i.e. as 'virtuous housewife'], this song is interpreted to the
> present day, and used as legitimation, confirmation, and instruction for the
> woman to be active as 'conscientious housewife' within her family, and to find
> her calling and life's task there. The poem was supposed to be a didactic song, a
> guideline for the married woman as to how she should behave if she was to
> earn the praise of her husband and sons.[89]

Of the latter, as represented by Toy, they write:

> He therefore explains away – as also happens in other commentaries – all those
> places which might suggest (shameful thought!) religious or intellectual inter-
> ests, such as verse 26 and verse 30. The latter verse must be understood, with
> the help of the Septuagint, of her 'administrative capacity', or else it is a gloss;

---

[88] H. van der Sluis-van der Korst and D. van der Sluis, 'De deugdelijke huisvrouw
in opspraak. Een interpretatie van Spreuken 31:10–31', *Schrift* 69 (1980), 93–98.
[89] Van der Sluis-van der Korst and van der Sluis, 'De deugdelijke huisvrouw', 93:
'En zo wordt dit lied dan ook tot op de huidige dag uitgelegd en gebruikt als
legitimatie, bevestiging en leerdicht voor de vrouw om als 'degelijke huisvrouw'
binnen haar gezin bezig te zijn en daar haar roeping en levenstaak te vinden. Het
gedicht zou een didaktisch lied zijn, een richtlijn voor de getrouwde vrouw hoe
zij zich moest gedragen, wilden haar man en haar zonen haar loven en prijzen.'

the former verse refers to her (feminine?) friendliness with respect to children, servants and friends.[90]

Instead, they emphasize that the subject of the Song is a woman of strength, independence, and initiative, who is fully a match for her husband. They point out that much of the vocabulary used to describe her has an almost aggressive connotation,[91] and that she is certainly not restricted in her activities to the domestic scene.[92] Interestingly, they also adopt David Rosin's suggestion that the Song was originally a eulogy spoken at a specific woman's graveside, which recounts the various stages of her married life.[93]

In a concluding section the authors also point out that earlier Jewish interpreters had understood the Valiant Woman to be a symbol of the Torah or the Shekinah. They themselves also defend a symbolic interpretation, in addition to the literal one, but in their view the Valiant Woman represents Wisdom.[94] They appear to have come to this conclusion independently, because they refer neither to Edmond Jacob nor his predecessors, though they unwittingly repeat some of their arguments. Unlike them, however, they take a further step by seeing the Valiant Woman as a symbol of the divine:

> In our treatment of this song of praise – which is no more than an initial exploration – we have come to a topic which is preeminently worth investigating, namely the expression of the divine by means of 'feminine' images. One of the attempts to do this, already in biblical times, was the song in praise of the woman in Proverbs 31, which we take to be symbolic.[95]

[90] Van der Sluis-van der Korst and van der Sluis, 'De deugdelijke huisvrouw', 93: 'Hij verklaart daarom, zoals ook in andere commentaren gebeurt, al die plaatsen weg, die zouden kunnen wijzen op – o schande – religieuze of intellectuele belangstelling, zoals vers 26 en vers 30. Het laatste vers moet met behulp van de Septuaginta geïnterpreteerd worden met 'administratieve kwaliteit', of het is een glosse; het eerst genoemde vers slaat op haar (vrouwelijke?) vriendelijke natuur ten aanzien van kinderen, dienaren, en vrienden'.
[91] Van der Sluis-van der Korst and van der Sluis, 'De deugdelijke huisvrouw', 95–97.
[92] Van der Sluis-van der Korst and van der Sluis, 'De deugdelijke huisvrouw', 97.
[93] Van der Sluis-van der Korst and van der Sluis, 'De deugdelijke huisvrouw', 95,96.
[94] Van der Sluis-van der Korst and van der Sluis, 'De deugdelijke huisvrouw', 97–98.
[95] Van der Sluis-van der Korst and van der Sluis, 'De deugdelijke huisvrouw', 98: 'We zijn bij de behandeling van deze lofzang – een eerste verkenning nog maar – gekomen bij een onderwerp, dat meer dan de moeite waard is onderzocht te

Although Van der Sluis-van der Korst and Van der Sluis do not elaborate on this last point, they are clearly suggesting an approach which was to become prominent in later feminist treatments of personified Wisdom in Proverbs.

In some ways it is surprising that feminists in general have not paid more attention to the Song of the Valiant Woman, since it depicts such a strong, independent, and enterprising female figure. But in other ways it is not surprising, because there is also another side to this powerful heroine. Denise Carmody puts it well:

> Today this text is bound to make feminists feel ambivalent. On the one hand, there is a recognition of all the competence and hard work that domestic management can entail. This ideal wife is busy, efficient, and productive. She probably would be a demon of energy, and the implication is that she cares for her family's every need. As well, she is wise, kindly, concerned for the poor, and beloved by her husband and children. To efficient management she adds qualities of mind and heart. This record is no mean accomplishment, and such a woman undoubtedly would be strong and self-confident.
>
> On the other hand, much of her status seems auxiliary. The text implies that her diligence supports her husband's more public affairs, her care enables her children to live well, perhaps even to be spoiled. This woman is not property, but she is a good investment. With her as a helpmate, a husband will get a good return. The last lines of the text also are jarring. Why need charm be deceitful? Does a good wife have to be a plain-Jane? Why does the author insinuate a fear of beauty? Can we not praise beauty as a gift of God and so love it that it has little temptation to be vain? …
>
> In a single text, then, we find the ambiguity of the heritage bequeathed women by the Hebrew Bible. Even at its moment of high praise, the Bible reflects a man's world. From the Eve created as the helpmate of Adam to the good wife who eases the life of her senatorial husband, woman is the second sex. This patriarchal view is simply not acceptable.[96]

Despite this ambiguity, most feminists choose to emphasize the aspects of strength and independence ascribed to the Valiant Woman in the Song. The most notable example is Claudia Camp, who argues in her 1985 monograph, *Wisdom and the Feminine in the Book of Proverbs*, that the Valiant Woman completely overshadows her husband, and in fact

---

[95] (*Continued*) worden: namelijk de verwoording van het goddelijke door middel van 'vrouwelijke' beelden. Een van de pogingen die al in bijbelse tijden zijn gedaan is de ons inziens symbolische lofzang van Spreuken 31 op de vrouw'.
[96] D.L. Carmody, *Biblical Woman: Contemporary Reflections on Scriptural Texts* (New York: Crossroad, 1989), 73.

dominates both the private and the public spheres of her world. She writes, for example:

> [The husband] is a man who is "known in the gates", but the poem wastes no time describing his talents. The impression is given instead that his position among the elders flows from the energy and capabilities of the wife in the home.[97]
>
> The woman not only runs the household but, in effect, defines and identifies it.[98]
>
> I would suggest that, in fact, the female image in Prov. 31 defines not only the home itself but also indicates the proper identity and character of the public domain as well, namely, one that finds its bearings in home and family life.[99]

Camp goes so far as to say that the repeated reference to the Valiant Woman's husband as her *baʿal*, literally 'master' or 'owner' (verses 11, 23, 28), comes close to irony. In fact, she writes: 'It would be difficult to describe more aptly the woman of worth in our poem' than in Pedersen's description of the dominant position of the *baʿal* in Israelite society.[100] In the Song of the Valiant Woman, the wife seems to have assumed the central position usually ascribed to the husband.

Furthermore, Camp argues that the portrait of the Valiant Woman at the end of the book of Proverbs balances the portrait of personified Wisdom in Proverbs 1–9, and that these two female figures provide an editorial frame and hermeneutical key to the entire book.[101] She refrains, however, from interpreting these figures as divine.[102]

There is less restraint on this point in the work of the Swiss Catholic scholar Silvia Schroer, who takes over from Camp the idea that the personification of Wisdom at the beginning and at the end of Proverbs constitutes an editorial frame. She argues that the Song contains: 'quite a large number of comparisons and phrases in the text which leave no doubt that this woman is closely associated with God and the divine Wisdom'.[103] In fact, the text makes it clear that 'the Valiant Woman

---

[97] C. Camp, *Wisdom and the Feminine in the Book of Proverbs* (Decatur GA: Almond, 1985), 91.

[98] Camp, *Wisdom and the Feminine*, 91.

[99] Camp, *Wisdom and the Feminine*, 92.

[100] Camp, *Wisdom and the Feminine*, 91.

[101] Camp, *Wisdom and the Feminine*, 186–191.

[102] Camp, *Wisdom and the Feminine*, 190.

[103] S. Schroer, 'Die göttliche Weisheit und der nachexilische Monotheismus', in eadem, *Die Weisheit hat ihr Haus gebaut. Studien zur Gestalt der Sophia in den biblischen Schriften* (Mainz: Matthias-Grünewald-Verlag, 1996), 27–62, specifically

represents Chokmah, and as the latter's representative she is entitled to attributes which are otherwise reserved for YHWH alone'.[104] Schroer writes that many studies have shown that: 'the Chokmah in the frame of the book of Proverbs is a divine figure',[105] and that: '[f]rom a form-critical point of view, Chokmah speaks as a deity, or as the God of Israel'.[106]

However, this is not to be understood as a challenge to Israel's monotheism:

> Personified Chokmah is not an attack on the ancient Israelite conviction that YHWH is the God of Israel – a conviction which was never fundamentally called into question in the wisdom tradition. Nor is it an attack on the belief – first explicitly formulated after the Exile – that besides YHWH no other deities exist at all. And the biblical authors appear not even to have considered it necessary to defend, in apologetic fashion, the 'correct' monotheistic understanding of Chokmah. Instead, personified Chokmah is the completely unpolemical attempt to put, instead and alongside of the masculine image of God, a feminine one, which connects the God of Israel with the experience and the life especially of women in Israel, and also connects the highest God with the sphere of domestic religion, and beyond that with the images and roles of the goddesses of the ancient Near East.[107]

---

[103] (*Continued*) 34: 'eine grössere Anzahl von Vergleichen und Wendungen im Text, die keinen Zweifel daran lassen, dass diese Frau in die Nähe Gottes und der göttlichen Weisheit gerückt wird.' This essay appeared first in G. Braulik, et al. (eds.), *Der eine Gott und die Göttin. Gottesvorstellungen im Horizont feministischer Theologie*, Quaestiones disputatae 135 (Freiburg i. Br.: Herder Verlag, 1991), 151–182.

[104] Schroer, 'Die göttliche Weisheit', 36: 'dass die tüchtige Frau die Chokmah repräsentiert und als deren Repräsentin Attribute verdient, die ansonsten JHWH allein vorbehalten sind'.

[105] Schroer, 'Die göttliche Weisheit', 39: '[d]ass die Chokmah in der Rahmung des Sprüchebuches eine göttliche Gestalt ist'.

[106] Schroer, 'Die göttliche Weisheit', 39: 'Formgeschichtlich betrachtet, spricht die Chokmah wie eine Gottheit oder wie der Gott Israels'.

[107] Schroer, 'Die göttliche Weisheit', 42: 'Die personifizierte Chokmah ist kein Angriff auf die alte israelitische und in der Weisheitstradition nie grundsätzlich in Frage gestellte Überzeugung, dass JHWH der Gott Israels ist. Sie ist auch kein Angriff auf den seit dem Exil explizit formulierten Glauben, dass neben JHWH überhaupt keine anderen Gottheiten existieren. Und die Verfasser scheinen es gar nicht für nötig erachtet zu haben, apologetisch das 'richtige', monotheistische Verständnis der Chokmah zu verteidigen. Die personifizierte Weisheit ist vielmehr der völlig unpolemische Versuch, an die Stelle des männlichen Gottesbildes und neben dieses Gottesbild ein weibliches zu setzen, das den Gott Israels mit der Erfahrung und dem Leben besonders der Frauen in Israel, den obersten Gott mit dem Bereich der Hausreligion und darüber hinaus mit der Bildern und Rollen der altorientalischen Göttinnen verbindet.'

Other feminists do not go as far as Schroer in assigning divine status to the Valiant Woman, or as far as Camp in assuming that the Song reflects a kind of matriarchal society in Israel. Instead, they are content to emphasize the relatively strong and independent status of the Valiant Woman within an otherwise traditional society. Two examples are Helen Schüngel-Straumann[108] and John Goldingay.[109]

Nevertheless, all feminist scholars need to wrestle with what from their perspective is the 'ambiguity' of the Song. Carol Fontaine and Athalya Brenner are good examples of the ambivalence this engenders. Fontaine, in her 1992 commentary on Proverbs lists first the positive and then the negative aspects:

> In all, she is the living embodiment of Woman Wisdom's teachings and attributes and does not rely on simple appearances (vv. 25–26, 30) … Just as Woman Wisdom began the book with promises of wealth, happiness, honor, and long life as the reward for following her prudent teachings, the Woman of Worth and her fine household represent the concrete fulfillment of those earlier promises and so make a fitting conclusion to the work … As seen earlier, the success of this woman is viewed from the perspective of what she provides for her husband and children. It is her fulfillment of the roles in the home assigned to her by society that causes her to be praised in the very gates of the city where Woman Wisdom first raised her cry.[110]

Brenner, in the context of an essay exploring the presence of a female voice in the book of Proverbs, advances the hypothesis that 'the *'ēšet ḥayil* poem (Prov. 31.10–31) is the single instance of a "mother's instruction to daughter" genre, the opposite and complementary number of the "mother's instruction to son" convention of chapters 1–9 and the first part of chapter 31'.[111] Yet this is a female voice which largely reflects

[108] H. Schüngel-Straumann, 'Die wahre Frau', *Christ in der Gegenwart* 33 (Nov. 1981), 383.

[109] J. Goldingay, 'Proverbs' in G.J. Wenham et al. (eds.), *New Bible Commentary. 21ˢᵗ Century Edition* (Downers Grove, IL: IVP, 1994), 584–608. He writes that the Song 'encourages the complete woman to make the most of and to push the boundaries of what a woman's role might mean in a patriarchal society'.

[110] C.R. Fontaine, 'Proverbs' in C.A. Newsom and S.H. Ringe (eds.), *The Women's Bible Commentary* (London: SPCK; Louisville, KY: Westminster/John Knox, 1992), 152. See also her earlier commentary on Proverbs in J.L. Mays et al. (eds.), *Harper's Bible Commentary* (San Francisco: Harper & Row, 1988), 495–517, specifically 516–517.

[111] A. Brenner, 'Proverbs 1–9: An F Voice?' in A. Brenner and F. van Dijk-Hemmes (eds.), *On Gendering Texts. Female and Male Voices in the Hebrew Bible* (Leiden: Brill, 1993), 127.

patriarchal values: 'The image is that of a woman overworked in the service of her husband and sons (sic!), undoubtedly the reflection of prevailing social norms'.[112] It may be true, as Camp has argued, that language describing the Valiant Woman echoes that describing personified Wisdom in chapters 1–9, but she is still relegated to the domestic sphere:

> She lives to advance male interests and male well-being. In so doing, however, she ultimately subverts the male order by becoming its focal point and essential requisite. Or so the F voice imagines, or so it hopes. Appearances aside, it seems to say, in ancient Israel as in many other cultures, ancient and latterday, men have the authority. Nevertheless, women can gain power while formally appearing to defer to M authority … The final victory and perhaps revenge – so whispers the secondary muted voice – is the woman's, for she is the actual controller of the family … Whether males find 'her' physically and sexually attractive or not (v. 30), 'she' is the ultimate winner. The price for her implicit victory is explicit complicity in the system, the perpetuation of its values, the introjection of its ideology. Thus is male dominance preserved while being overcome'.[113]

Another way for feminists to deal with the Song is to show that it has been an empowering text for women in the past. Such is the approach of Shulamit Valler, in an essay entitled 'Who is ʾēšet ḥayil in Rabbinic Literature?', in which she examines the way the Song has been interpreted in a number of medieval Jewish midrashim.[114] She summarizes her conclusions as follows:

> The attribution of such wisdom, in addition to other virtues such as bravery and intelligence, to an ʾēšet ḥayil, i.e. the ideal woman, highlights the actuality of a liberal conception of woman and womanhood among the sages. Two major models, or concepts, of the ideal woman have been revealed by our reading of the midrashic texts on the biblical ʾēšet ḥayil passage. The first concept is that of the ideal woman as a spiritual leader who is close to God and carries out his will; the second describes her as a political leader and diplomat. Both concepts place the ideal woman far beyond the narrow circle of her home and family. Both praise her activities within the wider circles of society, community and nation. Both expand the image of ʾēšet ḥayil obtainable in the biblical passage'.[115]

---

[112] Brenner, 'An F Voice', 129.

[113] Brenner, 'An F Voice', 129.

[114] S. Valler, 'Who is ʾēšet ḥayil in Rabbinic Literature?' in A. Brenner (ed.), *A Feminist Companion to Wisdom Literature* (Sheffield: Sheffield Academic Press, 1995), 85–97.

[115] Valler, 'Who is ʾēšet ḥayil,' 96–97.

Our final example of a feminist treatment of the Song is found in an article written by the South African scholar Madipoane Masenya, entitled 'Proverbs 31:10–31 in a South African Context: A Reading for the Liberation of African (Northern Sotho) Women'. Reflecting on recent scholarship on Proverbs 31, she writes 'It is disturbing to note that little has been done regarding the reading of this poem from a feminist/women's liberation perspective'.[116] Masenya's contribution toward filling that gap is of particular interest because her feminism is quite different from that of her counterparts in Europe and North America. For one thing, she looks upon the Valiant Woman as an ideal to be emulated by contemporary women in Africa, despite its patriarchal setting. She writes 'A sceptical reader may ask what a poor Northern Sotho woman may benefit from a male elitist text. I wish to argue that though the text does have oppressive elements, it also contains liberative or life-giving elements'.[117] For another, she includes among the normative features of the Valiant Woman that she manages the family (a position of power),[118] cares for the needy,[119] and works hard'.[120]

It is also noteworthy that Masenya has a rather positive appreciation of the role of the husband in the Song:

> The portrait of a family (household) that the poet presents in this paean is that of husband and wife, children and servants. Something interesting and also making sense in the light of the patriarchal environment of the poet is that, of all the members of the household of the Woman of Worth, the husband is the one who is foregrounded by the poet (vv. 11, 12, 23, 28). From the picture we are given in this poem we assume that according to ancient Israelite mentality (and the Northern Sotho one), the ideal family is the one which has man, woman, and children'.[121]

It is a testimony to the pluriformity of feminism today that this feminist reading of the Song advocates largely conservative social values.

This is perhaps also the place to mention an entirely different kind of commentary on the Song, written by women and for women, which also reflects more traditional values. These are popular books, written in a

---

[116] M. Masenya, 'Proverbs 31:10–31 in a South African Context: A Reading for the Liberation of African (Northern Sotho) Women', *Semeia* 28 (1997), 55–68. Here, 60.

[117] Masenya, 'Proverbs 31', 63.

[118] Masenya, 'Proverbs 31', 63–64.

[119] Masenya, 'Proverbs 31', 65.

[120] Masenya, 'Proverbs 31', 65–66.

[121] Masenya, 'Proverbs 31', 66.

readable and sometimes humorous style, and standing outside the profes-
sional guild of biblical scholarship, which relate Proverbs 31 to the lives of
women today who accept this part of Scripture as normative for their
lives. I am thinking in particular of three recent English-language examples of this genre: two in the evangelical Christian tradition, written by
Marsha Drake[122] and Liz Curtis Higgs,[123] and one in the tradition of
Orthodox Judaism, written by Tzipporah Heller.[124] The genre also exists
outside of the English language.[125]

C. Other studies (1980–2000)

Turning now to the more traditional scholarly studies of the Song, we
observe that a veritable torrent of publications has appeared in the last
two decades. I will simply list the most significant ones in chronological
order, and for each one note very briefly its main point or some salient
features'.[126]

(1) Murray H. Lichtenstein, 'Chiasm and Symmetry in Proverbs 31'.[127]

The two poems of this chapter (1–9 and 10–31), though perhaps originally independent compositions, manifest not only thematic and verbal
links, but also striking stylistic and structural analogies, especially in their
chiastic patterns. The acrostic form of the Song does not prevent it from
having an intricate and balanced rhetorical structure. *Kîšôr* means
'dexterity'.

---

[122] M. Drake, *The Proverbs 31 Lady and Other Impossible Dreams* (Minneapolis:
Bethany House, 1984).

[123] L. Curtis Higgs, *Only Angels Can Wing It: The Rest of Us Have To Practise* (Nashville: Thomas Nelson, 1995). See also Lane P. Jordan, *Twelve Steps to Becoming a
More Organized Woman. Practical Tips for Managing Your Home and Your Life Based
on Proverbs 31* (Peabody MA: Hendrickson, 1999).

[124] T. Heller, *More Precious Than Pearls. Selected Insights into the Qualities of the Ideal
Woman, Based on Eshes Chayil* (Jerusalem/New York: Feldheim, 1993).

[125] E.g. G. Karssen, *Een vrouw naar mijn hart* (Amsterdam: Buijten & Schipperheijn,
1977), written in Dutch.

[126] In this time period we also note the intriguing monograph by F.M. Biscoglio,
*The Wives of the Canterbury Tales and the Tradition of the Valiant Woman of Proverbs
31:10–31* (San Francisco: Mellen Research University Press, 1993), which does
not deal with the biblical text itself, though it does draw heavily upon the sub-
stance of chapter 5 of the present volume. See also A.R. Larsen, 'Legitimizing the
Daughter's Writing: Catherine des Roches' Proverbial Good Wife', *Sixteenth
Century Journal* 21 (1990), 559–574, which deals with a poetic rendering of the
Song by a scholarly Frenchwoman in the sixteenth century.

[127] M.H. Lichtenstein, 'Chiasm and Symmetry in Proverbs 31', *CBQ* 44 (1982),
202–211.

(2) Al Wolters, 'Nature and Grace in the Interpretation of Proverbs 31:10–31'.[128]

The various interpretations of the relationship of the 'religious' verse 30 to the 'secular' rest of the Song follow basic paradigms (worldviews) construing the relationship between 'grace' and 'nature'.

(3) Otto Plöger, *Sprüche Salomos (Proverbia)*.[129]

A classical historical-critical treatment, marked by openness to conjectural emendations, a blunder on verse 19 (distaff and spindle are taken as *weaving* implements), and an interesting parallel to the Song from India.

(4) J.P. Lettinga, 'Een bijbelse vrouwenspiegel'.[130]

Offers some novel proposals with respect to syntactical subordination in verses 16a and 28a. Interprets *saḥar* in verse 18 as 'housekeeping' rather than 'trading', and *kîšôr* in verse 19 as 'dexterity'. Polemicizes with the Van der Sluis couple.

(5) Al Wolters, '*Ṣôpiyyâ* (Prov. 31:27) as Hymnic Participle and Play on *Sophia*'.[131]

The unusual verbal form in verse 27 can be explained as a 'hymnic' participle, and as a deliberate bilingual play on the Greek word *sophia*, 'wisdom'.

(6) Thomas P. McCreesh, 'Wisdom as Wife: Proverbs 31:10–31'.[132]

The Song functions both as a summary of the book of Proverbs and, together with Woman Wisdom of Proverbs 1–9, as its frame. The Valiant Woman is primarily a symbol, perhaps deliberately presented as a riddle, of Wisdom. Her striking similarity to Ruth may not be accidental. Lichtenstein's rhetorical analysis is to be accepted.

(7) Y. Levin, ' "The Woman of Valor" in Jewish Ritual (Prov. 31:10–31)'.[133]

An account of the Song's use in various Jewish liturgical contexts. The custom of reading it at the beginning of the Sabbath arose in fifteenth-century mystical communities.

---

[128] Chapter 2 of the present volume, originally published in *Calvin Theological Journal* 19 (1984), 153–166.
[129] O. Plöger, *Sprüche Salomos (Proverbia)* (BKAT XVII; Neukirchen: Neukirchener Verlag, 1984), 376–431.
[130] J.P. Lettinga, 'Een bijbelse vrouwenspiegel', in *Bezield verband. Opstellen aangeboden aan prof. J. Kamphuis* (Kampen: Van den Berg, 1984), 119–125.
[131] Chapter 3 of the present volume, originally published in *JBL* 104 (1985), 577–587.
[132] T.P. McCreesh, 'Wisdom as Wife: Proverbs 31:10–31', *RB* 92 (1985), 25–46.
[133] Y. Levin, ' "The Woman of Valor" in Jewish Ritual (Prov. 31:10–31)', *Beth Mikra* 107 (1986), 339–347. [In Hebrew.]

(8) Dorothée Metlitzki, 'A Woman of Virtue'.[134]

The song is the climax of Proverbs, summing up its teaching about wisdom. The Valiant Woman is a woman of strength, of 'virtue' in the sense of *virtus*, a quality of worth and valour in both man and woman.

(9) Ellen Louise Lyons, 'A Note on Proverbs 31:10–31'.[135]

Lyons sees the Song as very early (premonarchical), though she does not refer to Crook, who had made a similar point in 1954.

(10) Antonio Bonora, 'La donna eccellente, la sapienza, il sapiente (*Pr.* 31, 10–31)'.[136]

Detailed philological study of both the MT and the LXX of the Song. The Valiant Woman represents simultaneously a flesh-and-blood woman, Wisdom, and the sage. The Song therefore recapitulates the entire book of Proverbs. Lichtensteins's rhetorical analysis is to be accepted. *Ṣôpiyyâ* may well allude to *sophia*.

(11) Al Wolters, 'Proverbs 31:10–31 as Heroic Hymn: a Form-critical Analysis'.[137]

From a form-critical point of view, the Song is a 'hymn', and represents an adaptation of traditional 'heroic' poetry in praise of warriors.

(12) Maryse Waegeman, 'The Perfect Wife of Proverbia 31:10–31'.[138]

The Valiant Woman has striking Greek parallels, especially in Xenophon's *Oeconomicus*. Unlike her, however, the Greek counterparts do not engage in profit-making business ventures.

(13) Claire Gottlieb, 'The Words of the Exceedingly Wise: Proverbs 30–31'.[139]

Proverbs 30 and 31 together constitute a collection of 'Massaite wisdom literature', exemplifying a 'mixed-genre text', and constituting

---

[134] D. Metlitzki, '"A Woman of Virtue", A Note on Eshet Ḥayil', *Orim. A Jewish Journal at Yale* 1 (1986), 23–26.

[135] E.L. Lyons, 'A Note on Proverbs 31:10–31', in *The Listening Heart. Essays in Wisdom and the Psalms in honour of Roland E. Murphy* (JSOTSup 58; ed. K.G. Hoglund *et al.*; Sheffield: Sheffield Academic Press, 1987), 237–245.

[136] A. Bonora, 'La donna eccellente, la sapienza, il sapiente (*Pr.* 31, 10–31)', *Rivista Biblica* 36 (1988), 137–164.

[137] Chapter 1 of the present volume, originally published in *Vetus Testamentum* 38 (1988), 446–457.

[138] M. Waegeman, 'The Perfect Wife of Proverbia 31:10–31', in K.D. Schunck and M. Augustin (eds.), *Goldene Äpfel in silbernen Schalen. Collected Communications to the XIIIth Congress of the I.O.S.O.T., Leuven 1989* (Frankfurt/Main: Peter Lang, 1989), 101–107.

[139] C. Gottlieb, 'The Words of the Exceedingly Wise: Proverbs 30–31', in K.L. Younger, Jr., et al. (eds.), *The Biblical Canon in Comparative Perspective* (Lewiston NY: Edwin Mellen, 1991), 277–298.

an appropriate conclusion to the book. Chapter 31 is a unitary literary text, consisting of advice given by the queen-mother. The Valiant Woman is the feminine equivalent of the 'mighty man of valour', and has many ancient Near Eastern parallels. She is not an unattainable ideal; Ruth (canonically placed next to the Song) is an example. *Ṣôpiyyâ* may be playing on both Greek *sophia* and Egyptian *sb3yt*, 'instruction' or 'wisdom'.

(14) Arndt Meinhold, *Die Sprüche. Teil 2: Kapitel 16–31*.[140]

The Valiant Woman is primarily the symbolic representation of personified Wisdom, balancing the picture of Woman Wisdom in Proverbs 1–9. These two framing female figures provide a hermeneutical key to the entire book.

(15) Jutta Hausmann, 'Beobachtungen zu Spr 31,10–31'.[141]

A surface reading of the Song reveals an unrealistic, unattainable ideal. A deeper reading reveals that it is really about Wisdom, recalling Woman Wisdom of Proverbs 1–9. Both levels constantly interact.

(16) Duane A. Garrett, *Proverbs, Ecclesiastes, Song of Songs*.[142]

The Song displays a chiastic structure centered on verse 23 and the theme 'Public respect for husband', thus highlighting 'the central message of the poem: this woman is the kind of wife a man needs in order to be successful in life'. Garrett does not cite Lichtenstein, who also discerned a chiastic structure to the Song, albeit a quite different one.

(17) Al Wolters, 'The Meaning of *Kîšôr* (Prov. 31:19)'.[143]

Kîšôr's meaning is most probably 'doubling spindle'.

(18) R.N. Whybray, *Proverbs*.[144]

The Song is hymnic in character, late in date, and recalls the figure of Wisdom in chapters 1–9.

(19) André Lelièvre and Alphonse Maillot, *Commentaire des Proverbes, Tome II: Chapitres 19–31*.[145]

---

[140] A. Meinhold, *Die Sprüche. Teil 2: Kapitel 16–31* (Zurich: Theologischer Verlag, 1991), 521–530.

[141] J. Hausmann, 'Beobachtungen zu Spr 31, 10–31', in J. Hausmann and H.-J. Zobel (eds.), *Alttestamentlicher Glaube und Biblische Theologie. Festschrift für Horst Dietrich Preuss* (Stuttgart: Kohlhammer, 1992), 261–266.

[142] D.A. Garrett, *Proverbs, Ecclesiastes, Song of Songs* (Nashville: Broadman, 1993), 246–252.

[143] Chapter 4 of the present volume, originally published in *HUCA* 65 (1994), 91–104.

[144] R.N. Whybray, *Proverbs* (Grand Rapids: Eerdmans, 1994), 425–431.

[145] A. Lelièvre and A. Maillot, *Commentaire des Proverbes, Tome II: Chapitres 19–31* (Paris: Les Editions du Cerf, 1996), 347–362.

The Valiant Woman is both a human workhorse and the personification of the Fear of the Lord/Wisdom. Verse 30b is rendered, 'Cette
femme est la Crainte-du-Seigneur!' The large initial letter with which
some Hebrew manuscripts write ṣôpiyyâ (verse 27) supports the suggestion that it alludes to *sophia*. Woman Wisdom and the Fear of the Lord
frame the book. Perhaps the Song is a marriage sermon addressed to the
bride.

(20) Ignatius G.P. Gous, 'Proverbs 31:10–31 – The A to Z of Woman
Wisdom'.[146]

Cognitive psychology can help us understand the function of the
acrostic form of the Song. The latter provides the necessary security to
allow readers to experience the unsettling aspects of the Valiant Woman
here described, and thus to dare test wisdom in the real world of
experience.

(21) Tom R. Hawkins, 'The Wife of Noble Character in Proverbs
31:10–31'.[147]

A survey of recent scholarship on the Song. Points out some of the *dis-
similarities* between the Valiant Woman and Woman Wisdom in Proverbs
1–9. Discusses the Song's applicability today.

(22) Raymond C. Van Leeuwen, 'The Book of Proverbs. Introduction,
Commentary, and Reflections'.[148]

The Song is heroic and hymnic in character, the meaning of *kîšôr* is
'doubling spindle', and ṣôpiyyâ alludes to *sophia*. Wisdom and fear of the
Lord come to expression in the everyday.

(23) Jana K. Riess, 'The Woman of Worth: Impressions of Proverbs
31:10–31'.[149]

Neither the traditionalist nor the feminist readings of the Song are sat-
isfactory. Instead, the Valiant Woman should be read as the embodiment
of the basic theme of Proverbs: the fear of the Lord is the beginning of
wisdom. As such, her portrait is prescriptive for both men and women
today.

(24) Roland E. Murphy, *Proverbs*.[150]

---

[146] I.G.P. Gous, 'Proverbs 31:10–31 – The A to Z of Woman Wisdom', *Old Testament Essays* 9 (1996), 35–51.

[147] T.R. Hawkins, 'The Wife of Noble Character in Proverbs 31:10–31', *BSac*
153 (1996), 12–23.

[148] R.C. Van Leeuwen, 'The Book of Proverbs. Introduction, Commentary, and
Reflections', in *The New Interpreter's Bible*, vol. 5 (ed. J.J. Collins; Nashville:
Abingdon, 1997), 259–264.

[149] J.K. Riess, 'The Woman of Worth: Impressions of Proverbs 31:10–31', *Dialogue. A Journal of Mormon Thought* 30 (1997), 141–151.

[150] R.E. Murphy, *Proverbs* (WBC 22; Nashville: Thomas Nelson, 1998), 243–250.

Lichtenstein's rhetorical analysis is to be accepted, as well as the play on *sophia* in verse 27. Perhaps the Valiant Woman alludes to Woman Wisdom in Proverbs 1–9, but this cannot be proved.

(25) Bruce K. Waltke, 'The Role of the "Valiant Wife" in the Market-place'.[151]

The Song is heroic, but not hymnic in character. A structural analysis employing syntactic, poetic and thematic criteria can go beyond the rhetorical analysis of Lichtenstein and others, and show further aspects of the Song's intricate literary patterning. The Valiant Woman does not represent Woman Wisdom. Ṣôpiyyâ may be a trilingual pun.

(26) Richard J. Clifford, *Proverbs. A Commentary.*[152]

The Song is hymnic and heroic in character, has a chiastic structure and is symbolic of Woman Wisdom.

Concluding Observations

In looking back over the flood of scholarly literature on the Song of the Valiant Woman which has appeared in the last two decades of the twentieth century, we can discern five foci of interest which dominate this period, and which, in large measure, distinguish it from the centuries which preceded it. Perhaps we can tag these five foci with the following catchwords: feminism, literary analysis, symbolic reference, canonical shape, and cultural comparison.

It is feminism which can be said to be the most vigorous ideological impulse in contemporary biblical studies, and it has already begun to leave its mark on studies of the Song of the Valiant Woman – especially in the contributions by the Van der Sluises, Camp, Schroer, Fontaine, Brenner, and Masenya. However, the quantity and extent of feminist work on this pericope has so far been relatively restricted. We can expect much more in the future.

Literary analysis has been primarily rhetorical analysis. This has effectively demolished the old shibboleth that the acrostic form does not allow for meaningful literary arrangement within the Song. Lichtenstein's

---

[151] B.K. Waltke, 'The Role of the "Valiant Wife" in the Marketplace', *Crux* 35 (1999), 23–34.

[152] R.J. Clifford, *Proverbs. A Commentary* (OTL; Louisville KY: Westminster John Knox, 1999), 271–277.

breakthrough analysis has been followed by McCreesh, Bonora, Murphy, and Clifford, while it has been refined and expanded by Waltke. Garrett's alternative stands largely alone. Lichtenstein's work has also made it respectable again to see chapter 31 as a single literary unit, as was commonly done before the advent of modern historical criticism (see Brenner and Gottlieb). A different type of literary analysis is Wolters' form-critical identification of the Song as both hymnic and heroic. He has been followed, on one or both of these points, by Whybray, Van Leeuwen, Waltke and Clifford.

The symbolic reference of the Valiant Woman to Wisdom has suddenly become popular again, beginning already with Jacob in 1971. With or without reference to him, or to the long sub-tradition which had equated the Valiant Woman with Wisdom in the centuries before, most recent commentators are adopting this view. Among their number are the Van der Sluises, Wolters, Camp, McCreesh, Bonora, Meinhold, Fontaine, Hausmann, Brenner, Whybray, Lelièvre-Maillot, Gous, Van Leeuwen, and Clifford. Murphy is a bit cautious on this point.

The position and function of the Song within the canonical shape of Proverbs has also attracted a great deal of attention in recent years. Whereas the Song was formerly considered simply one of a series of loosely attached 'appendixes' to Proverbs, it is now widely viewed as integral to its overall structure, either as a concluding summary or as part of an editorial frame (together with Woman Wisdom in chapters 1–9) which sets the hermeneutical parameters for the collections in between. The former view is that of Metlitzki, Bonora and Gottlieb, the latter that of Camp and McCreesh (who seem to have come to it at the same time and independently of each other), followed by Meinhold, Hausmann, Whybray, and Lelièvre-Maillot.

Finally, we have seen a number of cultural comparisons. The Valiant Woman has been compared to similar figures in India by Plöger, in Greece by Waegeman, and in the ancient Near East by Gottlieb. It is this fifth focus of interest in recent studies which perhaps preserves the greatest continuity with the mainstream of biblical studies before 1980. We find a similar continuity with that tradition in Lyons' isolated attempt to fix the date of the Song.

Relatively rare are new studies which focus on philological or theological issues – staples of earlier eras of the history of interpretation. Wolters provides the main exception to this general rule, although Lettinga and Plöger also contribute.

There is, however, one characteristic which is shared by almost all recent commentators on the Song: a widespread ignorance of the history of its interpretation. Although there are some signs of an awakening historical interest (Levin and Valler), there are still numerous examples of contemporary biblical scholars reinventing the wheel with respect to the understanding of this portion of Scripture. The recent rediscovery of the Valiant Woman as the personification of Wisdom is only one example among many. It is my hope that my rough sketch of the history of interpretation will help to combat that widespread ignorance, and lead to greater engagement with the exegetical tradition on the part of contemporary exegetes. There is here a wide and promising field which lies open for further investigation, and which can lead to renewed appreciation for the exegetical riches of the past – not least in the areas of philology and theology.